The House of Stuart

MAURICE ASHLEY

The House of
STUART
Its Rise and Fall

J. M. Dent & Sons Ltd

LONDON, MELBOURNE AND TORONTO

Illustrations

Acknowledgments

MY FIRST ACKNOWLEDGMENT must be to Professor Gordon Donaldson D.Litt., F.B.A. on three counts: he introduced me to a former pupil of his, Mr A. W. Napier, who meticulously went through the Scottish part of my book and saved me from several errors, particularly about times and dates. Secondly, Professor Donaldson answered a number of questions I put to him about Scottish history, some general and others detailed. Lastly, I have drawn upon his excellent books about Scottish kings and Scottish history: I particularly admire his book on the Scottish Reformation.

I am also grateful to Mrs Caroline Bingham, a deep admirer of the Stewarts, who has written some first-class biographies; I have enjoyed especially her biography of King James V. She was also good enough to show me her collection of illustrations and to lend me some of them.

I should also like to thank Professor Geoffrey Holmes for some valuable suggestions which I have incorporated into Chapter 17.

Finally, I must convey my thanks to Miss Pat Entract, the Picture Editor of *The Listener*, a friend and former colleague of mine, who selflessly helped me with the arduous task of collecting the numerous illustrations that adorn this book.

Note on Dates and Abbreviations

IN 1582 POPE GREGORY XIII introduced a new Calendar which was adopted by most European countries, but not by Scotland or England until 14 September 1752. In this book dates in Great Britain during that period are given according to the old Calendar; dates outside Great Britain are in accordance with the Gregorian Calendar.

The following abbreviations are used in notes: *S.H.R.* = *Scottish Historical Review*; S.H.S. = Scottish History Society; S.T.S. = Scottish Text Society.

Foreword

'THE STUARTS? AN UNLUCKY FAMILY,' King Louis XVI of rance is reputed once to have exclaimed, 'I wish to hear no more of them.' In fact he did wish to hear more of them, for when in 1793 he was about to be executed by the French revolutionaries, he was anxious to discover how King Charles I had behaved on the scaffold so that he might die with equal dignity.

Since then a great many people have wanted to know about them: the English Stuarts are a perpetual source of curiosity. Hundreds of books have been devoted to them and their portraiture is also vast. Hardly a liberal arts university in Great Britain or the United States of America fails to boast a professor or two who lectures about their lives and times and, subsidized by academic funds, delves deeper and deeper into their careers, distributing praise or blame.

Much of my long life has been occupied in reading and writing about them, though only publishers have subsidized me, enabling me in a good year to earn almost as much as an unskilled labourer from my exertions.

I started my researches when I was a fledgling history graduate working for four years as an assistant to Winston Churchill, then, among his many other activities, writing a biography of his ancestor, the first Duke of Marlborough. In the course of my work I copied out in long hand some of Queen Anne's letters to the ineffable Sarah Marlborough, which were at that time in the archives in Blenheim palace, but have recently been sold to the British Library. Churchill thought more highly of Queen Anne than I did, but he did not much care for Sarah. Recently I have written biographies of Charles II and James II and I commented on William III in a book on the Glorious Revolution of 1688.

Now I have felt that I would like to widen the framework and learn more about the Scottish Stewarts, who reigned over the northern kingdom longer than their descendants did over England and also about the three Jacobite Pretenders, often the figures in romantic novels. It is fascinating to realize that two of the Hanoverian kings, who replaced the Stuarts on the thrones of England and Scotland, were attracted by their history. George III granted a pension to the last would-be Stuart King; George IV bought up many of their letters and memoirs. In this book I try to assess the characters and achievements of all the Stewart or Stuart monarchs and look for common denominators.

I have always believed, even in these days of deutero-Marxism, that individual personalities can influence the course of history. For instance, I think we owe more to the sterling qualities of our present Queen than is generally realized. Our own history might easily have developed differently had others than the Stewarts or Stuarts ruled over Scotland and England or claimed to reign over them for a period of more than four centuries. At any rate here is my panorama.

Maurice Ashley
1979

Prologue: the Battle of Bannockburn and After

FROM THE HEIGHTS OF Stirling castle, once a wooded stronghold guarding the main route from the Lowlands into the Highlands of Scotland, one can still look down, when the sky is clear, upon the low-lying land where many of the fiercest contests of the Middle Ages were fought. Of these the battle most endearing to Scottish pride was that of Bannockburn, which was won on midsummer day 24 June 1314; for it in fact decided, though it did not conclude, the war for the independence of Scotland.

The origins of that war can be traced back to the time when the ancient line of Scottish kings, stemming from Kenneth MacAlpin, suddenly died out. In 1290, nearly 450 years after he began to reign, the seven-year-old granddaughter of King Alexander III of Scotland, who was also the daughter of the King of Norway, was recognized as the rightful successor to the vacant throne, though, since a ruling queen was then thought to be inconceivable, her future husband would have become King of the Scots. But the Maid of Norway, as she was known, died mysteriously in the Orkneys, possibly of sea sickness, on her way to Scotland. This afforded the opportunity for the brother-in-law of Alexander III, King Edward I of England, who was a bold expansionist, eager to unite England, Wales and Scotland into one island kingdom, to assert the right to arbitrate on the rival claims for the legitimate succession. Even before the Maid's death Edward had invoked the help of the Pope in arranging a marriage between her and his eldest son, Edward of Carnarvon, the first English Prince of Wales, who was six. The Scots might have acquiesced, provided that their laws and liberties were respected. In any case Edward's offer to arbitrate was accepted. Upon the advice of 104 auditors or assessors he pronounced in favour of John Balliol, who undoubtedly had the best hereditary claim to become the new Scottish monarch. But before the King of England named him, he required all the candidates for the Crown to acknowledge him as their overlord. They consented, though unwillingly, in order to win his vote in the competition. Indeed they had little choice, for Edward was utterly determined to impose his authority on a divided country: so he was reluctantly recognized as 'superior and lord paramount' of the northern kingdom.

John Balliol, crowned king on St Andrew's day, 30 November 1292, was not a strong character, but it is wrong to say that he sold the pass and betrayed the independence of his kingdom. In fact he defied Edward on more than one occasion and refused him military aid when he was fighting against France. Infuriated, the English King rode north in the spring of 1296 to chastise his disobedient vassal. Thus the war began.

The only serious rival to John Balliol as the rightful heir to the throne of Scotland had been Robert Bruce Lord of Annandale, who was already in his eightieth year when the Maid of Norway perished. This Robert died on Maunday Thursday 1295, but neither his son, also named Robert, nor his grandson, yet a third Robert, who was twenty-two in 1296, had acknowledged John Balliol's right to be king. That was why when King John called out the host to resist Edward I's invasion neither of the Bruces answered the summons: for they demanded the Crown themselves. In the history of Scotland 1296 was a year of disaster. At the end of March Edward stormed and sacked Berwick on Tweed, then a frontier town inside Scotland; in the same month he procured the defeat of the Scots at the battle of Dunbar; and then the governors of Edinburgh and Stirling castles quickly abandoned them to the English invaders. In July John Balliol, who was no soldier, surrendered his title and kingdom into the hands of his conqueror, who in return allowed him in due course to find refuge from the toils of public life on his English estates.

The community of the Scottish realm felt its humiliation profoundly. During the winter there were many scattered instances of unrest. It was left to the relatively obscure second son of a knightly family from the Lowlands, by name William Wallace, to head a concerted rising against the English occupation. He was, however, inspired by greater men, who included, according to English chroniclers, the Bishop of Glasgow and the hereditary Steward of Scotland, whose first name was James; they also took up arms, but were compelled to capitulate to the English in western Scotland during July. But on 11 September 1297 Wallace himself defeated an enemy army in the battle of Stirling bridge, drove it out of the land, and harried the north of England. Though he was hailed as a hero, he did not crave the kingship for himself; instead he was chosen the sole Guardian of Scotland to govern in the name of the absent John Balliol. Wallace's triumph was brief. Just over a year later a formidable army, led by Edward I in person, overwhelmed Wallace and his followers at Falkirk, ten miles south-east of

Stirling bridge, where the armoured cavalry and Welsh long-bowmen were victorious over the Scottish spearmen. Wallace became an outlaw, ultimately to be handed over to the English by Sir John Stewart of Menteith, the Keeper of Dumbarton castle; in 1305 Wallace was brutally executed in London.

For five years after the battle of Falkirk the English held sway over much of the Lowlands, commanding nearly all the castles there while Edward was absorbed in his war against France. Robert Bruce, the young Earl of Carrick, replaced Wallace as Guardian together with John Comyn Lord of Badenoch, known as the Red Comyn, a neighbour of Bruce's because he had estates in Galloway, and was the nephew of John Balliol. They still governed the kingdom nominally on behalf of the illustrious but absentee King John, who at this period was allowed to remove himself to France. But Bruce did not remain Guardian for long. In 1302 he astonishingly entered the service of Edward I. As he was not only Earl of Carrick but was to become Lord of Annandale, owned a house in London and was married to Elizabeth de Burgh, daughter of the rich Earl of Ulster, when his father died in 1304 Robert Bruce became an affluent and prominent nobleman. We do not know how it came about that this Scottish champion, as he grew to be in the chronicles of later times, was, in the words of his latest biographer, 'the only leader of the first rank to desert the national cause' at the outset of the fourteenth century. Was he jealous of John Comyn with whom he had evidently quarrelled as Guardian? Did he believe that the cause of independence was hopeless after Wallace's defeat? Did he wish to safeguard the English estates that he was about to inherit? Did he seek the favour of Edward I? At any rate soon after his father's death Robert the Bruce, realizing that Edward I had not long to live and had a weakling son and that the cause of Balliol, who remained comfortably in exile abroad, was impossible, again changed his attitude and aspired in defiance of the English to become King of the Scots himself.

So Robert Bruce, now thirty, revived his grandfather's claim to the succession. The time was opportune for direct action. Bruce rapidly proved himself to be an inspiring leader, ambitious, quick-tempered and at times ruthless but patient and imaginative and firm of purpose. Venerating the Scottish saints from St Columba to St Andrew, he loved his country devotedly and possessed all the assurance of an aristocrat born to rule over it. Edward I, he recognized, was an old man likely to lose his grip and John Balliol, the exile, he perceived to be a failure. But he felt he needed the help of John Comyn, who had been his fellow Guardian and was the same age as himself. Comyn was invited to meet him in a Franciscan church in Dumfries in order to discuss revolutionary tactics against the English; and Bruce offered Comyn rewards if he would back him. When he refused to agree to these proposals, the two men quarrelled and suddenly the Bruce in a fit of anger stabbed him to death.

Political murders were almost the stock-in-trade of magnates in early Scottish history. So although the Comyn family was infuriated and the Pope excommunicated him for sacrilege, Bruce actually received the support of William de Lamberton the Bishop of St Andrews, the senior bishop in the Scottish Church, who had himself been a joint Guardian with Comyn. Robert Bruce was also sponsored by the next senior bishop, Robert Wishart of Glasgow. Thus blessed by the clergy, Bruce and his adherents seized castles, exacted fealties, and thrust Englishmen across the borders. Six weeks after the death of the Comyn, on 25 March 1306, Robert Bruce was crowned King at Scone. Unhappily for him, Edward I had taken away from Scone the Stone of Destiny on which earlier kings had been enthroned. But the tradition was also that at the ceremony of coronation the Earl of Fife was always present. Although the current Earl of Fife was not available, his sister, the Countess of Buchan, a girl of twenty, rode to Scone to represent her family. A second ceremony was performed on Palm Sunday when she placed a golden circlet around Robert Bruce's head. English chroniclers wrote that she aspired to become his mistress.

As soon as Edward I learned the news of the usurpation he gave orders that the rebel Scots were to be punished. Bruce was overwhelmingly defeated in the field by the English and forced to flee the country. No one knows for certain where he hid, maybe in the Orkneys or the Hebrides or Ulster, whence his wife came. All his supporters who were captured were hanged; his womenfolk were seized; his wife, his elder sister and her young daughter were put into prison; another sister and the Countess of Buchan, who had crowned him, were hung up in cages in Roxburgh and Berwick castles to be mocked at by passers-by; the two bishops who sponsored him were fettered in irons.

But it was not long before Robert the Bruce achieved his revenge. By the spring of the following year he was back in the Lowlands to defeat the English commander there at the battle of Loudon hill in Ayrshire. Edward I, who was in his sixty-ninth year, died two months later on 7 July 1307 while still directing operations against the Scots. His son, Edward II, a spoiled youth of twenty-three, perforce had to hurry back to London. For four years the Scots were left alone so that the Bruce was able to assert his authority over rival magnates and gradually consolidate his position. Though abortive invasions by the English took place in 1310 and 1311 it was not until seven years after Edward I died that the war for Scottish independence was resumed in earnest.

King Edward II, having temporarily overcome his difficulties in England, where the leading barons had obliged him to capitulate to their constitutional demands in a drawn-out civil war, at last resolved to fulfil his father's ambition to subject Scotland to English supremacy. Unlike his father, however, Edward was faced with a kingdom which, if by no means completely united (several Scotsmen of standing served with the English army), now had a ruler who was firm and effective. Though Robert Bruce was still excommunicated by the Pope, the Scottish clergy acknowledged his right to the Crown. Most of the castles left garrisoned by the English at the time of Edward I's death had been retaken one by one, usually being scaled by ladders placed against the walls and assaulted during the hours of darkness. Even the rock-girt castle of Edinburgh fell in March 1314 to a bold attack at night directed by one of Bruce's ablest officers, Thomas Randolph Earl of Moray. Only Berwick and Stirling castles, both of immense strategic value, remained occupied by English partisans when the campaign of 1314 opened. Stirling, which had an anglophile Scottish military governor, Sir Philip Mowbray, was besieged for months by Robert Bruce's brother Edward, normally a reckless soldier, who found the castle hard to subdue; eventually, without his brother's agreement, he had consented to a treaty with Mowbray which provided that if an English army failed to relieve the castle by midsummer next it would be surrendered to the Bruces. For this reason it was Edward II's aim to relieve Stirling and then to conquer the rest of the country.

The campaign started in June because it was not until then that the English could be sure to find sufficient forage to feed their horses. So Robert Bruce had ample time to complete his preparations. Aware that the primary objective of his enemy was to save Stirling, the King posted his army in Torwood, five miles south of the town, where over three centuries later the Scottish general, David Leslie, was to defy Oliver Cromwell. On receiving the news that the English host had reached Edinburgh King Robert withdrew his men from Torwood into the New Park, a hunting preserve fenced in by King Alexander III and thickly wooded, which lay to the west of the former Roman road that crossed it on its south-east corner and led from Falkirk to Stirling. Bruce's army consisted of four 'battles' or brigades of infantry under the command of himself, his brother Edward, his nephew, Thomas Randolph Earl of Moray, and Walter the sixth High Steward of the Royal Household.

Walter the Steward was called 'the Beardless' by the poet, John Barbour

Archdeacon of Aberdeen, who wrote two generations later but is the only fourteenth-century Scottish author to describe the coming battle; so it is reasonable to assume that Walter was then sixteen or seventeen years old. His father, James, as has been noticed, a feudal superior of William Wallace, who had risen against the English in the summer of 1297, had fought with Wallace at the battle of Falkirk, and had earlier been Guardian after the death of the Maid of Norway. He was one of the first of the great men of Scotland to recognize Robert Bruce as king. Walter was his second son, but his elder brother, Andrew, had met his death when he was very young, while his father followed him into the unknown in July 1309 so that the youthful Walter became heir to vast estates in the neighbourhood of Renfrew and elsewhere, including the Isle of Bute, Teviotdale, Lauderdale and parts of Lothian, as well as being one of the monarch's hereditary household officers and traditional counsellors. In Renfrewshire he collected his men to join the Scottish army, but his 'battle' was really under the command of his cousin, James Douglas, also known as the Good Douglas, who had distinguished himself as an officer in the Bruce's service earlier in the year. If Walter the Steward, though one of the greatest men in the kingdom with an exceptionally loyal and honourable background, was then a mere youth, it is understandable why he was put in command of one of the King's four brigades, but was in fact only nominally in charge of it.

What was the character of the army led by Robert the Bruce in which Walter the Beardless served? The Scots have always been first-class soldiers; they were accustomed to fighting on foot as they had done under Wallace at Stirling bridge and Falkirk. The infantrymen wore helmets to protect their heads, leather or quilted coats, shields and gloves of plate to cover their hands and wielded twelve-foot spears. They also had personal weapons such as a sword, an axe and a dagger. These spearmen were formed into schiltroms, hollow squares or, more precisely, ovals, consisting of up to 500 men. Each 'battle' contained two, three or four schiltroms. Besides his infantry Bruce had 500 light horsemen and a number of archers.

The aim of the King of the Scots was to impede the advance of the English upon Stirling. He therefore posted Moray's brigade near the kirk of St Ninian's, which lay beside the Roman road; he placed his own brigade at the entry to the New Park where the road crossed it; his brother Edward was stationed to the south of the Earl of Moray, while the Steward's brigade was positioned immediately in support of Moray. The baggage, together with army servants and poorly equipped volunteers, was left in a hollow to the north-west of the park. On either side of the road the King ordered 'pots' or pits a foot across and the depth of a man's knee to be dug and camouflaged;

they were the medieval equivalent of a mine-field, though far less effective. Thus, should the English climb up the road to Stirling castle they could be attacked on the flank by the Scots distributed in or near the New Park, most of them hidden from view among the trees.

The Scottish infantry numbered some 6,000 to 7,000 men contained in the four 'battles'. The English infantry — since they were divided into ten 'battles' — may have been two or three times as numerous. However, for victory Edward II did not rely so much on his foot soldiers as on his heavily armoured cavalrymen mounted on war-horses and armed with lances. The lowest estimate given by an English chronicler who wrote about ten years after the battle — and this no doubt was the correct one — was that the English had some 2,000 cavalry while Edward also had a number of archers chiefly from Wales.

The English army concentrated at Berwick about 17 June; by the 19th it was in Edinburgh and on the 22nd it marched twenty miles north to Falkirk. To reach Stirling from Falkirk Edward II and his army had to cross the Bannock burn, a tributary of the river Forth, which ceases to be navigable at Stirling. The Bannock burn was easy enough to ford and on the afternoon of Sunday 23 June a contingent of 300 cavalrymen was sent forward either on reconnaissance or to let the garrison at Stirling castle know it was relieved. Clearly the force commander, Sir Robert de Clifford, did not realize that the Scottish brigade under the Earl of Moray barred the route to Stirling. Moray let the English squadron, which had ridden uphill from the burn, move around him before he and his men came out of the wood to surprise them. Vainly Clifford ordered his heavy cavalry to thrust back the schiltrom posted by St Ninian's, a mile and a half from Stirling, but the mounted knights could make little impression on the Scottish spearmen, just as the French cavalry at a later date was to be held off by the Spanish tercios. The brigade under the nominal command of Walter the Steward was ready to come to the rescue of Moray's men — indeed started to do so — but in the end it did not prove necessary to deprive them of the glory of repulsing the English.

Facing the southern end of the Scottish line another and larger force under the command of King Edward's young nephew, the Earl of Gloucester, but with the more mature Earl of Hereford, the hereditary Constable of England, as his colleague, attacked Robert Bruce's own brigade on the south-eastern edge of the New Park in the neighbourhood of the Borestone, where a statue of the Scots King, erected in the twentieth century, today marks the site of the battle. Here the English were also brought to a halt, the Scottish soldiers aiming their spears at the enemy's horses: Gloucester, for example, was knocked off his steed during the fighting. Hereford's nephew, Sir Henry de Bohun, one of the armoured knights, nearly succeeded in felling the King of the Scots with his lance, but Bruce swerved away from him, pierced his helmet with his axe and split his head in two. After these significant setbacks the English drew off with the intention of renewing the battle on the following day.

Most of the area east and north-east of the New Park, that was bounded by the Roman road, the Bannock burn and the river Forth (about two miles by three in extent) and was known as the Carse, was a stretch of marshland covered with streams which were fed by tidal water. It was not an inviting place on which to encamp, but almost certainly Edward II brought the bulk of his army across the burn during the night. After all, it was midsummer and patches of dry or drier land were to be found to the south of the Carse. Conceivably Edward and his commanders hoped that the Scots, outnumbered as they were, would not resume the battle at all, but accept the fact, which was true enough in theory, that Stirling castle had been relieved by the arrival of the superior English army within three miles of it.

But learning that the enemy was dispirited after its repulses the day before, Robert the Bruce had no intention of retreating. The Scots prepared religiously for battle on the 23rd, a Sunday and the eve of the birthday of St John the Baptist; they had partaken of the Mass and confined their diet to bread and water. Early the following morning they heard the Mass and knelt in prayer at sunrise. When Edward received the intelligence of their devotions, he asked one of his Scots lieutenants, Sir Ingram de Umfraville, who, like the Bruce and James the Steward, had once been a Guardian, why they prayed and whether they would fight. The English King supposed that they knelt to ask for mercy. 'Not of you,' retorted Sir Ingram. In fact King Robert delivered an eloquent speech reminding his men that it was a day of rejoicing when they were to fight 'with the saints of Scotland for the honour of their country.' It was then that Walter the High Steward and his cousin, James Douglas, received the distinction of knighthood.

The Scots assumed the offensive soon after dawn, led by Edward Bruce's brigade, followed by that of Moray and of Sir Walter Steward with the King's own brigade in reserve. Once again the English cavalry was unable to resist the leading Scottish schiltrom as the array of spearmen again attacked their horses. The young Earl of Gloucester and the veteran Sir Robert de Clifford were both killed. Seeing the success of Edward Bruce's brigade, his brother ordered the other brigades forward and they all fought side by side with the Steward's brigade to the left of the line. When Edward's archers shot at the spearmen on the right flank they gave the only check to the Scots offensive. Robert Bruce then threw in his light cavalry and the bowmen were scattered.

At this point the King of the Scots realized that the battle had been won, while seeing the Scottish soldiers everywhere victorious, even the servants guarding the baggage excitedly came out of their hollow in search of spoils. Imagining that they were another Scottish army, the English began to panic. Edward II himself got away safely; he might have thrown himself into Stirling castle, but preferred to ride behind the back of the enemy army and hasten for home. Many of his followers were less fortunate, being trapped or drowned in the Forth and the Bannock burn. Though the English losses were not excessive, it was a signal victory.

To the military historian the battle is of importance for two reasons. The first is that the English pikemen and halberdiers appear to have taken littleeor no part in the battle. On both days the mounted knights headed the charges, no doubt expecting the infantry to do the mopping up and on the second day the bulk of Edward's foot soldiers must have been cramped upon the boggy ground lying between the Forth and the Bannock burn behind the dry land on which their cavalry was fighting. Secondly, the Scots spearmen showed that they were more than a match for the English chivalry; it was only when the archers were thrown in against them that they were harassed for a time. The English were to digest the lessons of the battle; Edward II's son, Edward III, was to win his famous victory over the French at Crécy thirty-two years later not with his armoured knights, who fought dismounted, but with his archers. On the other hand, the Scots failed to profit from what they learned in the battle. Nearly 200 years later excellent Scottish armour and heavy swords were to prove cumbersome when employed against the English infantry at the battle of Flodden.

The victory of Bannockburn did not end the war; in fact it only began it. It was not before another nine years that a lengthy truce was agreed nor for another fourteen years that a definitive treaty was signed between Scotland and England. Both sides carried out raids across the border. In 1315 Robert Bruce penetrated as far as York while his brother opened a second front in Ulster and was actually crowned King of Ireland at Dundalk in May 1316. When in 1319 Edward II besieged Berwick, which had surrendered to the Scots in the previous year, Robert Bruce did not seek battle, but invaded northern England, thus forcing the English to abandon the siege. In 1322 Edward II again crossed the Tweed, but was compelled to withdraw by an effective scorched earth strategy.

Meanwhile the Scottish community of the realm was concerned over the succession, for Robert Bruce, now King beyond question, had no son. After the battle of Bannockburn his daughter, Marjory (by his first wife, Isobel of Mar) had been released along with his second wife, Elizabeth de Burgh, and his sister, Christian; they were exchanged for high-ranking English prisoners taken in the battle. But the Scots, still absorbed in their war with England, did not want their next ruler to be a queen. A parliament that met at Ayr in April 1315 had therefore resolved that Robert's brother, Edward, 'a vigorous man, highly skilled in warlike deeds', should succeed if the King had no legitimate son. At about the same time Walter the Steward was married to Marjory Bruce (who had waived her hereditary right to the throne in favour of her uncle) as a kind of insurance in case Robert and Edward both died without heirs. It was an outstanding honour for Walter the Beardless, who had fought honourably for the King at Bannockburn, to be thus taken into the royal family; he must have been a young man of exceptional promise. He was by then about eighteen and his bride was older, perhaps twenty. The marriage did not last long. In March 1316 Marjory was thrown from her horse and her son, Robert, was born from her dead body. This Robert was in time to become the first Stewart King of Scotland.

In October 1318 Edward Bruce was killed while still fighting in Ireland. Meeting at Scone in December a parliament therefore acknowledged Robert, the two-year-old grandson of King Robert I, who was destined to be the seventh High Steward, as heir presumptive to the throne. His father, Walter, lived for another eleven years after his only child's birth and developed into one of the Bruce's most trusted officers and counsellors. In 1319 after he had been appointed governor of the town and castle of Berwick Walter repulsed Edward II, who was trying to besiege it with 8,000 men. Earlier during the winter of 1316–17, when Robert Bruce joined his brother in the campaign in Ireland, Walter was named along with his cousin, Sir James Douglas, as the two lieutenants responsible for protecting the kingdom during their absence. In April 1320 Walter's name appeared after those of five earls as one of the principal signatories of the Declaration of Arbroath, a letter of protest addressed to Pope John XXII, who had renewed the excommunication of the Scottish King and attempted to compel him to make peace with England. In this letter Walter, along with other magnates, barons and freemen declared:

For so long as but one hundred men of us remain alive, we shall never under any conditions submit to the domination of the English. It is not for glory or riches or honour that we fight, but only for liberty, which no good man will consent to lose but with his life.

A modern historian has observed that this declaration demonstrated 'the strength of the sense of national identity that the wars of independence generated', stressing 'the ultimate justification for their insistence on the political independence of the kingdom'. Whatever the truth of that claim may be — and it has been accepted by most Scottish historians in recent times, just as Magna Carta was, or used to be, acclaimed the cornerstone of English liberties — the Declaration of Arbroath has certainly become a document precious to Scottish nationalists.

Before Robert Bruce died on 7 June 1329 he again invaded Ireland and successfully carried out campaigns in the north of England, which compelled the Council of Regency in London (Edward II having been murdered in 1327) to agree to a treaty, ratified by an English parliament at Northampton on 4 May 1328, recognizing the independence of Scotland under 'the magnificent prince, the Lord Robert, by the grace of God, King of the Scots, our ally and dear friend'. In the same year Pope John XXII at last released the Bruce from excommunication. One other triumph greeted the closing years of the great Scottish King. His second wife, Elizabeth de Burgh, unexpectedly after twenty-two years of married life, gave birth to a son, who was christened David. When he was four years old this precocious infant was wedded at Berwick on Tweed to Princess Joan of England, known as Joan of the Tower, the young sister of the new king, Edward III. Joan's French mother, Queen Isabelle, had intended to bring the Stone of Destiny, which had been carried away to Westminster by Edward I, as a kind of wedding present, but the Londoners prevented her from taking it. About a year after the marriage Robert I died, leaving instructions that his heart should be carried into battle against the Saracens. It was Walter the Steward's cousin, Sir James Douglas, who took the embalmed heart to Granada; it was brought back to be buried at Melrose, Robert Bruce's favourite abbey.

The birth of David Bruce meant that Walter Stewart's son, Robert, ceased to be the next heir to the throne. A parliament, meeting in July 1326 at Cambuskenneth near Stirling, had laid it down in an entail that he could only claim the succession if David died without heirs. As Robert was eight years older than David — although David was his uncle — the chance of Robert becoming King seemed remote. Nevertheless when Sir Walter Stewart died on 9 April 1326, still in his early thirties, he left his son with every prospect of becoming one of the richest and most powerful landowners in Scotland, clearly bound to be appointed a Guardian of the realm when his uncle was still a minor. Furthermore since in fact David Bruce, despite two wives, was to have no legitimate children, Robert, the seventh hereditary High Steward, was destined to become the founder of the Royal House of Stewart.

One of the latest and best of the many lives of King Robert I is G. W. S. Barrow, *Robert Bruce and the Community of the Realm of Scotland* (1965). For the battle of Bannockburn see W. M. Mackenzie, *The Battle of Bannockburn* (1913); J. E. Morris, *Bannockburn* (1914); Sir Herbert Maxwell, 'The Battle of Bannockburn', *S.H.R.* xi (1914); A. J. Becke, appendix B to the *Complete Peerage* xi (1949); J. D. Mackie, review of this in *S.H.R.* x/vii (1950); Sir Philip Christison, 'Bannockburn 23rd and 24th June 1314 A Study in Military History', *Proceedings of the Society of Antiquaries of Scotland* xc (1959); and there is a detailed account in Barrow, op. cit., which on the whole I have followed. Morris and Maxwell usefully discuss the original sources. The main points of controversy are where the English army was stationed on 24 June and what part the English infantry played in the battle. There is now pretty general agreement about the numbers which fought on each side and on the fact that the Scots took the offensive on 24 June. The quotation about the declaration of Arbroath is taken from David Daiches, *England and the Union* (1977).

2

The Early Stewarts and
Medieval Scotland

WHO WERE THE EARLY STEWARTS, the ancestors of Walter the Beardless and his only son, Robert, the first Stewart King? It used to be thought that they had come over from Normandy to England with William the Conqueror before migrating to Scotland, but modern research, completed only half a century ago, has shown conclusively that they came from Brittany and arrived in England at the outset of the twelfth century.

In the middle of the eleventh century the lord or local magnate of the little town of Dol, which lies fourteen miles south-west of St Malo, was named Rhiwallon, whose *dapifer* or steward was called Alan. But it was not this stewardship which gave the future Scottish Stewarts their name. Alan had three sons, the youngest of whom was loyally named after his father's master and became a monk. The eldest son, called after his father, succeeded him about 1180 as the *dapifer* of Dol. But the second son, named Flaald, evidently both aspiring and enterprising, settled in Monmouthshire on the borders of Wales about 1101 just after Henry I, the youngest son of William the Conqueror, became King of England.

After the turmoil that prevailed during the reigns of the first two Williams from Normandy, England was prospering. The scholarly Walter Map was to declare that 'no one but an idiot was poor in those days', while his contemporary Peterborough chronicler wrote of Henry I that 'he was a good man and was held in great awe. In those days no man dared to wrong another. He made peace for man and beast.' Henry I may not have been exactly a good man, for he appears to have been responsible for the murder of his brother and predecessor, William the Redbeard, who had in fact been successful in procuring peace on the borders of Scotland and Wales. And as it was on the border of south Wales that Flaald settled, he had come to the right place at the right time. His son, Alan fitz Flaald, no doubt inheriting his father's adventurous spirit, must have been a wealthy man, for besides owning his father's property on the borders of Wales, he held an extensive fief in Norfolk, where he founded a priory, and also had a manor or manors in Yorkshire. Moreover his two younger sons, William and Walter (the eldest returned to Brittany as *dapifer* of Dol) acquired lands in Shropshire near the frontier with Wales, where they were the tenants of the Earl of Shrewsbury. It has been suggested that the third son, Walter fitz Alan, may have met David I King of the Scots at the Court of King Henry I of England when they were both young men; alternatively, he could have encountered the future Scottish monarch when they were both fighting for Henry I during his Welsh campaign of 1114. At any rate Walter left the castle he guarded at Oswestry in north Shropshire somewhere around 1140 and followed David to Scotland, where he had become King in 1124.

Walter fitz Alan then changed countries, as his grandfather had done before him. It was an auspicious moment in history: life had become tempestuous on the borders or 'marches' of north Wales where castles like that at Oswestry were liable to be frequently attacked and sacked by belligerent Welshmen. On the other hand, David I had thrown off the feudal yoke to which his brother and predecessor, King Alexander I, had been subjected by Henry I of England. Since, after Henry's death in 1135, caused by an excess of hunting and eating too many eels, the succession to the English throne had been violently contested between the widowed Empress Matilda, David I's niece and Henry I's only legitimate child, and Count Stephen of Blois, Henry I's favourite nephew, in a prolonged civil war, David was able to fish profitably in these troubled English waters. By the end of his reign he had acquired Cumberland and Northumberland as well as the honour (or lordship) of Lancaster. Before he died in 1153 David had officially appointed Walter fitz Alan as the high Steward at his Court (although Walter had settled in Scotland at least ten years earlier) and thus it was that the fitz Alans were transmuted into Stewards or Stewarts.

The ancestors of the Stewarts were upcoming men who seized all their opportunities in life. The fact that they were Bretons by origin was a distinct advantage to them. When in the last decade of the eleventh century the future King Henry I of England was struggling for survival against two of his brothers, his base was the celebrated and beautiful island town of Mont-St-Michel, still a favourite haunt of tourists, lying near the border of modern Brittany. The Bretons were then Henry's allies and it is likely enough that Walter Stewart's father fought for Henry when he was a young man. We are told that the Bretons were 'Celts of the Cymric branch, of the same race and speaking the same language, with only dialectical differences, as the Cymri of Wales'. It may therefore well have been the policy of Henry I to settle Bretons to guard the borders of Wales and equally it may have been the policy of David I to settle Bretons in Cumbria (or modern

Strathclyde), where many Welsh or Cymri were to be found. At any rate David I gave to his High Steward, Walter, lands both in Renfrew and Paisley in south-west Scotland, as well as in Lothian, in return for the obligation to provide, when required, five mounted knights for his wars. Thus Walter Stewart became one of the most wealthy and influential lairds in the Lowlands.

After the death of David I his grandson, Malcolm IV, who was only eleven, succeeded to the throne of Scotland. Since Henry I had married David I's sister (though he was not notably faithful to her) the young Malcolm was related to King Henry II, one of the outstanding English monarchs of that age, who came to the throne in 1154, and through parentage, marriage and inheritance was also the effective ruler of much of France, dwarfing his overlord, the French King, in the multitude of his possessions. His kinship with this powerful English ruler made little difference to Malcolm IV's own fortunes: he was compelled to surrender Northumberland, Cumberland and Westmorland, which had been cleverly acquired by his grandfather when the English were distracted by their war of succession; the only compensation Malcolm received was the earldom of Huntingdon in England.

When Malcolm was seventeen he accompanied his formidable relative, who in his late twenties was both restless and overwhelmingly ambitious, upon a military expedition to France in which he tried to extend his already vast territories as far south as Toulouse. Whether Walter Stewart accompanied his young master upon this campaign, which in fact proved fruitless, is uncertain, but at any rate soon after Malcolm returned to Scotland in 1160 he granted a charter to Walter confirming him in all the feudal territories bestowed on him by David I and also confirming him in his stewardship, which was transformed into a hereditary office as a reward for the services Walter had already performed for two Scottish kings. Walter celebrated the receipt of this munificent charter by founding a monastery near Renfrew, which he endowed for the benefit of the souls not only of David I and Malcolm IV but also for the soul of Henry II, who certainly stood in need of the prayers of the faithful. Walter lived on to defend Renfrew against an invasion by a Scottish rebel from Argyllshire, married an heiress, and died full of years, honours and riches in 1177.

What was the nature of the office of Steward which had thus become hereditary in the family of the fitz Alans? The previous holder of the office retired from his duties to become a monk in England, which suggests that he did not regard them as vital. But because it was to be made hereditary after Walter successfully passed through a period of trial at the royal Court its importance was enhanced, although its scope was smaller than that of the similar office at Court in England which boasted not only a High Steward but a steward of the household as well. In Scotland the duties of the hereditary Steward were to supervise the running of the royal household, fix the wages of the King's servants, such as the butlers, cup-bearers and scullions, and to suggest remedies for any defects unearthed.

Two other offices in the King's household, those of the Constable and Marshal, were either hereditary then or at least became hereditary later, but the principal posts, those of Chancellor (who had always been a cleric) and of Chamberlain, who was, as it were, the Treasurer or Minister of Finance – for he was responsible both for the King's domestic expenditure and the royal income in general – were filled by merit. The Steward was responsible to the Chamberlain and he had to obtain his agreement for any improvements he had in mind in the administration of the royal household. The Steward did not, as in England, preside over the judicial court of the household – the Constable did that – but both the Steward and the Marshal and other royal officials attended the court. When the Steward was absent a 'sufficient knight' was appointed as his deputy. As the royal Court was peripatetic in the early Middle Ages – for Scotland had as yet no capital – and as the landed properties of the fitz Alans were scattered right across the Lowlands, the hereditary Steward could not be with the Court all the time and often had to leave his duties to a deputy.

When Walter, the first hereditary High Steward, died in 1177 he was replaced by his son, Alan, who died in 1204; next succeeded Alan's son, another Walter, who died in 1246 and then came Walter's son, Alexander, who died in 1281. Little is known of the careers of the second and third High Stewards, although each of them appears to have grown wealthier, fattening his patrimony, except that Alexander the fourth High Steward served under King Alexander III of Scots against the King of Norway by name Hakon. Alexander III had aimed to acquire the Western Isles and the Isle of Man from the Norwegian ruler. To safeguard them King Hakon organized a large-scale amphibious expedition to assert his rights over these islands. His ships were wrecked in an October storm (in 1263), his soldiers were defeated in the battle of Largs, in which Alexander Stewart fought for his King, and the Norwegian monarch died in the Orkneys – also belonging to Norway – on his way home. His successor sold the Western Isles (or Hebrides) and the Isle of Man to the Scottish King, but it was left to a Stewart king 200 years later to acquire the Orkneys for Scotland.

The reign of Alexander III, who had come of age in 1262, was a flourishing one. Although married twice, he had no son: that was why after his death in 1286 the magnates of the realm, including James, the fifth High Steward, recognized, if reluctantly, his daughter's young daughter, the Maid of Norway, as their future Queen; James Stewart was appointed along with five others, two of whom were bishops, to act as Guardians of the realm during theeMaid's minority. After her death – or even before – James threw in his lot with the Bruces, who, he believed, were better qualified to govern the country, and he remained loyal to them both after King Edward had decided in favour of John Balliol's right to succeed and during the time when Edward, as the Hammer of the Scots, sacked Berwick, occupied Roxburgh, which James himself was compelled to surrender, and defeated Robert Bruce.

But James Stewart had picked the right side and it has well been said that 'throughout the vacillating and tortuous policy of Robert Bruce James flits like a shade, like a ghost behind the arras, never far away'. Soon after Robert I had consolidated his position as king, James died, leaving his son, by his wife, Cecilia, daughter of the Earl of Dunbar and March, Walter the Beardless, the sixth High Steward, one of the greatest men in Scotland. After the victory of Bannockburn it was Walter who was sent to Berwick to escort back to Edinburgh Robert Bruce's second wife, who was a niece of Walter's mother, and Marjory, the Bruce's daughter by his first wife, after they had been exchanged for noble English prisoners captured during the battle. Next year Marjory was to marry Walter; historians have romantically envisaged the young couple falling in love on the way home. More likely it was a marriage of convenience, Robert Bruce deliberately selecting his High Steward as a young man of promise to be one of his leading servants and commanders and, hopefully, the father of an heir apparent to the Scottish throne.

What was the character of the kingdom of Scotland over which the Stewards were soon to rule? At first sight it was not an attractive land, for it was covered by thick forests and woods of oak and fir, huge wastes of moor and bog, swiftly running rivers which frequently overflowed, poor roads and a cold and wet climate; in the winter, noted an Italian visitor, 'the sun illuminates the earth little more than three hours'. But the rivers were navigable for long distances and recognized routes linked the centres of life. As today, the lakes and mountains had the beauty of grandeur and throughout the country were to be found fertile fields and excellent pasture on which cattle could graze, though they covered only about a fifth of the whole area. The poorest land lay in the north and the richest in the south. This contrast was one of the characteristics that divided the Highlands from the Lowlands. In fact two-thirds of Scotland was occupied by the Highlands, the dividing line running from north-east to south-west, roughly from Inverness on the Moray firth to Dumbarton on the firth of Clyde.

Nevertheless the Highlands were the least populated part of Scotland. Out of a total population of 400,000 fewer than half lived in the Highlands. Because the communities that dwelt there in the Middle Ages were geographically isolated they consisted of extremely hardy and independent men and women impossible to control from afar. Gordon Donaldson has observed that 'the monarchy was one of the few things shared by the races on both sides of the Highland line and the belief in its antiquity helped to give cohesion to the country'. But here he is writing of the early modern period, for it was not until then that the Scottish kings, the later Stewarts, were able to maintain some degree of law and order in the Highlands. Up till that time loyalty to the clan and its chieftains was the only loyalty known there; as John Major wrote, 'war rather than peace' was 'their normal condition'. Militarily they were almost impregnable if they retreated into the mountains. No royal army could operate there for long: it could not be supplied from the sea; virtually no roads existed. A navy was necessary to reach the Western Isles. On the mainland a mobile force, living off the country, like the small armies to be led in later times by James Graham Marquis of Montrose, could sometimes outmanoeuvre better armed and more sophisticated troops operating far from their bases.

Throughout the kingdom the small population was widely scattered; few nucleated villages — in England evidence of co-operative arable farming — existed. The farmhouses or steadings were situated at considerable distances from one another. Not only the cottages but the castles for the most part of this period were built of wood and earth, easily erected and easily destroyed. Mixed farming was almost universal, though more sheep farming was to be found in the Lowlands and more cattle farming in the Highlands. The burghs came into being as the streets or gateways leading to the castles, either royal or baronial, and under their protection markets grew up. Many of the burghs, especially on the east coast, were close to the sea so that commerce gradually developed in them, based on the exchange of goods with countries in western Europe. By and large Scotland, like England, was predominantly an agricultural country throughout the Middle Ages: its chief crops were oats, barley, peas and beans. Although cheese and oatmeal were the staple foods and ale the usual drink, meat and fish were plentiful. At Martinmas (11 November) cattle were salted to provide food for the winter. Most people tailored their own clothes, generally of a rough white or grey cloth. To keep warm, wood and peat were used as fuel, though coal was discovered in outcrops fairly early in Scottish history.

Hardly any industries existed. Cloth manufacture was not, as in England, a rural industry but was confined to the burghs. Exports consisted principally of wool, hides, and fish in barrels or smoked. In exchange iron to shoe horses, leather to make saddles and oil to light lamps were imported together with wines and a few other luxuries. Foreign trade developed with the Netherlands, France and the Baltic countries, which in return bought raw wool and smoked fish. A large colony of Flemings settled at an early stage in Aberdeen which then, as now, was one of the most flourishing towns in the country. But because of constant wars between the two parts of the island little trade was done with England: this fact militated against the rapid expansion of commerce. No recognized capital existed before the sixteenth century. Law courts might meet and parliaments be held in a dozen different places. In so far as any recognized political or legal centre existed it was at Scone, east of Perth, where kings were crowned, successions declared, and parliaments or great councils gathered periodically.

About the exact spread of languages in medieval Scotland it is difficult to be precise. It has been stated that more than half of the Scots spoke Gaelic, that it was the language of the majority north of the Forth and Clyde, and that it was also the language in Galloway where Carrick, the earldom of Robert Bruce, was situated. Robert himself spoke two languages, Gaelic and Norman French, while, as has been noticed, the Stewarts came from the borders of north Wales where a language closely akin to Gaelic was spoken, though only one Stewart King (James IV) knew Gaelic. In Lothian and other parts near to England 'quaint English' (as a chronicler called it) or what is now known as Scots, a Scottish form of English, was the common language. Undoubtedly by the time of Bannockburn Scots was slowly ousting Gaelic and it continued to make progress in the more civilized parts of the kingdom. Although Scottish historians are not always willing to accept this, linguistic differences were one factor which divided the Highlands and the Lowlands. In addition, of course, Latin was the academic language and French was often spoken at Court.

As in England, society was feudal, that is to say the tenants-in-chief held their lands of the King in return for providing the service of armed knights, though this service was gradually commuted for money rents. But the bulk of the population had little security of tenure from their landlords. Peasants were required to do boon work and harvest work and sometimes weekly work on the demesne lands – the lands directly cultivated by their lords. Even then their tenure was usually only for one year, although what were called 'tacks' for three to five years might be granted in return for money rent. A man's position in the tenurial pyramid did not determine his

political standing. Anyone who held a barony was a baron; anyone who held
a lordship was a lord. Thirteen earldoms existed, which carried with them
possession of the areas to which their titles referred. For example, the Earl of
Carrick's lands lay in Carrick and the Earl of Moray's lands lay in Moray.
Knighthood was a military rank; as has been seen, Walter the High Steward
was knighted when in command of a brigade at Bannockburn. Bishops and
abbots also held their lands by virtue of their offices.

About the character of ordinary Scots it is dangerous to generalize,
especially as they clearly differed according to whether they lived in the
Highlands or the Lowlands. Foreign observers and contemporary historians
thought that they were warlike rather than industrious. The historian, John
Major, went so far as to say that farmers did not cultivate their lands, but
had a horse and weapons ready to fight for their landlords at any time. In the
Highlands one suspects that the women did most of the work. The Spanish
ambassador, Pedro de Ayala, writing towards the end of the sixteenth
century, considered that the Scots spent all their time in wars and 'when
there is no war they fight one another'. He added that the women were
'courteous in the extreme . . . very bold . . . absolute mistresses of their
houses and even of their husbands'. But it is difficult to believe that
Scotland was a matriarchal society.

In parliaments, which rarely met for more than a few days and might be
summoned anywhere, lay peers, spiritual peers and burgesses were all
represented: they met together in a single chamber presided over by the
King. Parliament was the highest court in the land – though it could also
enact laws and vote taxes, normally on the recommendation of the king,
regent or guardian. General Councils also consisted of all three Estates, but
they could be called at shorter notice and were not hampered by judicial
formalities. A Privy Council, in which the Chancellor was the most
important functionary, dealt with day-to-day affairs on behalf of the King.

Though judicial decisions were take by parliaments, justices went on
circuit or what were known as 'ayres'. The more active Stewart monarchs
went on ayres themselves. Royal justice was administered locally by sheriffs
of counties appointed by the King, but baronial courts handled civil and
criminal cases at the grass roots, from which appeals might go to the
sheriff's court and thence to the justice ayre. Sheriffs were masters of all
trades, as they were the financial, administrative, judicial and military
officers of the monarchy.

Foreign policy was the concern of the King himself, although parliaments were often consulted about questions of national significance, such as
declarations of war and peace. Special ambassadors were sent to conduct

negotiations with foreign countries. Relations with England, France and the Papacy were of the first importance. At times in the Middle Ages Scottish kings recognized the kings of England as their overlords. Malcolm III (1058–93) had accepted both William I and William II as his overlords, not willingly but because he was beaten in war. William the Lion, King of the Scots from 1165 to 1214, was defeated in the north of England, taken a prisoner, and compelled to acknowledge Henry II's feudal superiority over himself and his kingdom. But whenever the kings of England were weak or in difficulties over their widely flung possessions the Scottish kings would repudiate any claim by them to feudal superiority and even, as Alexander III was able to do, extended their own authority over Northumberland and Cumberland. Although Edward I could point to plenty of precedents, Robert the Bruce refused to recognize the overlordship of the English King once he himself was secure on the Scottish throne; and after Edward II was defeated it was agreed that the 'marches' or boundaries between the two kingdoms should be governed by earls or barons entrusted with this duty by the two Kings. The borders of Scotland were divided into a west march, a middle march, and an east march. When frontier differences arose they were referred to a mixed commission. None the less the frontier was rarely settled or at peace and the towns of Berwick and Roxburgh often changed hands. Whenever the Scots invoked the help of the French against the English, they would offer in return to stir up trouble for the English (at war with France on and off for a hundred years) by carrying out raids across the border. It was during the war of independence from England that the Scottish-French alliance was first concluded: and this alliance, known as 'the Auld Alliance', continued to be the foundation of Scottish foreign policy until the Stewart kings became kings of England.

No portrait of medieval Scotland would be complete without reference to the Church. The lives of ordinary Scotsmen were spent under the shadow not only of the castle but of the local kirk. In the time of Robert Bruce no archbishop existed and the twelve bishops were all equal in authority, although the Bishop of St Andrews was the senior. By a Bull published at the end of the twelfth century the Scottish Church was made a special daughter of Rome, subject directly to the Pope. Through the influence he possessed the King either nominated the bishops or gave his approval to those elected by the cathedral chapters.

Parish priests – rectors and vicars – were possibly relatively better off than those in England. Not only were parish churches endowed with lands, but tithes (or teinds) had to be paid both on crops and on the offspring of animals as well as on milk, butter, cheese and eggs, while mortuary dues

and oblations of various kinds had also to be found. Tithes, it is true, were
often diverted to support abbeys and other religious houses, but they were
supposed to provide vicars with an adequate living wage. Beside the secular
clergy in charge of parishes were a great many monks and friars gathered
together in monasteries and other religious houses, for the most part
adequately endowed by the King and the nobility. By the thirteenth
century some twenty friaries existed, many in the burghs, and more than a
hundred hospitals, leper houses and alms houses administered by the
Church. Both the Cistercians or white monks and other orders, cloistered or
not cloistered, engaged in arable or sheep farming; an abbey at Kelso, for
instance, kept 7,000 sheep. The regular clergy have been described, too, as
'the greatest shipowners in the country'; they also speculated in the purchase of imported goods. By the time of the Reformation the Church owned
half the wealth of the kingdom. It is true that the king could tap some of
these riches by appointing his servants and illegitimate sons as bishops,
abbots or priors, but this concentration of so much of the national income in
the hands of the clergy presented many problems to the Stewart rulers of
Scotland.

The thirteenth century was a golden age in the history of Scotland.
Relations with England were on the whole peaceful and the frontier
between the two kingdoms was defined along the Tweed-Solway line. The
Norwegians had been defeated and the Western Isles acquired. Commerce
was beginning to flourish and the construction of ships, made out of the
oaks and firs that abounded in the kingdom, started to develop. A rudimentary navy coped with pirates. But the long war of independence during
the first third of the fourteenth century left Scotland exhausted, while
the ambitions of the three English Edwards brought constant wars. Dark
and troubled days lay ahead as the first Stewart King grew to manhood.

For the ancestors of Walter the Beardless see J. T. T. Brown, 'The Origin of the
House of Steward', *S.H.R.* vol. 2 (1927). The most recent books on the Stewart
kings of Scotland are Gordon Donaldson, *Scottish Kings* (revised 1977) and Caroline
Bingham, *The Stewart Kingdom of Scotland 1307–1603* (1974). The duties of the
Steward are discussed in Mary Bateson, 'The Scottish King's household and Other
Fragments', *S.H.S. Miscellany II* (1964). For the general history of medieval
Scotland Ranald Nicholson, *Scotland: the Later Middle Ages* (1974) and W. Croft
Dickinson, *Scotland from the Earliest Times to 1603* (revised and edited by Archibald
A. M. Duncan, 1977) are the latest and best surveys. Selected documents are to be

found in W. C. Dickinson, G. Donaldson and Isabel A. Milne, *A Source Book of Scottish History* (1953). The best of the books which give a nineteenth-century view of medieval Scotland is Patrick Fraser Tytler, *History of Scotland* (1845). For social and economic history see I. F. Grant, *The Social and Economic Development of Scotland before 1603* (1950) and W. C. Mackenzie, *The Scottish Burghs* (1949).

3

The Two Roberts

THE TWO ROBERTS – Robert II (1371–90) and Robert III (1390–1406) – the first two Stewart Kings of the Scots, are usually uncharitably dismissed as nonentities. It is admitted that they were amiable and likeable men who had the good of their country at heart, but it is contended that they were incapable of standing up to their nobility and, being thus unable to enforce law and order, failed to govern the kingdom adequately.

Yet the art – or science – of history requires one to place one's picture in the framework of past time. In western Europe the fourteenth century was an era of conflict and unrest everywhere. During the last years of his long reign King Edward III of England was obliged to try to secure the future of his dynasty through marriages with the aristocracy and by sharing the richest estates of his realm among his sons and relatives. Indeed he was always sensitive to baronial pressure and at the end of his reign allowed the government to be virtually taken over by his son, John of Gaunt, Duke of Lancaster. After Edward died his grandson, Richard II, was defied by the magnates of the realm known as the Lords Appellant who seized all power. In France Charles V, a sedentary ruler, was succeeded by a child King who later went mad and was dominated by his uncles. In Castile Pedro I was overthrown by Henry of Trastamara and other nobles. As neither of the Roberts came to the throne until they were in their middle fifties (about the same age as Robert I had reached when he died) it was hardly surprising that they found difficulty in withstanding their nobility – who in any case regarded them merely as the first among equals – and rather than engage in pointless wars with England preferred to look for peaceable methods of governing.

Before he became King the first Robert Stewart, son of Walter the Beardless acted as Guardian for Bruce's son, David II, during his minority and afterwards. But as Robert the Steward himself was only a stripling when David II succeeded, other Guardians had first to struggle with the problems of the time. Edward Balliol, the son of John Balliol, a more ambitious man than his father, promptly invoked the help of Edward III to secure the Scottish throne for himself instead of letting it be inherited by Robert Bruce's son, in return for a promise that Edward should receive his homage for the kingdom of Scotland. The first Guardian of the Bruce's son, Thomas Randolph Earl of Moray who had fought so bravely at Bannockburn, was thus as once confronted with a threat to internal peace; before he could cope with it he died, just eight months after David's coronation. The second Guardian, Donald Earl of Mar, was defeated and killed by Balliol in 1332. Sir Andrew Moray, the brother-in-law of Robert Bruce, who replaced the Earl of Mar as Guardian of the realm, was captured by Edward Balliol at Roxburgh on the border. Then the fourth Guardian, Sir Archibald Douglas, in attempting to relieve Berwick, besieged by the English, was defeated and killed at the battle of Halidon hill. Robert the Steward, who fought in that battle, managed to escape to Dumbarton, where David II and his Queen had been sent for safety. So successful were Edward Balliol and his English sponsors that he was crowned at Scone and able to hold a parliament in Edinburgh. David II and his wife fled to France, Balliol handed over much of the Lowlands to Edward III, and thus, after all, the Balliols succeeded in ousting the Bruces.

It was not until 1334, when the exiled David II was aged ten, that Robert the Steward and John Randolph Earl of Moray (son of the hero of Bannockburn) became his joint Guardians. Both relatively young, they overran south-west Scotland; but Edward III called up a large army which forced Robert the Steward and other nobles to agree to a pacification at Perth in August 1335. Thus Robert was compelled to abandon his Guardianship, but another Guardian, Sir Andrew Moray (for the second time), who had been released on the payment of a ransom, carried on guerrilla warfare against Balliol and the English with a fair amount of success.

When Moray died in 1338 Robert Stewart, who was still only twenty-two, was once more appointed Guardian. Now in the absence of Edward III, who was fighting in France, Robert secured the surrender of Perth, where he was able to summon a parliament. In 1341 Edinburgh castle was wrested from the English; in that same year David II at the age of seventeen returned from France to take up the duties and pleasures of kingship. Thus Robert Stewart's second and by no means unprosperous tenure of office drew to an end. Even then as David II's heir presumptive he was the most notable figure in the land after the King. It was through his influence that Sir William Douglas, who had played a leading part in fighting the English during David's absence in France, was pardoned for killing a rival in a feud

over possessions on the borders. As a reward for his loyalty David II
presented the Steward with the earldom of Atholl in 1342.

Then came the crux in David's reign. The Scots had concluded an
offensive and defensive alliance with the French. So when Edward III
overran Normandy and won the battle of Crécy in 1346, the Scots felt it was
their duty to assist their ally by invading England. A battle was fought at
Neville's Crosssnear Durham in which the Scots, formed into three
brigades, though they appear to have taken the English by surprise, were
overwhelmed by arrows from the opposing bowmen. David II himself was
wounded and made a prisoner, John Randolph Earl of Moray was killed,
and four other earls were captured. Altogether fifty Scottish barons were
killed or imprisoned. The third brigade, led by Robert the Steward, along
with the Earl of March, withdrew safely from the field.

Both English chroniclers and later Scottish historians have made a
mockery of Robert the Steward by saying that he turned tail, returned to
Scotland, 'and thus led off the dance, leaving David to caper as he wished'.
Still, if the Steward had not got back to Scotland with the remnant of the
royal forces, drawn off in good order, Edward III could, by exploiting his
victories over the Scots as well as the French, have achieved the aim of
destroying Scottish independence, won with so much heroism by David II's
father.

For eleven years David remained a close prisoner in the Tower of London
except for one brief visit to Scotland on parole. During that time Robert
Stewart was acknowledged as ruler of Scotland on David's behalf; he was
entitled the King's Lieutenant, appointed sheriffs, and tried to maintain
order as best he could. But the task was arduous. In the first place, Edward
Balliol, though confined to an island off Galloway, still claimed to be the
rightful King and had a nuisance value; secondly, the capture of so many
earls and barons at Neville's Cross meant that the normal machinery of
government was unable to function properly; lastly, the Popes, now exiled
from Rome to Avignon, imposed demands on the Scottish Church which
weakened it considerably. In the light of these handicaps Robert did not
manage too badly. By marrying his eldest daughter to the semi-
independent magnate, John MacDonald of the Isles (the Western Isles) he
staunched trouble in the Highlands, while by holding on to Edinburgh,
Stirling and Dunbar castles he prevented English penetration beyond the
Forth. When, at the beginning of 1356, Edward III invaded Scotland for
the last time, intending to claim the Crown for himself, a scorched earth
strategy forced him to withdraw. At no time was Robert the Steward
disloyal to David II.

Negotiations for David's release from imprisonment in London were initiated by David himself. In 1350 he had informed Pope Clement VI that Edward III was demanding, among other things, homage, military service against France, and the recognition of himself as David's heir if the Scottish King died childless. These terms were still unacceptable. Two years later Edward III modified them by asking for a large ransom and the succession of one of his younger sons to the Scottish throne if David had no direct heir. When David himself presented these terms to a Scottish parliament, meeting at Scone in 1352, they were unanimously rejected. It was not until 1357 when Robert the Steward dispatched an impressive embassy to the English Court that it was agreed by Edward that in return for the large payment of 100,000 merks, guaranteed by hostages to be sent to London, David would be restored to the throne without any political conditions except for a ten-year truce. Before the King returned home the Steward persuaded the three Estates to endorse the terms of the treaty.

Unquestionably David himself would have been perfectly willing to consent to the Scottish throne being handed over after his own death to Edward III or one of his sons, though he was not prepared to do homage to the English King during his own lifetime, as the two Balliols had done. If the Plantagenets had become kings of Scotland as well as of England and Wales, whatever paper guarantees were given, Scotland would almost certainly have been ruled from London, as it was to be from the time of James VI onwards. David was happy that if he had no children a member of the English royal line should follow him as Scottish king. Indeed he proposed this to a parliament in March 1364. But in the words of John Major, 'the three Estates used no delay in rejecting the propositions of the King of the Scots, declaring that there was not lacking a rightful heir to the kingdom and one mature in years after his decease and that they would be no party of his disinheritance'.

Although Robert the Steward had been scrupulously faithful to him, David clearly did not want his nephew to become the next king. This is shown by the fact that he soon stopped paying his ransom, which would have given the King of England an admirable excuse to impose political demands on Scotland. Furthermore he abandoned his English wife, Edward III's sister — another highly provocative step — and married his beautiful mistress, Margaret Logie, a Drummond by birth, in the hope that she would give him an heir; then when she failed to do so, he planned to marry another of his mistresses. It is hardly surprising that Robert the Steward resented this behaviour, demonstrated against it on his own behalf, and briefly suffered imprisonment at the behest of David's second wife.

Whether it is true, as has lately been argued, that in spite of his long absences in London and in spite of his bleeding his kingdom to meet his ransom, while keeping much of the money to pay for his own extravagances, David II was a worthy successor to his father may be questioned. At any rate when he died in Edinburgh at the age of forty-seven Robert II inherited many difficult problems.

The chronicler, John Fordun, described the first Stewart King of Scotland as 'tall and modest, liberal, gay and courteous and for the innate sweetness of his disposition generally beloved by true-hearted Scotsmen'. Another chronicler, the author of the *Book of Pluscarden*, wrote: 'he was right noble, handsome and had a fine figure and was amiable and popular with everyone. In his time there was great fruitfulness and plenteousness of wealth, peace and prosperity and friendly unity among the magnates of the realm.' Apart from hunting, which was to be a passion with all the Stewarts down to the time of James VII, his chief hobby was women. He was twice married: first to Elizabeth Mure, who had been his mistress, and then to Euphemia, daughter of the Earl of Ross; he had thirteen children and at least eight illegitimate children so that, as has recently been observed, 'the nobility of Scotland looked destined to be saturated with prolific Stewarts'. The monkish chroniclers could not approve of that. The author of the *Book of Pluscarden* added to his words of praise 'Because he begat many children outside the bonds of wedlock they therefore did not turn out as well in the end . . .

> In bastards' character three stamps receives
> They're always pompous, lecherous and thieves.'

Robert Stewart's popularity was clearly shown in the parliament of 1364 when David II's proposal that Edward III should be his heir was unanimously rejected. Understandably Robert had stood up for his rights, which had been solemnly affirmed in the reign of his grandfather, Robert the Bruce. Though David II made Robert swear to be faithful after he had recorded his remonstrances, it was only when his right to succeed was in peril that the Steward resisted the Bruce's son. He was no great soldier, as was shown by his conduct at the battle of Neville's Cross. He realized that after the spasmodic wars against England what Scotland needed was an interval of peace. The previous reigns had seen not only battles and rebellions but also floods and pestilences. Robert felt genuine concern for the common people.

To describe his reign as prosperous is an exaggeration, but the peace that he sought stimulated commerce and opened up trade with England. Although he ratified a treaty with France seven months after his coronation, the truce with England, concluded during the previous reign, still had thirteen years to run. The new King saw to it that the ransom money for David II, which had to be paid annually even after his death, was punctually met. The English therefore had no cause of grievance against the Scots, while the death of Edward III, which took place in 1377, left a boy of ten, Richard II, as King. It was not until the year after the truce expired in 1385 that Richard, provoked by the unruly behaviour of the Scottish lords of the marches, followed in his grandfather's footsteps and invaded Scotland.

To start with, Robert II relied very much on his own rapidly expanding family to help him in governing his kingdom. His brother, another Robert Stewart Earl of Fife and Menteith was appointed his Chamberlain to administer the royal finances. By 1377 seven out of the sixteen earldoms were held by the monarch or his relatives. It has been noticed that his eldest daughter had been married to the powerful and independent Lord of the Western Isles. His Constable, John Dunbar Earl of Moray, also became one of his sons-in-law. Because he was so anxious to keep the peace at home and abroad Robert II is usually described as feeble and lacking in energy. But it should be remembered that when the warrior king, Edward III of England, reached Robert II's age at his accession, he adopted exactly the same policy of intermarriage with and bribery of his magnates to maintain quiet at home.

Nevertheless Robert found it harder and harder to maintain law and order in his turbulent kingdom; he earnestly wanted to do so, but unrest on the borders and in the Highlands had long been endemic and proved almost impossible to repress. So too was the habit of the Scottish nobility of murdering one another, usually with impunity. When in 1382 one of the King's own nephews (Sir John Lindsay) killed one of his sons-in-law (Sir John Lyon) he escaped punishment. It may be recalled that the Bruce himself had committed murder in a church and though excommunicated by the Pope, was promptly crowned King. Nearing seventy, Robert II found the strain of office severe; so he assented to his eldest son, John Earl of Carrick, being appointed specifically as his Lieutenant of the Realm to enforce order.

The undeclared warfare on the borders with England, together with disputes between subjects of the two kingdoms at sea meant that as soon as the long truce expired both sides had to prepare for war. In August 1383 Robert II ratified a defensive agreement with France; so seriously did the French rulers take it that in May 1385 the experienced French admiral,

John de Vienne, came to Scotland with over a thousand knights and men-at-arms to helpihim. It was arranged that the Scots and the French should invade England, but as soon as an army under Richard II's uncle, John of Gaunt Duke of Lancaster, appeared, the allies withdrew across the frontier and allowed Edinburgh to be set on fire by the enemy. Once again a scorched earth strategy frustrated King Robert's opponents. After they retired the northern counties in England were sacked and plundered by the Scots in revenge. A truce followed which only lasted until June 1388. In that year the Scots alone (the French contingent having left in disgust, the scorched earth policy not being to the taste of the French chivalry) again crossed the border to inflict a severe defeat on Henry Percy, younger son of the Earl of Northumberland, in August at Otterburn or Chevy Chase, forty miles north-west of Newcastle.

By now the first Stewart King had reached the age of seventy-two and had virtually ceased to be in active control of the country. A General Council, held at Edinburgh on 1 December, decided that as neither he nor his eldest son, John Earl of Carrick, who had experienced the misfortune of being violently kicked by a horse, was capable of maintaining internal and external order, Robert's second son, the Earl of Fife and Menteith, should be appointed as Guardian of the realm for the time being. By now Archibald the Grim third Earl of Douglas — the Black Douglas — and George Douglas Earl of Angus — the first of the Red Douglases — had become the most militant magnates in the kingdom, just as the Dukes of Lancaster and Gloucester were during Richard II's minority in England. Though the first Stewart had thus lost command over his secular lords, the author of the *Book of Pluscarden* wrote kindly of him at the end of his reign: 'Thus was the kingdom pacified after much tribulation and abode in the most blissful prosperity for years and years.'

After a brief illness Robert II 'gave up the ghost, paying the debt of nature'; and he lay 'honourably entombed at Scone', having died on 19 April 1390, leaving the kingdom, so this chronicler declared, 'in quiet, freedom, fruitfulness and peace'. But John Major, writing in the next century, felt compelled to say: 'I cannot hold this aged King . . . to have been a skilful warrior or wise in counsel.' To be a man of peace was not thought highly of in the Middle Ages.

Robert II's eldest son, John Earl of Carrick, took after his father in character and looks. He was tall with a florid countenance and a long white beard which 'gave a look of singular sanctity to his appearance'. He never fully recovered from the kick he had received from a horse belonging to Sir James Douglas of Dalkeith — the Douglases were rarely agreeable to the

Stewarts. He must also have been mentally hurt by the fact that the three Estates of the realm had removed him from the office of Lieutenant responsible for law and order after he had held the position for only four years. But he started his reign with a flourish. He decided that John was an unpropitious name for a Scottish monarch: King John II of France had been captured by Edward III at the battle of Poitiers to die a prisoner in London; King John of England had been humiliated by his barons into sealing Magna Carta and lost all his treasure and jewels in a whirlpool just before his death; John Balliol (could he be called King John I of Scotland? – Scottish historians don't usually do so) had his reign cut short and withdrew into exile in France. So John changed his name to Robert after his father and grandfather. He was married to Annabella Drummond, a niece of Margaret Drummond, King David II's second wife, evidently a lady belonging to an attractive family. Another Margaret Drummond was to be the mistress of King James IV. The Drummonds may be compared to the Villiers family which was to provide favourites for the English Stuart kings in the seventeenth century.

Like his father, Robert III was prolific in spite of the horse's kick. He had three sons and four daughters and at least two illegitimate sons, both of whom were, like his second legitimate son, named James. Some of his enemies claimed that Robert himself was illegitimate because his father had been living with his mother 'in canonical incest' (that is to say they were related) before a dispensation was procured from the Pope to put matters right. Like his father, Robert III showed care for ordinary people. When during his coronation in August 1394 the ripening corn was trodden down by the crowds attending the ceremony he insisted that the monks who were growing it should be compensated.

For seven or eight years after Robert III's succession the country, particularly the Highlands, continued to be in a state of discord. Robert's brother, Alexander Stewart Earl of Buchan, a ferocious character known as 'the Wolf of Badenoch', started the ball rolling by setting on fire the town and cathedral of Elgin in the neighbouring county of Moray to the anger of the Bishop there, whom he had been blackmailing. Buchan got off scotfree. John Lord of the Isles, the husband of Robert III's sister, Margaret, was also prominent in defying law and order. In Aberdeenshire Sir Robert Keith tried to kidnap his aunt, but was frustrated in battle by her husband. The county of Angus, famed for its beef, was devastated by Highland robbers known as 'caterans'. The only solution that the King could find when the Highland clans clashed was to preside over a mortal combat between thirty warriors on either side, an episode celebrated by Sir Walter Scott in his novel, *The Fair Maid of Perth*, but this solution was ineffective in bringing anarchy to a halt. In 1397 the three Estates demanded that an expedition should be dispatched by the King to the Hebrides to impose peace and stop the destruction, arson and slaughter there. Everywhere the sheriffs were ordered to arrest offenders while the justices on circuit were told to make sure that the sheriffs were doing their duty.

In 1398 Robert III, imitating the example set by Richard II of England, introduced the title of duke. Robert's eldest son, David Earl of Carrick, was created Duke of Rothesay and his brother Robert Earl of Fife was made Duke of Albany. The King relied principally on these new dukes to help him govern the kingdom. A General Council, meeting in January 1399, blamed the chaotic state of the country on the King 'and his officers' particularly the Duke of Albany. The three Estates therefore asked that the Duke of Rothesay should be appointed the King's Lieutenant for three years to punish the guilty and reward the penitent: he was provided with the counsel of twenty-one wise men. But Rothesay had little success in the performance of these duties. Indeed he managed to annoy the Earl of March by jilting his daughter in order to marry the wealthier daughter of the third Earl of Douglas, whereupon March moved into England and joined the Percys of Northumberland, who were still smarting over their defeat at Otterburn, and together they began laying waste the border country.

After the close of the fourteenth century the situation in the Lowlands was complicated by the fact that the first Lancastrian King of England, Henry IV, who had usurped the throne of Richard II, was induced by the aggrieved Earl of March to lend him his support against Robert III and his eldest son. Henry therefore demanded the homage of the Scots King and marched with an army on Edinburgh. However, the King of England was more of a diplomat than a general, who needed to consolidate his position in his own country before engaging in foreign adventures. He rapidly withdrew from Scotland and peace negotiations were opened.

Soon after this Rothesay's three-year term of office as royal lieutenant expired. His mother and his father-in-law were now dead while the Prince was left without any powerful friend. His father was persuaded that he had failed in the task that he had been allotted, had been foolish and corrupt, abandoning himself to obscure 'evil courses'. So Robert III ordered his brother, the Duke of Albany, to arrest his son and confine him until he mended his ways. Rothesay was placed in custody at Falkland castle in Fife, where he died in March 1402: nobody knows for certain what happened to him, but his father exonerated David's uncle from the crime of murder. The parallel with the fate of Richard II of England, who was incarcerated in

Pontefract castle, where he had perished two years earlier, is quite extraordinary: both of them were said to have starved themselves to death; both were in all probability murdered.

Now Robert III was left with only one legitimate son, James, who was eight. In that same year the frontier war with England was renewed; the English raided Lothian, to which the Scots retorted by laying waste Northumberland. At the Battle of Homildon hill, fought in Northumberland on 14 September 1402, the Scots were defeated by Henry Percy, who thus avenged the battle of Otterburn fourteen years earlier, and the Duke of Albany's son, Murdoch Stewart, was taken prisoner as well as the fourth Earl of Douglas, who bore the nickname of the Tyneman, which meant the Loser. Whether through fear of the English or of the ambitions of the Duke of Albany, three and a half years later Robert III resolved to send his only surviving son to France there to be educated in safety. If the King had aranged this more secretly, all would have been well. As it was, the boy James, after some adventures, embarked on a ship from Danzig, which was captured by English freebooters off Flamborough head. The news was brought to Robert III as he was supping at Rothesay castle. According to the author of the *Book of Pluscarden*, he gave way 'to piteous sighs and bitter grief'. In the spring of 1406 'by reason of the fierce anguish of his heart he was, at it were, half-dead and his spirit drooped so that he never took food with good heart until he have up the ghost to the Most High at the castle of Bute'. This was on Palm Sunday, 4 April 1406. Before he died he asked that his body should be buried 'deep in a midden' and that his epitaph should be: 'Here lies the worst of kings and the most wretched of men in the whole realm.' He was in fact entombed in the abbey church at Paisley in front of the high altar.

A nineteenth-century historian was to observe that because Robert III's nature 'was sweet, pacific and indolent' he was unable to 'overawe and control the fierce passions and resentments of the barons'. This verdict was largely based upon that of the abbot, Walter Bower, who wrote in the fifteenth century. Bower also said that 'in the days of this King there was in the realm great fertility of victuals but the greatest discord between the magnates and the nobles because the King, weak in body, nowhere exercised rigour'. Yet it needs to be emphasized that, as in England, these were the days of what has been called 'bastard feudalism', when new loyalties or affinities were cutting across the old, undermining the monarchy by creating lordships which overawed the courts of law and royal officials. Since the King no longer commanded his earls and barons through feudal tenure he had to purchase their loyalty as best he could by pensions and bribes. That is what Robert II, Robert III and the unfortunate Duke of Rothesay all attempted to do. It can be argued, as one Scottish historian has done, that in the dread of making anyone their enemies they made no one their friends. One of the paradoxes of medieval history is that kings who were anxious to be considerate to the poor, to avoid foreign wars, and to promote trade and economic well-being, were rarely at the same time sufficiently strong to overcome the anarchy created by mighty subjects, who were undisciplined and selfish. Thus, as John Major wrote, Robert III was 'a good man, but in no way a good king'. The same thing could be said of the first Stewart monarch. When James, the third Stewart king, at last returned from his captivity in England a different story was to unfold.

The chronicle of John of Fordun, who wrote during the reign of Robert II, was edited and translated by W. F. Skene; its continuation by Walter Bower, who wrote the *Scotichronicon* in the reign of James II, has not yet been translated from the Latin. The *Liber Pluscardensis*, a chronicle largely founded on Bower, was edited and translated by Felix H. Skene (1880). John Major, who wrote his *History of Greater Britain* in 1521, was edited and translated by Archibald Constable, S.H.S. (1892). The leading modern authority for the period of David II and Robert II and III is Ranald Nicholson: besides his book on the *Later Middle Ages* he has written on *Edward III and the Scots* (1965) and on 'David II, the Historians and the Chroniclers', *S.H.R.* xlv (1966). His spirited defence of David II, who used to be dubbed one of the worst of the Scottish kings, has not yet been generally accepted, though to call him 'a petulant and impulsive boy who was unable to bridle his nobles and allowed lawlessness to prevail', as Agnes Muir Mackenzie did in her book, *The Rise of the Stewarts* (1935), is an exaggeration.

4

James I and the
Unification of Scotland

KING JAMES I, who had been born at Dunfermline in July 1394, was not yet twelve years old when he was lodged in the Tower of London as a prisoner of the English Crown in honourable captivity. Here, as he recalled later, he lived 'a deadly life full of pain and penance' and he bewailed his misfortune, envying the freedom of the birds and beasts and even the fishes in the sea. He continued to suffer in discomfort and sorrow for eighteen years; he had reached the age of twenty-nine when he was at last permitted to return to Scotland to be crowned.

James remained a prisoner so long for two reasons: one was that both the first Lancastrian Kings of England were involved in hostilities with France, defensively in the case of Henry IV, offensively in the case of Henry V. The French had been angered by the overthrow of Richard II, who had been married to a French princess, whom Henry IV promptly packed off home, so angry that they gave their recognition to a pseudo-Richard II, a pretender known as the Mammet (or impostor) who turned up in Scotland where he was treated seriously and did not die until 1419. A Scottish-French alliance had been twice renewed during the reign of Robert III and though intermittent truces were agreed the Scots were always ready to strike across the border when the King of England was absent fighting in France. Some prospect of James I's release came about towards the end of Henry IV's reign after the Scots King started writing letters to his uncle, the first Duke of Albany, the fourth Earl of Douglas and others on his own behalf. But the succession of Henry V in 1413 put an end to his hopes of release: the new King of England was actually to take James with him to France after his victory at Agincourt so as to persuade the Scots who were in the service of the French monarch to change sides. 'But the Scots', we are told, held 'the King in small esteem' and remained loyal to the Dauphin, Charles VI's son, the future Charles VII.

The other reason why James's release was long delayed was that the Regent or Governor of Scotland, his uncle, Robert Stewart Duke of Albany, failed to exert sufficient pressure on his behalf. In February 1416, four months after Agincourt, Albany procured the release of his own son and heir, Murdoch, who had been taken prisoner at the battle of Homildon hill, in return for a ransom of £10,000; but when in July 1415 the Scots broke a six-year truce by raiding across the English border, in order to help the French, that action was well calculated to diminish the chances of James's release. After being generously treated by Henry IV, James was thrust back into the Tower by Henry V and, though later allowed out for a short time, was sent back there again in 1416, the year when Murdoch Stewart was freed. In the following year the Duke of Albany, still at war with England, besieged Berwick while the fourth Earl of Douglas, one of the closest of Albany's associates, besieged Roxburgh, both in English hands; though neither siege succeeded, war was endemic along the frontier. Four years later Archibald Earl of Wigtown, Douglas's son, and James Stewart Earl of Buchan, Albany's son, were fighting against the English in France where they defeated a small force at the battle of Baugé, killing Henry V's brother and heir presumptive, the Earl of Clarence. Naturally exacerbated, Henry V determined to hang on to the possession of the Scottish King, who was obliged to accompany him again to France that year. Previously James had been present at Henry V's wedding to Princess Catherine of France, daughter of Charles VI, then recognized as heiress apparent to the French throne. Only just over another year later James attended the funeral of Henry V, who died unexpectedly at the age of thirty-five when his ambition to be the ruler of both France and England was within reach of fulfilment. A year earlier the octogenarian Duke of Albany also died. Thus a real opportunity for James's return was created. On 4 December 1423 a treaty with the regency in England (Henry VI was a baby) was signed in London providing for James's release in return for a payment of 60,000 merks (about £45,000) spread over six years; nobles were to be sent as hostages to England to guarantee the payment of this large sum, euphemistically described as the reimbursement of the expenses of James's long stay with two Lancastrian Kings.

What sort of man had James Stewart grown to be during his sojourn in England and visits to France? He was of middle height, strong and broad-shouldered with a tendency to stoutness — 'oppressed by his excessive corpulence' was the way it was expressed by one who met him later in life. His portraits show him to have been dark with auburn hair, thick eyebrows, a pointed beard, fine eyes and a sensitive and intelligent look. He was an athlete, capable, according to John Major, of throwing the hammer further than anyone, while he excelled in drawing the bow, wielding the lance, in horsemanship, wrestling and running. At the same time he was a trained musician, sang beautifully, accompanying himself on the harp, composed music and became skilful in writing Scottish poetry. Many of his works and songs were still remembered as 'the best of their kind' in the sixteenth century. It is doubtful if James acquired his artistic tastes from proximity to Henry V, who was a tough soldier and religious fanatic rather than the chivalrous prince of Shakespeare's plays, but he emulated the English King's athleticism. He could also have learnt at the Court of the two Henrys the need to have an adequate income, the importance of royal displays to dazzle the multitude, and the necessity of disciplining the nobility.

While James was in exile his uncle, the Duke of Albany, had been so much the Regent that he assumed royal prerogatives, having his own great seal struck and publishing charters in his own name. The Duke was in fact one of the most remarkable of the Stewart rulers of Scotland. Although he did not bear the title of king, he governed the country for fourteen years, which was longer than James I was to do. Contemporary chroniclers praised him highly, especially because of his care for the poor. Walter Bower Abbot of Inchcolm wrote, for instance, that 'he sought the blessings of the common people beyond measure', while a distinguished modern historian tells us that 'in the second year of his governorship he was to be found with a concourse of nobles supervising the narrowing of a street in Ayr to prevent the encroachment of sand'. He did not hold parliaments, which required the presence of the King, but he regularly summoned General Councils to meet at Perth, where his authority was never questioned. He employed the fourth Earl of Douglas to maintain peace in the Lowlands and his own nephew, Alexander Stewart Earl of Mar, an illegitimate son of the Wolf of Badenoch, to take care of the Highlands. He also appointed his second son, John Stewart, to be Earl of Buchan, which lies in north-east Scotland. When his nephew Donald Lord of the Isles menaced the peace of the Highlands by seizing the royal borough of Inverness and threatening to sack Aberdeen and when the Earl of Mar failed to subdue him, Albany himself recovered Dingwall castle, a key post in the earldom of Ross, west of the Moray firth, and in the following year, 1412, raised three armies with which he compelled the Lord of the Isles to hand over hostages and swear on oath to keep the peace. He created his son, the Earl of Buchan, also to be Earl of Ross, thus extending the Stewart possessions in the Highlands. It was during Albany's governorship that Bishop Wardlaw of St Andrews founded the first Scottish university there, while Albany was to accept the advice of the theologians of the university about which Pope should be recognized as the Great Schism in Catholic Europe moved towards its close.

Thus Albany cared for both the safety and spiritual well-being of his country.

Albany has sometimes been described as 'treacherous' and 'the usurper of the throne' because he did not work hard enough to bring about the release of his nephew from his confinement in England and because, it is assumed, he aspired to be King of the Scots in name himself. But, after all, he was the heir presumptive to the throne and could reasonably have considered that as he had proved himself to be a more capable ruler than either of the first two Stewart monarchs he was entitled to continue to govern the kingdom rather than hurry home a completely inexperienced young prince, who was suspected of being an anglophile. Albany was over eighty when he died and still in complete control – a medieval Churchill or Adenauer. His quality was demonstrated by contrast when his son, Murdoch, followed him as Governor and proved to be neither as efficient nor as popular as his father had been. In effect, Albany smoothed the way for the reign of James I, particularly by obtaining what has been called 'the Stewardization of the Highlands'.

As has been seen, James had in fact benefited greatly from his upbringing in England and France. He had been able to study the methods of Henry IV as an administrator and of Henry V as a general. He was in a relatively strong position because after the ransom treaty had been agreed he had married Joan Beaufort, the niece of Henry IV, with whom he had fallen deeply in love and to whom he was always faithful; at the same time he sealed a treaty with the English at Durham providing for a seven-year truce, but without committing himself to withdrawing the Scots, including his cousin, the Earl of Buchan, and the fourth Earl of Douglas, who had been fighting not unsuccessfully for the future Charles VII of France against the English. He announced that it was his first objective to secure law and order in his own kingdom before entering upon foreign adventures. On his return, according to Walter Bower, he exclaimed: 'If God grant me life and aid, even the life of a dog, throughout all the realm I will make the key keep the castle and the bracken bush the cow.'

Five days after his coronation at Scone on 21 May 1424 James met his first parliament in Perth and was compelled to ask it to vote taxes from the Church as well as the State to pay his ransom; this was hardly calculated to make him popular, but he evidently hoped to offset this drain on the national income by stimulating economic growth, descending to minutiae. A new coinage was promised; the export of metals was subjected to tax and later forbidden completely; fines were imposed on fishing for salmon in the closed season; heather was not to be burnt after March; and when rooks' nests were found on trees they were to be cut down. This parliament also passed laws aimed at preventing rebellions and suppressing marauding companies. To increase his military strength the King sought statutes to promote archery, while footballers were fined for playing football. To facilitate the passage of so many measures a committee or commission was appointed to consider the articles put forward by the King and transmute them into effective legislation.

At the second parliament of the reign, which met during the following March this comprehensive programme was extended. Here, though further regulations were passed, for example imposing fines on those who destroyed dovecotes and rabbit warrens and on stalkers who slew deer, more attention was concentrated on the reform of the law. New law courts were set up to relieve pressure on litigation and it was enacted that poor men were to be provided with advocates for whose services they did not have to pay. The third parliament called by the King, which again gathered in Perth, conveniently situated as it was between the Lowlands and Highlands, and therefore intended by James to be his national capital, introduced what came to be known as the Court of Session, the highest court in the land after parliament, which was to be presided over by the Chancellor himself and to be held three times a year.

It used to be thought that not only was James I an innovator in matters of justice but that he also attempted to reform parliament. The suggestion was that when he lived in England he had been impressed by the existence of two Houses of Parliament with the Commons, which were composed of knights of the shire and burgesses, and the Lords containing the secular and spiritual peerage. In fact, of course, in those days the House of Commons had comparatively little influence and though the right of members to petition the Crown, particularly on questions of trade, was accepted, they were usually summoned to vote taxes to pay for war or to meet extraordinary royal expenditure. A proposal was put forward in the Perth parliament of 1428 that the peers of the realm should be called by the king's writ, while the small barons and representatives of the burghs should be excused attendance and instead commissioners chosen in each shire, which should be responsible for the expenses of their representatives, should constitute a Lower House. The latest view, however, is that this revolutionary scheme was put forward not by the King but by the magnates of the realm 'at the instigation of their lesser neighbours and dependents', hoping that their influence over the King could thus be increased because they would have a say in the choice of the shire commissioners. At any rate the scheme was never put into effect and after 1430, when James became confident of his secure hold on his kingdom, parliaments were called less frequently.

The difficulty about evaluating the work done by James I's parliaments in passing innumerable statutes on questions of justice, finance and economic affairs, often going into such detail as how to organize wolf hunts and what was the right time of the year to eat partridges, is first to decide whether the Government itself was really responsible for initiating these measures and secondly how far they worked in practice. Clearly the sheriffs were the maids-of-all-work in these matters and their activities could only be checked from time to time by the justices on ayre. The Chamberlain could be expected to enforce some of the economic regulations and bishops' officers be made liable for attending to matters of health and charity. But investigation of the functioning of administration, as distinct from the simple enactment of new laws, during the Middle Ages has taught us that statutes were frequently dead letters. What James I really did was to put forward a programme of ideal reforms and also to aim at checking the evils of 'bastard feudalism' by tightening up royal justice. In the same way in the Church he wanted to mitigate the harm done to religious life by the growth of pluralism. Unquestionably James was thoroughly aware of the need for improvements in every side of public life, particularly in the maintenance of justice. But it is likely that he was in too much of a hurry to put things right, having been in exile for so long, and that he overburdened the sheriffs and other royal officials with fresh duties. He also built up some resentment among the ruling classes who came to regard him as a tyrant or autocrat. Indeed European rulers who have tried to reform abuses, ranging from Henry II of England to Cardinal Richelieu in France, have invariably provoked angry reactions from the nobility.

After his return to Scotland James I showed at once that he meant to take a firm line with his earls, barons and knights. It is likely that his own resentment over the behaviour of the Albany family was pent up, that he could neither forgive nor forget what his late uncle had done, first in bringing about the mysterious death of his elder brother and then in failing to work harder for his earlier release from his imprisonment by the Kings of England. Yet at first he did not reveal his intentions. It is true that even before his coronation he had ordered the arrest of the second Duke of Albany's eldest son, Sir Walter Stewart, who had been appointed Keeper of Dumbarton castle by his grandfather, but as Walter was obviously lawless and had even disobeyed his own father, his arrest and imprisonment on Bass rock did not necessarily mean that James was proposing to revenge himself on the whole Albany family. But less than a year later, while his second

Parliament was in session, he struck out fiercely. Murdoch Stewart Duke of Albany, his wife Isabella, his father-in-law, Duncan Earl of Lennox, his secretary, Alan Otterburn, and his youngest son, Alexander Stewart, were all placed under arrest and in May 1425 James, supported by most of the other earls in the kingdom, presided over their trials. The only member of Murdoch's family who had escaped arrest was his son, James; he attacked the burgh of Dumbarton, killing the King's uncle, John Stewart, who had replaced Walter as the Keeper, and thence fled to Ireland. No record of the trials survives, but as the death penalty was pronounced on Murdoch, Lennox, Alexander and Walter Stewart, it is reasonable to assume that they were condemned for conspiracy, treason and corruption. After all, the behaviour of Walter and James, two of Murdoch's sons, amounted to open rebellion; and since Alan Otterburn was speedily released, it may well have been because he had provided damning evidence against his master.

Another purpose of these trials was no doubt to reduce the territorial power of the Duke of Albany and his relatives. For between them they held not only large estates in the Lowlands, covering the earldoms of Lennox, Menteith, Streathearn and Fife, while Murdoch's brother, killed in France during the previous year, had been Earl of Buchan and Ross in the Highlands. The first Duke of Albany had built himself one of the most formidable castles in the kingdom in Menteith, not far north of Stirling, where it guarded one of the main routes into the northern Highlands. Falkland castle in Fife, on the way to Perth, also belonged to Albany, and Lennox held the castle of Inchmurrin near Loch Lomond. Thus clearly if all these Stewarts had banded together, Stirling could have been menaced from the north and east and the King's effective dominion have been confined to the southern Lowlands. That surely is what James I must have feared. At any rate Sir Walter Stewart was put to death on the day the trial was concluded; Lennox, Albany and Alexander Stewart were beheaded on the following day. The widowed Duchess of Albany was taken from Doune to be imprisoned in Tantallon castle in the Lowlands.

The forfeiture of the estates of these condemned men therefore not only enlarged the income of the Crown but enhanced the security of the Government. It is hardly likely, as one or two chroniclers hinted, that greed was the main motive of James in bringing his relatives to trial. Murdoch, after all, was the heir presumptive to the throne and in view of his father's obvious ambition for the kingship might well have been suspected of planning to overthrow his cousin, egged on by his three sons, all of whom were reckless and dangerous men, before James had consolidated his own position. But such evidence as remains does suggest that James was thought to have been unnecessarily brutal, particularly since Lennox was an old man of eighty. The tragic episode should certainly have warned other Scottish nobles of the perilous results of conspiracy or rebellion.

Having eliminated any threat to the throne in the Lowlands and southern Highlands, four years later James decided himself to go north and impose order there. The first Duke of Albany had relied upon his nephew, Alexander Stewart Earl of Mar as his military commander in the north. James had also, to begin with, depended upon him and had visited Aberdeen in 1424 to confirm Mar's charters. The King now raised an army and accompanied by the Queen, who had so far presented him only with daughters, who were left behind, rode by way of Aberdeen to Inverness, where he summoned all the Highland chieftains to meet him; they were headed by the young Alexander Donald Lord of the Isles, who had just succeeded his father and had provocatively called himself Earl of Ross, a title that had been held by John Stewart Earl of Buchan, Murdoch's younger brother. Heavy fines were imposed on chieftains who failed to appear; those who came were interviewed one by one in the castle. Three of them were executed; a number of others were imprisoned in various castles; the young Lord of the Isles was sent to Perth. But he had not learnt his lesson. Next year, having escaped, he set fire to Inverness; once more James I had to move north, captured Alexander somewhere in Lochaber and carried him off this time to prison in Tantallon. His overthrow provoked widespread unrest and disorders throughout the northern Highlands.

In 1431 James summoned a parliament and asked it to provide money to pay for a third expedition to the Highlands. The Estates were reluctant to do so unless they were certain that the yield from the taxes they granted was assigned to the specific purpose for which it was required; and they asked the King to release the Lord of the Isles, who was in effect the uncrowned King of the Highlands, so that he could be pressed to exert his authority to restore order on James's behalf. Scottish historians are divided over whether it was politic of the King to release his obstreperous prisoner for the third time and, in general, doubt was expressed about the wisdom of his ruthless conduct in Inverness. A recent verdict is that 'the Highland episode reveals the arbitrary streak in James I's political behaviour and his cupidity' (because he would not allow the proceeds of the taxes raised to be taken out of his own hands). Still his decision worked. James's English Queen Joan intervened on behalf of Alexander Lord of the Isles and after 1431 there was no serious trouble for the time being in the Highlands.

James's marriage to Joan Beaufort adds a romantic note to a reign largely concerned with internal dissensions and hopeful reforms. He fell in love with her in 1423 when he was in captivity at Windsor castle and saw her walking in the gardens. *The King's Quair* or *King's Book*, a poetic allegory written after the style of Chaucer, was either compiled by James or inspired by him and is certainly autobiographical. In it he speaks of 'the fairest and freshest young flower that ever I saw' when he first glimpsed his future wife in the Windsor garden while the nightingales sang. He imagined himself transported to the Court of Venus, who promised her help in winning his love and then sent him on to the palace of Minerva, who told him his love must be founded on virtue. After their marriage James showered presents on Joan, who herself was very generous. They had only one son but six daughters and were happily married. The Queen possessed some political influence and was consulted by her husband on matters of State. After James's death she married another Stewart, Sir James Stewart of Lorne, by whom she had three sons.

One reason why James was able to devote so much of his time to domestic affairs was that throughout almost the whole of his reign peace with England prevailed. That was not because the Scots liked the English; a future Pope, Aeneas Silvius, who came on a mission to Scotland towards the end of the reign, noted that 'nothing pleases the Scots more than the abuse of the English'; but James had an English wife, while in England the King, Henry VI, was a minor. The Lord Protector, Humphrey Duke of Gloucester, was not highly competent and his elder brother, the Duke of Bedford, who was an abler man, was completely absorbed in trying to keep and even extend Henry V's conquests in France. It is true that many Scottish mercenaries fought on the side of Charles VII, who was not crowned King of France until 1429, but Scotland was not officially at war with England. After the Duke of Bedford had in 1424 defeated a Franco-Scottish army at the battle of Verneuil, where two Scottish earls, the fourth Earl of Douglas and James I's cousin, John Stewart Earl of Buchan and Ross, were killed, the English were much less worried by the Scottish help given to the future King of France than they were by that fascinating daughter of God, Joan of Arc. Although in 1428 James promised to renew the 'Auld Alliance', marry his three-year-old daughter Margaret to Charles's equally youthful son, and send 6,000 troops to fight in the French army, these arrangements were not immediately carried out – Princess Margaret did not sail to France until 1436 – and the truce with England was renewed at the end of 1430 for another five years. Before then Joan of Arc inspirited Charles by relieving Orleans and the Duke of Bedford died. The French prospects had thus brightened so much and the English were so hard pressed in France that James decided not to renew the truce with England further, but to lay siege to Berwick and Roxburgh, two of the frontier fortresses that remained in English hands.

James was also able to benefit from the distractions in England to avoid paying over large sums that were owing to the Lancastrian monarchy since his release. Out of the total of 60,000 merks only 9,500 merks were ever paid. Though to guarantee security for these payments noble hostages had been dispatched to England, as promised, James was not unduly concerned about them; on the contrary, it was quite convenient for him to send away members of powerful families who, if left in Scotland, might have moved in opposition to him. For their part, the English had no wish to antagonize the Scottish King when they were up to their ears in the interminable war against France. Thus much of the money provided to meet James I's ransom found its way into his own coffers and was used for such extravagances as building himself a new palace at Linlithgow, reconstructing the castles in Edinburgh and Stirling, buying himself jewels, French and German wines, tapestries and royal barges. He also invested in bombards (stone-throwing machines) and other up-to-date weapons of war, which he brought over from Flanders at a heavy cost. But James was more of an aesthete than a soldier. When in August 1435 he enlisted a large army and tried to batter down Roxburgh castle by cannonade, he was compelled to abandon the siege after a fortnight and leave his expensive new engine and other military apparatus to be acquired by his enemies. His disappointment was profound; he relieved his anger at the failure by summoning a General Council to Edinburgh and promoting there such anti-English regulations as forbidding the purchase of English cloth and ordering English merchants to pay for their Scotch salmon in gold.

James's other main problem abroad was with the Papacy. The election of Martin V in 1417 had brought the Great Schism, when at one time there were three Popes, to an end, but Martin's position was precarious and he was confronted by a conciliar movement which attempted to overrule him. The theologians at St Andrews university, founded when James was a prisoner, supported Martin V, though it had received generous gifts from his rival, Benedict XIII. James vainly tried to persuade Martin to allow him to move the university to Perth, which he aimed to make his capital city. It was not until the end of March 1432 that James confirmed the university's foundation by charter; he then exempted it from royal dues. He was in fact a religious man who displayed a flattering, if somewhat belated, interest in the theological faculty at the university.

James's attempt to remove the university to Perth was symptomatic of his desire to exercise firmer control over the Church; he tried to obtain a concordat with the Papacy which would define clearly his rights in nominating to vacant sees and other benefices. In this effort he received the help of John Cameron Bishop of Glasgow, who was his Chancellor. But the Papacy was alienated by regulations passed by the parliament at Perth which prohibited clerics from going abroad without the permission of the King and banned the purchase of benefices by the clergy or the raising of pensions on them. An example was made of William Croyser the Archdeacon of Teviotdale, a great pluralist, who was deprived by parliament of his benefice on the ground that he was a traitor. Eugenius IV, who succeeded Martin V in 1431, intervened on his behalf; he also sent over a Nuncio to reform the Scottish Church. But no settlement had been reached before James's death on 21 February 1437.

James was assassinated. Two Stewarts were involved in the murder plot against him, his youngest uncle, Walter Earl of Atholl, who was then about seventy-three, and his grandson, Sir Robert Stewart, who was the King's domestic chamberlain. The principal conspirator was Sir Robert Graham, who had been arrested at the time when the second Duke of Albany and his relatives were condemned to death, but had managed to escape from imprisonment at Dunbar into the Highlands to nurse his grievances against the King ever since. Robert Stewart betrayed his trust by admitting the conspirators into the Blackfriars monastery at Perth where James was then residing. He was unarmed and undressed and so easily overpowered. His Queen was wounded and a page boy killed. The causes of the murder are not known with certainty, but Robert Graham claimed he had delivered the kingdom from a cruel tyrant, though it has also been suggested that the aged Earl of Atholl aspired to become the regent for James's son and heir, who was only six. The Scottish people as a whole did not regard James as a tyrant; a hue-and-cry was raised; his murderers were relentlessly hunted down and after being tortured were beheaded in Edinburgh.

Scottish historians are divided over James I's character and career. In a recent book it is stated that he was an autocrat, sometimes cantankerous and vindictive and that his rule was 'totalitarian', which seems anachronistic. James's modern biographer balances his judgment by writing that

> Whatever his faults as a man and a ruler, James was in the main pious, chaste and upright, and he sought with untiring industry to give Scotland domestic peace and firm government. If the purpose of his foreign policy was to abstain from war, he was successful on the whole.

The historian, John Major, who wrote eighty-four years after James's

death, having commended his virtues (by which were meant his piety and
chastity) asserted that he had excelled in the administration of justice and
had tamed the 'Wild Scots', that is to say the Highlanders. To an outsider it
does not seem that there was really such a profound difference in the
character and careers of the first three Stewart Kings except that James was
much younger than his immediate predecessors when he began to govern
and was therefore much tougher and more ruthless. Like them, he had
compassion for the poorer people in his kingdom. For example, when
people murmured because of a tax imposed to pay for his daughter Margaret's marriage to the Dauphin, 'he ordered', Major tells us, that 'the
money collected should be returned to the common people'. Major considered that 'the Stewarts preserved the Scots in the blessings of peace, and
maintained the kingdom that was left to them by the Bruces in undi-
minished state'. It is not easy to differ from that verdict.

James I's long poem, *The King's Quair*, was edited for the S.T.S. by Dr W. W.
Skeat (1911). *The Life and Death of James the First* consists in part of a Latin
chronicle, the *Scotichronicon*, with interpolations, and partly of an English translation of an account of James's murder by someone who accompanied his daughter
Margaret to France. Both were edited by Joseph Stapleson for the Maitland Club
(1837). A modern biography, *James I King of Scots* by E. W. M. Balfour Melville
was published in 1936. The recent book mentioned is the volume by Ranald
Nicholson referred to in Chapter 3.

5

James II – a King Cut off
in His Prime

AT THE AGE OF SIX James II was crowned in Holyrood abbey – it was not yet a palace, although his great-grandfather, John of Gaunt, had been lavishly entertained there. The new King was to be known as James of the Fiery Face because he had on one cheek a broad red mole as a birthmark, which gave him a somewhat sinister look as he grew to manhood. His father's murderers were all dead including his aged uncle, his only genuine rival for the succession. What happened now was that much manoeuvring for position took place, the question which was first fought over being who was to be Lieutenant-General or in effect Guardian for the King. In the end Archibald fifth Earl of Douglas, the son of Archibald the Loser, who had been killed in battle in France, was selected by the Council of the Three Estates for the post. Two years later Alexander Lord of the Isles, whom James I had compelled to submit to his authority, was appointed Justiciar to keep order in the Highlands and in return was accepted as Earl of Ross, the territory that stretched right across the north of Scotland as far as Inverness; it had been claimed by John Stewart Earl of Buchan, but he had been killed in 1424. John Cameron Bishop of Glasgow, who had been James I's Chancellor and chief Minister (he has been described as 'the able Minister of the ablest of the Stewarts'), was retained in office while Queen Joan, who had been vigorous in hunting down her husband's assassins, was permitted to look after her son, given an income of 4,000 merks a year, and assigned Stirling castle as her residence, but she was not chosen as Regent: the Scots would not have cared to be ruled by an Englishwoman.

Thus James II, unlike his father, was brought up in Scotland and had ample opportunity to study the seamy side of Scottish political life. Unlike the two Roberts he was to become the effective ruler of his kingdom when he was a young man. But at first he was the victim of intrigues and counter-intrigues. His mother naturally aimed to take him to Stirling as the castle there had been allotted to her, but the Keeper of Edinburgh castle, Sir William Crichton, who had been a trusted servant of James I and was also sheriff of Edinburgh, was anxious to avoid losing control of the boy King and wanted to hold him there. However, Queen Joan enterprisingly managed to smuggle him out of the castle and carry him away to Stirling where he was enthusiastically greeted by the Keeper, Sir Alexander Livingston of Callendar.

Both Crichton and Livingston tried to enlist the help of the Guardian, the fifth Earl of Douglas, but when he refused to back either of them, they came to an agreement with one another which virtually amounted to a coup d'état. The Queen Mother and her second husband, another Stewart known as Sir James, the Black Knight of Lorne (reputedly more interested in her money than her looks) were imprisoned until Joan, frightened about the fate of her new husband, separated from her in a dungeon down below, agreed to hand over her son to Livingston's care, lend her son the castle, and convey to Livingston the income of 4,000 merks that had been granted her. Crichton replaced Cameron as Chancellor and assented to these arrangements.

Meanwhile the Earl of Douglas, who had proved disinterested in the welfare of the kingdom, died of plague; he was not replaced as Guardian or Lieutenant-General, though his son, the sixth Earl, a conceited but inexperienced youngster, optimistically aspired to that post, but was quickly frustrated. The Livingstons and the Crichtons were not going to stand for that, though they still distrusted each other. Indeed Crichton succeeded in kidnapping the King, when he had reached the age of nine, while he was playing happily in the garden at Stirling, and carried him off to Edinburgh; Livingston swallowed the insult, preferring to take it lying down. While James was in Edinburgh again Crichton invited the young Earl of Douglas and his brother David to a feast at the castle. As they were finishing their meal armed men came in and seized them, led them out to the castle wall and struck off their heads. Crichton told James, when he pleaded for their lives, that they were traitors. It was a searing experience for the boy King, which he never forgot.

Whatever they may have been charged with, it seems certain that the next Earl of Douglas, known as James the Gross because of his bulkiness, who had been the great-uncle of his predecessor, connived at these shocking proceedings and thus was able to inherit the vast Douglas estates. He did not enjoy them for long. Two and a half years later he died; his eldest son, William, the eighth Earl, succeeded and also became Earl of Avondale, an earldom he obtained through marriage, arranged (with a papal dispensation) by his father, to his cousin Margaret of Galloway when she was eleven years old, after he himself had been divorced. William also became Lord of

Bothwell and Galloway. The acquisition of all these earldoms and lordships had made this young nobleman the richest and most influential figure in the Lowlands; so it was natural enough that by 1444, with the aid of the Livingstons, he assumed the title of Lieutenant-General that had been held by the fifth Earl.

When James attained the age of fourteen, nominally the age of discretion, on 16 October 1444, the manoeuvring for political position was intensified. A new character entered the stage in the person of James Kennedy Bishop of St Andrews, a nephew of James I, who had appointed him Bishop of Dunkeld, and was in high favour with the Pope Eugenius IV. To start with, Kennedy allied himself with Crichton, who still controlled Edinburgh, the Queen Mother, and James Douglas third Earl of Angus (the Red Douglas) and for a short time he replaced Crichton as Chancellor, but then yielded place to James Bruce, who had succeeded him as Bishop of Dunkeld. Thus arose contests for power between the Black Douglases and the Red Douglases, between Kennedy and Bruce, between the Crichtons and the Livingstons and between the Homes and the Hepburns, baronial families whose estates lay near the English border, and also between the Lindsays and Ogilvies, baronial families in the southern Highlands. When the Queen Mother died in July 1445 Kennedy thought it wise to withdraw from the fray, while the Black Douglases organized raids to ravage his lands and properties. Kennedy, it is related, 'solemnly cursed his enemies with mitre and staff, book and candle' though as 'a man of singular virtue and prudence he held himself very quiet awaiting upon a better future'. By retiring into St Andrews castle he evaded capture himself. So young William Douglas became virtually supreme in the kingdom, but his attention was for a time diverted from domestic squabbles because hostilities with England had been renewed.

The war with England turned out to be brief and of little significance. Raids were carried out by both sides across the borders, setting fire to each other's castles; honour being satisfied, a truce was concluded in November 1449. The ruling classes in England were in far too much trouble of their own to be concerned much over Scotland. They were being steadily defeated in France where soon nothing remained of all Henry V's conquests except Calais. His son, Henry VI, after he had grown to manhood was cultured and amiable, but soon showed that he possessed little capacity for government; had it not been for the determination of his wife, Margaret of Anjou, he might quickly have lost his throne. As it was, events were moving fast towards civil war. So while the English, divided among themselves, were fighting their losing war in France, the French King, Charles VII, was glad enough to strengthen the family ties with Scotland. Two of his allies, the Dukes of Burgundy and Guelders (in the Netherlands), were involved in the negotiations: on 3 July 1449 James II married Mary of Guelders in Holyrood abbey after she had been promised a handsome dowry.

James was now nineteen and a married man. Like his father, he deeply resented the way in which he had been treated during his minority and was particularly angered by the manner in which the Livingstons had behaved towards his mother. But unlike his father, he proved himself a fighter, a soldiers' king, strong and courageous, a man of action, a man of the sword and the chase. First he turned his attention to the Livingstons who were accused of peculation. Their 'itching fingers', it has been said, 'had grasped one lucrative post after another: Comptroller, Chamberlain, and Warden of the Mint, the Captains of the castles of Stirling, Dumbarton, Doune and Methven — all were Livingstons'. Since the Comptroller and the Chamberlain were responsible for the royal finances their opportunities for embezzlement were legion. At the first parliament over which James II presided, held in January 1450, two of the Livingston family, including the Comptroller, were condemned for treason and not only hanged but beheaded; other Livingstons and their friends were sent to prison. Their powerful ally, the eighth Earl of Douglas made no attempt to save them; on the contrary, he lent the King money and departed on a pilgrimage to Rome. James was in desperate need of funds. He had promised his wife an unusually large income; indeed his want of money was one of the motives for his attacking the Livingstons so swiftly, although he was also moved by indignation over their treatment of his mother. Furthermore, taking advantage of William Douglas's absence in Rome, James, wrote a chronicler, 'besieged all the castles of the Earl and slew many of his free tenants'. When Douglas returned to Scotland in the spring of 1451 a temporary agreement was concluded. The Earl resigned all his lands into the King's hands and the King restored them to him as well as all his offices except the earldom of Wigtown, which he had assigned to one of his loyal servants.

What had in fact been a capitulation by James to a powerful subject merely induced Earl William to defiance. Allying himself with the Earl of Crawford, known as the Tiger Earl, and the young John Donald Lord of the Isles and Earl of Ross, who had succeeded to his father's dominance over the Highlands in May 1449, Douglas challenged the King's authority, even attempting to kidnap his Chancellor, William Crichton. But James, though compelled to climb down for the time being in 1450 and 1451, was only awaiting an opportunity to bring his mightiest subjects to heel. In February 1452 he sent for the Earl, giving him a safe conduct to Stirling castle, where a confrontation took place. James demanded that Douglas should break his alliance or 'bond' with Crawford and Ross. When after supper on 21 February Douglas refused, James exclaimed 'false traitor! if you will not, I shall'. He then struck him down with a knife; one of his courtiers, Patrick Gray, who also had his grievances against the Douglases, pole-axed his head and beat out his brains. The King then wisely removed his Court to Perth.

Stunned and infuriated by James's breach of his solemn word and the laws of hospitality, the murdered Earl's brother and heir and his younger brother, Hugh Earl of Ormonde, marched on Stirling, renounced their fealty and set fire to the town. The Earl of Crawford rose in rebellion against the King in the southern Highlands; Archibald Douglas Earl of Moray, twin brother of the ninth Earl of Douglas, joined in the insurrection; and the Lord of the Isles did what he could to help by seizing Inverness and other castles in the north and dispatching a hired fleet to raid and devastate Renfrew, Arran and the Isle of Bute. This was the crisis in James II's reign. The whole country was aflame and the nobility split asunder. But the young King did not flinch. That June he summoned a parliament to meet in Edinburgh where it cleared his name of treachery on the ground that Douglas had renounced all claims to personal security and by entering into a conspiracy against his monarch had justifiably been killed for committing treason.

Once again, as had happened several times before in Scottish medieval history, periods of violence were interspersed with temporary settlements. The Earl of Crawford was restored to his estates, which had been forfeited, on promise of good behaviour; the Lord of the Isles was left unmolested; and most extraordinary event of all, the ninth Earl of Douglas forgave James for his brother's murder and promised to make no bonds in the future. In return James permitted him to marry his brother's widow, promising to procure him a papal dispensation for the purpose, and allowed him to retain all the Douglas estates. Not only all that, but James sent Douglas on a mission to England on his behalf.

The exact reasons for this astonishing patching up of friendly relations between the King and his mighty vassal are simply a matter of guesswork. But James was clearly a Machiavellian character. Did he deliberately buy a breathing space for himself? In the spring of 1455 as soon as the campaigning season opened, while Douglas was on his way back from England, the King took an artillery force to batter and destroy one of Douglas's principal castles at Inveravon. Then he returned to Edinburgh and with an enlarged army systematically raided most of the Douglas lands, finishing with the demolition of another of his castles at Abercorn, again making use of the latest cannon including perhaps the famous Mons Meg, which is still to be seen at Edinburgh castle. By now Douglas himself was in Scotland again but once he observed the strength of James's army he fled back to England, leaving three of his brothers to uphold his cause. They were defeated by the royalist army at Arkinholm on the river Esk. One was killed, one was captured and executed, and the third managed to escape to join his eldest brother in England. Other members or friends of the Douglas family were attainted for treason and all their lands were forfeited to the Crown. So before he had reached the age of twenty-five James had made himself master of his kingdom and by his ferocious treatment of the Black Douglases delivered a warning to all the other magnates of the realm of what their fate would be if they rose against him.

Because of the elimination of the Black Douglases the next four years of James I's reign were relatively peaceful and prosperous. Not only did the forfeitures enrich the Crown, but on 15 November 1455, after the King attained the age of twenty-five, he revoked all previous alienations of royal property except those bestowed upon the Queen and her second son. From then on the possessions of the Crown were to be divided into two categories, annexed lands, which were not to be alienated, and unannexed lands with which the King could do as he pleased. The motive for this division was to ensure that the King had adequate means to meet all normal expenditure; the arrangement therefore averted demands for fresh taxation except in times of crisis. That no doubt was why a parliament that met at Edinburgh during August 1455 acquiesced in the forfeiture to the Crown of all the lands and goods of the Black Douglases. Finally, all the grants of hereditary offices were revoked. Had that been the case in early medieval history, it is unlikely that the Stewarts would ever have become kings.

But James did not aim to enhance the strength of the monarchy by wiping out the nobility, which would scarcely have been feasible. He accepted the continuing domination of the northern Highlands by the Lords of the Isles, the Donalds or MacDonalds, who not only ruled the Hebrides but were Earls of Ross and had proved such a trial to James I. It was because James II accepted the situation that he was able to assert his authority in the Lowlands without interference from the Highlands. Furthermore he established various new earldoms, notably that of Huntly, created in 1445, whose family name was Gordon, and that of Argyll, whose family name was Campbell, both families destined to play a leading part in future Scottish and English history. To some extent James was thus building up a new nobility which was to balance the old. After three civil

Stewart Scotland.

View from Stirling castle over the area where many battles famous in Scottish history to place.

The inscription on the statue base reads:

ROBERT
THE
BRUCE
KING
OF
SCOTS
1306-1329

The modern statue of Robert the Bruce, marking the site of the battle of Bannockburn fought in 1314.

Above. A scene typical of the Scottish Highlands: Loch Duich in Ross.

Below. King Robert III (1390–1406): a contemporary seal.

The *Great St Michael*, a model in the Royal Scottish Museum, of James IV's 'monstruous' warship.

King James VI of Scots
(1567–1625) at the age of
twenty-seven: a painting
attributed to Adrian Vanson.

g James I of England after
ucceeded Queen Elizabeth
the throne: a painting of
at the age of fifty-five by
iel Mytens.

Kirk o'Field, Edinburgh, a contemporary sketch. *Top left:* Darnley's son, the baby Prince James in his cradle, with the legend 'Judge and avenge my cause, O Lord'. *Left centre:* the quadrangle of houses attached to St Mary, Kirk o'Field showing the house as a heap of rubble after the explosion contrived by Bothwell. *Top right:* Darnley and his servant lying dead in the garden. *Centre:* the town wall, on which Kirk o'Field backed. *Bottom left:* the bodies of Darnley and his servant being carried away

Henry Stuart Lord Darnley, second husband of Mary Queen of Scots.

James Hepburn fourth Earl of Bothwell, third husband of Mary Queen of Scots.

E·STVART·REYNE·DESCOSSE·
'FE·DE·FRANCOIS·SECOND
·ROY·DE·FRANCE·

Above. Mary Queen of Scots (1542–67) with her first husband, King François II of France: a medallion by an unknown artist.

Below left. Mary as Queen of France by Clouet and *right* Diana of Poitiers, her father-in-law's mistress, by Primaticcio: contrasts in beauty.

Right. Robert Stewart first Duke of Albany, brother of King Robert III and uncle of King James I, who ruled Scotland when James was a prisoner in England.

Below. King James I (1406–37) by an unknown artist.

Robert Regent, 1406.

IACOBVS·I·D·GRATIA·REX·SCOTORVM

Left. King James II (1437–60) by Jorg von Ehingen.

Opposite. King James III (1460–88) from an altar-piece by Hugo van der Goes.

Below. Mons Meg, an early cannon, brought from the Netherlands by James II, still to be seen at Edinburgh castle.

wars, as Professor Nicholson has pointed out, James had secured a triumph for his dynasty, but 'not necessarily for the people of Scotland as a whole'. The 1450s were a time of in-fighting, pestilence and famine that bore hardly on the poor.

The three Estates, which constituted parliaments or general councils, had supported the King during the civil wars; a parliament, which met at Edinburgh in March 1458, congratulated the monarch on his victories and praised God for his grace in sending 'our sovereign lord such progress and prosperity that all his rebels and breakers of his justice are removed out of his realm and no masterful party remained that may cause any breaking of the realm . . .' It was this parliament which followed in the footsteps of James I's parliaments by passing numerous economic, social and judicial regulations aimed at national recovery and progress after the wars at home and abroad ended. The King was asked by this parliament to promote 'the quiet and profit of the realm' and ensure that justice was done everywhere.

One notable achievement at home, in which James II took a part, was the foundation of a second Scottish university at Glasgow. The University of St Andrews, founded in 1413 by papal Bull (only the Pope and the Holy Roman Emperor could found a university), had received a royal charter from James's father in 1432, and another one confirming its privileges from James II in 1445. Soon after this James had asked the Bishop of Glasgow to set up a second university there. The Pope duly issued a Bull in 1451 and in 1453 the King took the new university under his protection. Both the universities had faculties of arts; theology and medicine were taught as well as law, in which St Andrews specialized. A higher proportion of the clergy of Scotland are believed to have obtained a university education than was the case in England. while in Scotland lawyers acquired their professional qualifications at the universities, unlike their English counterparts, who were required to join the London Inns of Court. The patronage that James II conferred on the universities was his most enduring contribution to the arts of peace.

But Scotland was allowed only two years of quiet after 1458 in which to seek its recovery from the burdens of war. On 10 July 1460 the Lancastrian King Henry VI of England was quickly and decisively defeated at the battle of Northampton by Edward Earl of March (the future Yorkist King Edward IV) and carried a prisoner to London, while his wife, Margaret, found refuge in Wales, having previously been a fugitive in Scotland. After a two-year truce had been concluded with the Lancastrians in June 1457, James could not resist what appeared to be a golden opportunity to retake the castles of Berwick and Roxburgh, still occupied by English garrisons. It was even rumoured that he intended to raise a host of 30,000 men with whom to invade England in alliance with the Lancastrians. In fact his aims were modest. In August 1459 he raided England with a few thousand men, but only stayed there for six nights. A year later he gathered together a larger army, which included such Highland chieftains as the Earls of Ross and Huntly, and with it laid siege to Roxburgh castle, where in August 1460 James's Queen arrived to watch the bombardment. Ironically enough on that very day James himself was killed accidentally by one of his own favourite cannon, which exploded when being fired to welcome her arrival. He was not yet thirty. His son, the future James III, was barely eight years old.

It was not inappropriate that James II should have been killed in war — Roxburgh surrendered a few days after his death — for he has gone down in Scottish tradition as a soldiers' king. He was careless of his personal comforts in time of war and would ride among his soldiers as if he were one of themselves sharing the food and drink they offered him. Like Robert the Bruce, he was a military leader who never knew when he was beaten and who yielded to his enemies only to strike at them again soon. He was rapid in decision and in action, sometimes too resolute and impulsive as when he knifed the eighth Earl of Douglas. Like his father, he was energetic and unscrupulous but scarcely a tyrant, though it has been said that 'a sense of power tended to breed despotism at home and dreams of conquest abroad'. He possessed more personal charm than his father, but was less concerned over the welfare of the common people. Finally, although he has been acclaimed for the destruction of the Black Douglases, in fact his son was left to cope with much the same sort of problems as he had, a restless nobility and troubled relations with the neighbouring English.

The principal literary sources for the reign are the brief contemporary 'Short Chronicle of the Reign of James II' known as the *Auchinleck Chronicle* (1819) and Robert Lindsay of Pitscottie, *Historie and Character of Scotland* (ed. A. J. G. Mackay), S.T.S. (1899). Anne I. Dunlop, *The Life and Times of James Kennedy* (1950) deals pretty extensively with the reign, but some of the conclusions have been questioned. On James II's marriage there is an article in *S.H.R.* xxv. E. F. Jacob, *The Fifteenth Century* (1961) touches on the relations between the Lancastrians, Yorkists and Scots.

[6]

The Enigma of James III

JAMES III PROVED TO BE an enigmatic king about whom Renaissance chroniclers and modern scholars have expressed a variety of opinions. Yet it is not too difficult to place him in the context of his dynasty. Like his father, James II, his childhood was excruciating because he was the plaything of rival groups of ambitious nobles. Like his great-grandfather, Robert III, he was a man of peace; like him too, he was to be harassed by his more martial brother, the Duke of Albany. He appears to have been bisexual, as was his great-great-grandson, James VI, his homosexual tastes obtruding themselves late in his life. Finally, like Charles I, he was a connoisseur of the arts, while in common with Charles II he was justifiably described as 'licentious'.

After his father's unexpected death the eight-year-old boy was quickly crowned not at Scone but in the abbey of Kelso, which was near to Roxburgh. At a fully attended meeting of parliament in Edinburgh on 23 February 1461 the three Estates appointed his mother, Mary of Guelders, Regent, but also gave her a council of lords, who included the Bishop of St Andrews, James Kennedy, a character prominent in the previous reign, and the Bishop of Glasgow together with the Earls of Angus, Argyll, Huntly and Orkney. Mary was a woman of distinction, who did not commit the same mistakes as the widowed Joan Beaufort had done after the death of her husband, James I. For instance, she did not marry again, while the accusation that she later took an adulterous lover, Adam Hepburn Master of Hailes was a slander. But two things appear certain: the first is that no love was lost between her and her Council, for the lords declared that 'there was little of good worth, either spiritual or temporal, that gave the keeping of the kingdom to a woman'. Secondly, the royal Court was rapidly divided by faction with the Queen Mother, seconded by Argyll, on one side and Kennedy, seconded by Angus, on the other.

In any case the Regency's problems were complicated by the continuing war in England between the Lancastrians and the Yorkists. Understandably the sympathies of the official leaders of Scotland, committed to an unbroken line of Stewarts, lay with the Lancastrians rather than the upstart Yorkists so that when King Henry VI's wife, the amazon Queen Margaret, came to Scotland in search of help, dangling various baits, such as the marriage of her young son to James III's sister, Mary, and the surrender of Berwick to the Scots, both the Queen Mother and Bishop Kennedy were tempted to back the Lancastrians. When, after the Duke of York's son, Edward, convincingly defeated Margaret of Anjou at the battle of Towton in 1461 and assumed the title of Edward IV, not only Margaret but her husband, Henry VI, a saintly nonentity, and their son, Edward Prince of Wales, returned to Scotland, their offers of rewards in return for assistance expanded to include not only Berwick but Carlisle. These offers, however, were mostly castles in the air. So Mary of Guelders, whom critics doubtfully called 'unstable' and 'capricious', resolved to negotiate with both sides. She needed to do so because Edward IV was already stirring up trouble for her in Scotland.

In James ninth Earl of Douglas, who had fled to England during the previous reign, Edward discovered a ready-made agent, whom he employed to negotiate with John Lord of the Isles and Earl of Ross to create embarrassments for the Stewarts in the Highlands. Edward IV contemplated occupying the Lowlands himself and founding a separate and smaller Scottish kingdom in the Highlands. Thus for a time Scotland was threatened with partition and the destruction of the Stewart line. During 1462 the Lord of the Isles, who had so recently put his Highlanders at the service of James II, seized and burned Inverness and occupied Crown lands in the neighbourhood. The Regent, however, did not allow herself to be intimidated. At the outset of the new reign she had replaced the governors of Stirling, Edinburgh and Dunbar with men whom she trusted. She retired to Dunbar to bargain with both the English parties. Berwick had already been handed over. Receiving fresh promises of attractive rewards from Margaret of Anjou, Mary took her son to besiege Norham, a castle on the English side of the Tweed. Although they were repulsed there, the conspiratorial Earl of Douglas made little progress in his attack on the Lowlands on behalf of Edward IV; and Douglas's brother, Lord Balveny, was captured and beheaded in Edinburgh for the crime of helping the English.

At the beginning of December 1463 the Queen Mother died; Bishop Kennedy, who virtually took over the Regency, hitherto pro-Lancastrian, realistically came to terms with Edward IV (who kindly gave him a pension) and a fifteen-year truce was arranged in June 1464 with the victorious Yorkist Government. In the summer of the same year the Bishop himself, accompanied by the boy King, went to Inverness and together with other Lords of the Council, managed to exact the submission of the Lord of the Isles, who had many enemies and few friends. Thus Bishop Kennedy, who had proved himself an able politician, ended his life in a blaze of glory. Kennedy's death on 24 May 1465 when he was in his late fifties, only eighteen months after the death of the Queen Mother, left James III, then thirteen years old, without any obvious governor on whom he could rely; he was thus destined to become the victim of struggles between competing members of the secular nobility.

The family of the Boyds, whose territorial power was centred on Kilmarnock in the western Lowlands and who were intermarried with the Kennedys, were in a strong political situation after the death of Bishop James Kennedy. Sir Alexander Boyd, the younger brother of Robert Lord Boyd, had been appointed Keeper of Edinburgh castle in 1464. In July 1466 the Boyds seized hold of the King while he was hunting in the neighbourhood of Linlithgow palace and carried him off to Edinburgh. In October of that year, when the first Parliament of the reign gathered there, James, who had reached the consentient age of fourteen, announced that it was his pleasure that Lord Boyd should be his governor and also the governor of his younger brothers as well as in charge of all the royal castles until he himself was twenty-one. Thomas Boyd, the eldest son of Lord Boyd, married the King's sister, Mary, and was created Earl of Arran, while Lord Boyd himself was given the post of Chamberlain, that is to say he took control of the King's finances. Unquestionably James was pressurized into these wide concessions, which he resented having to make.

For three years the Boyds clung to authority, ousting the Kennedys, who had been responsible for giving them their leg upwards. The Boyds do not appear to have done too badly by the King. At a Parliament held in 1467 the Lords of the Council were given the right to deal with judicial matters when a parliament was not sitting, thus in theory at least centralizing the administration of justice. The truce with England was honoured, allowing Berwick to be retained by the Scots. During 1468 a marriage was arranged between James and Margaret, daughter of Christian I, King of Denmark-Norway. In return for a promise of a third of the Scottish King's income for the lucky bride she was given a large dowry, guaranteed by the revenue received by King Christian from the islands of Orkney. Because of this commitment by the Danish-Norwegian King, who was up to his ears in debt, and because of the surrender in 1470 to the Scottish monarchy by the then Earl of Orkney of his castle in the islands and of his holdings in the adjacent Shetlands in return for compensation, before the end of James III's reign both the Orkneys and the Shetlands came under the full and undivided sovereignty of the Stewart kings.

The marriage of Princess Margaret of Denmark, then only thirteen years old, who proved to be charming and gentle but no beauty, to James III, aged eighteen, took place at Holyrood in July 1469. The King was now a man and this spelt the doom of the Boyds, just as his father's marriage had heralded the overthrow of the Livingstons. Lord Boyd, realizing what was going to happen, fled to England, while his son, the Earl of Arran, who had accompanied Princess Margaret to Scotland, was warned of his danger by his wife, James's sister, and wisely took the same ship back to Denmark. Later the King confiscated his earldom, compelled his sister to divorce her husband, and married her to Lord Hamilton, thus establishing another famous family in Scottish history. A parliament that met in November in Edinburgh forfeited all the Boyds' estates; Sir Alexander Boyd, the chief abductor of the King from Linlithgow, who failed to escape to safety, was condemned for treason and beheaded on castle hill. It is almost certain that James III himself, supported by two of his uncles, the Earl of Atholl and the future Earl of Buchan, had personally engineered this coup: the Stewarts thus punished the Boyds for the King's forced and humiliating tutelage.

During the next ten years the history of Scotland was one of progress. The three Estates met regularly in parliaments and when they were not in session the Committee of the Articles (foreshadowed in James I's reign), consisting of members of each Estate, handled any unfinished business and prepared Bills for the next parliament. The Lords of the Council continued to act as a court of appeal from the decisions of ordinary justices, that is to say the sheriffs and provosts of burghs. In 1472 Patrick Graham, the Bishop of St Andrews, successor to his uncle, James Kennedy, when he was on a visit to Rome, persuaded the Pope, Sixtus IV, to issue a Bull erecting his bishopric into an archbishopric, giving it authority over other bishops, including a new Bishop of Orkney. Although the establishment of a metropolitan archbishopric caused difficulties and was resented at first, it was obviously more satisfactory than the earlier arrangement under which all the Scottish bishops were directly responsible to the Papacy. In March 1473 the birth of the Duke of Rothesay, the future James IV, ensured the continuation of the Stewart dynasty; and when her second son was born in March 1476 Queen Margaret also had him christened James as an insurance against the death of her eldest son. The year before, as King Christian I had been unable to fulfil all his treaty obligations, the Scottish Parliament annexed the Orkneys and the Shetlands to the Crown. The truce with England was extended, sealed by a marriage treaty between the newly born baby prince and Edward IV's daughter, Cecily, both parties promising not to aid each other's rebels. In consequence of this treaty Edward disclosed the intrigues which, with the ninth Earl of Douglas as his agent, had been aimed during James's minority at carving out a separate Highland kingdom under the rule of John MacDonald, the Lord of the Isles. Earl John was summoned to Edinburgh, where he was punished for his indiscretions by the forfeiture of his earldom of Ross to the Crown. But James allowed him to retain his other lands upon promise of good behaviour. Such leniency was typical of the way in which James treated his nobility. In this case it contributed to the temporary pacification of the Highlands.

All these were positive achievements. On the negative side was the inability of the government to suppress lawlessness. That was scarcely a new problem. Bastard feudalism in England as well as in Scotland had undermined justice. Perjury and intimidation were all too common in the courts of law. The root cause of the trouble was lack of codified laws and the absence of trained and paid professional judges. What was novel was the charges made in parliaments specifically directed against the King himself for the failure of his government to maintain law and order throughout the realm. In 1471 a proclamation was issued by parliament ordering that whenever manslaughter took place complainants should present their case to the King so as to ensure impartial justice. In 1473 the spiritual lords begged the King to travel throughout the land to enforce justice, presumably by ayres; in 1474 legislation was passed relating to the 'great derision and scorn of justice'. Here the faults may indeed have been personal. The chronicler, Lindsay of Pitscottie, insisted that James 'loved solitariness' and 'delighted more in the playing of instruments than in the defence of the borders and the administration of justice'. James was also thought to be far too merciful: the three Estates begged him in 1473 to stop granting remissions and respites for acts of manslaughter.

The other accusation levelled against the King was that he was responsible for the debasement of the coinage. This is a more doubtful charge. It is highly probable that during the long period of comparative peace that followed the death of James II internal trade became more active, more imports were purchased and therefore a shortage of currency arose. The production of copper coins such as pennies, halfpennies and farthings, was clearly a sensible measure, while the belief that export of gold and silver can be prevented by law has rarely worked even in more sophisticated times. It was easy to allege that the minting of 'black money' was the wicked crime of royal favourites, but the truth was that the economic difficulties of the kingdom were caused largely by the falling off of demand from abroad for the limited selection of Scottish exports, particularly raw wool and hides. Kings were not always economic experts any more than are modern Prime Ministers.

The confiscation of the earldom of Ross, the growing power of the Campbells, who had been given the earldom of Argyll by James II, and quarrels between the Lord of the Isles and his illegitimate son, Angus Og, led to feuds and disturbances throughout the northern Highlands during 1478 and 1479. Similar feuds divided the magnates in the Lowlands, in which the King's uncles were involved. To maintain his authority James did not depend on the traditional ruling classes. Colin Campbell the first Earl of Argyll became his Chancellor, the royal physician, William Scheves, became Archbishop of St Andrews (in place of Patrick Graham, who after his scoop in obtaining the establishment of the archbishopric, had been excommunicated by the Pope in 1475 and later went mad) and Robert Cochrane, the Court architect, looked after the royal finances or at any rate was blamed for the unpopular black farthings. In addition James surrounded himself with a number of 'familiar esquires', including physicians, musicians and artists, who were envied as upstarts or 'men of mean lineage' and accused of distracting the royal attention from the proper tasks of government, especially in the year 1479, which the chroniclers described as one of 'theft, strife and slaughter'. The poet, Robert Henryson, asserted that James neglected his duties 'lying still in lusts, sloth and sleep'.

For these reasons the King's two brothers, Alexander Stewart the third Duke of Albany and John Stewart Earl of Mar, came to the conclusion that they could rule the country a great deal better than the King. When this belief became clear to James he was naturally displeased. Whatever the Duke of Albany's initial crime was – defiance or conspiracy – is not known for certain, though to dismiss the matter merely as a product of the King's suspicious nature is odd, for he was normally a clement monarch. At any rate he ordered the arrest of Albany. The Duke was imprisoned in Edinburgh castle, but managed to overpower his warders, climb over the high walls and down the precipitous rock on which the castle stands; later he escaped to France. The Earl of Mar, who was also arrested and imprisoned at Craigmillar, was less fortunate, for he soon died, probably accidentally, and Robert Cochrane, having been concerned in bringing about the arrest, was created Earl of Mar in his place.

During the next three years no parliament met; the Edinburgh Parliament was prorogued again and again, the likely explanation being that the King was unable to formulate convincing accusations against the absent Albany, which were highly necessary as the King of France, Louis XI, had intervened actively on Albany's behalf. When French intervention failed, the Duke, in order to regain his position in Scotland, went over to England where Edward IV, who had recently made peace with Louis XI, recognized Albany as Alexander IV King of the Scots in return for promises that he would do homage to him as his feudal superior and hand over to him Berwick and other parts of the southern borders of the Lowlands. This treasonable arrangement was called the treaty of Fotheringay. A three-day raid into England authorized by James III and carried out by Archibald Douglas Earl of Angus and Warden of the East March in a time of truce, during which Bamburgh castle was set alight, provided a reasonable excuse for Edward IV to order the invasion of Scotland by way of retaliation. He recruited a large army, which was put under the command of his brother, Richard Duke of Gloucester (the future Richard III) who, accompanied by the Duke of Albany in his capacity as pretender to his brother's throne, set out for Berwick during the summer of 1482.

James III was fully aware that war with England was imminent. Later chroniclers all agreed that James was an unwarlike monarch who spent his money on arts and crafts instead of weapons. The accusation was exaggerated. James is known to have bought artillery, laid out considerable sums on strengthening the defences of Berwick, and did not hesitate to take personal charge of the host he summoned to gather in Edinburgh to confront the English invaders. But the magnates, who joined him there, seized the occasion as an excellent opportunity to vent their resentment against the King for his methods of government and his patronage of Cochrane and the 'familiar esquires'. It has even been surmised that the young Earl of Angus had deliberately provoked the English by burning Bamburgh castle two years earlier so as to create this very opportunity. At any rate when the Scots army reached the village of Lauder, twenty-four miles south of Edinburgh, the decision was taken to defy the King, Angus volunteering to take the lead, thus earning the nickname of Archibald Bell-the-Cat, and lynch the royal favourites. Cochrane, who had been clad in black velvet with a heavy gold chain round his neck, and some of the familiars were hanged from Lauder bridge; then the King was sent into honourable captivity at Edinburgh castle under the care of one of his uncles. After that the host broke up and dispersed.

This rebellion against James III simplified the task of the Duke of Gloucester, who rode to Edinburgh, accompanied by Albany, with the intention of realizing the terms of the secret treaty of Fotheringay. But when Archbishop Scheves emerged as head of a provisional government he insisted that in return for the restoration of Albany to his offices and estates

the Duke must recognize his allegiance to James III. Albany then decided
not to reveal his ambition to become king in place of his brother, for, after
all, he might well be chosen as Lieutenant-General of the realm, which
would be nearly as good. The Duke of Gloucester left the Scots to settle
their own affairs, refrained from setting fire to Edinburgh, as was customary on these occasions, and returned to besiege Berwick, which surrendered
on 24 August 1482 and, rightly or wrongly, has been an English town ever
since.

Momentarily Albany had triumphed and had enlarged his supporters to
include James's three uncles, Buchan, Atholl and Andrew Stewart Bishop
of Moray, who nursed a desire to become Archbishop of St Andrews. They
also included Archibald Bell-the-Cat and the last of the black Douglases,
the ninth Earl, who had been languishing in England ever since the reign of
James II. James III was released from captivity and in return appointed
Albany Lieutenant-General, Warden of the Marches, and Earl of Mar. But
Albany was still dissatisfied. He sent off two of his friends to Westminster
to renew the secret agreement with Edward IV concluded at Fotheringay. A
parliament, called in Edinburgh on 2 December 1482, consisting mainly of
magnates, approved Albany's appointments, but when it met again in
March 1483 the whole atmosphere changed. Albany's underhand dealings
with Edward IV had leaked out and the loss of Berwick was blamed on the
Duke. He was compelled to confess to treason and promise to repudiate his
treaties with the English. Though James pardoned his brother, Albany was
obliged to give up his office of Lieutenant-General; after that he thought it
judicious to return to England and before he left he handed over his castle at
Dunbar to an English garrison. Another Anglo-Scottish war was, however,
not on the cards, for by now Edward IV was dead and his brother and
effective successor, Richard III, had too much to do to secure his own
position to worry about Scotland. In Albany's absence the Scottish Parliament resolved that he had forfeited his life and estates because of his treason
to his sovereign. Albany now shot his last bolt; accompanied by the ninth
Earl of Douglas, he came north with force of cavalry which struck hard
across the border. After a long-drawn-out battle at Lochmaben in July 1484
they were defeated by royalist troops. Once again Albany fled, this time to
France, where he was accidentally killed a year later. James took pity on the
Earl of Douglas, now getting on for sixty; he was merely confined to
monkish seclusion in an abbey. James's moderation after all he had been
through was remarkable.

Having thus overcome all his enemies, James aimed to secure peace at
home and abroad. According to Robert Lindsay of Pitscottie, 'the King

passed all Scotland at his pleasure in peace and rest'. He settled down at Stirling where he rewarded such of his familiars who survived the lynching at Lauder and he found an able new minister in William Elphinstone Bishop of Ross and later of Aberdeen. James concluded three-year truces first with Richard III and then with Henry VII, the first Tudor King of England, and he renewed the old alliance with France. He also entered into negotiations with Pope Innocent VIII, who was elected in Rome after the death of Sixtus IV. Both these Popes exerted all their influence to induce Scottish noblemen, both lay and spiritual, to be obedient to their King. Innocent VIII sent the Bishop of Imola as *legate a latere* to Scotland who 'dealt out excommunications and interdicts with a liberal hand'. By way of a return visit Archbishop Scheves headed a mission to Rome to ask the Pope to allow a delay of eight months before disposing of ecclesiastical vacancies on account of the distance between Rome and Scotland. The Pope consented to this request, which provided the Stewart monarchy with a valuable hold over the Church. For it thus gave time to it to make its own recommendations for vacancies and also to draw upon the revenues of unoccupied bishoprics, abbacies and priories until new incumbents were appointed. This large concession or 'indult' hardly proved wise from the point of view of the Papacy, for the corruption and nepotism that were engendered by it were among the causes of the overthrow of Roman Catholic supremacy in Scotland during the following century. The Stewarts had a foretaste, as it were, of becoming heads of the Scottish Church.

Another concession extracted from Innocent VIII contributed indirectly to James III's subjugation and death. The wealthy priory of Coldingham in the Lowlands had originally been a dependency of the Benedictine priory of Durham in northern England, but at the beginning of James's reign all the English monks had been ejected from Scotland and the baronial family of the Homes, who dominated the district, managed to get one of its members intruded as prior so as to exploit the endowments and properties for their own benefit. James asked the Pope to suppress the priory and have its revenues transferred to the royal chapel at St Andrews. The Homes and their friends and neighbours, the Hepburns, were soon up in arms and pointedly absented themselves from a parliament that met in 1488. Other members of the nobility were angered by a plan to negotiate royal marriages with the new Tudor dynasty in England; they also blamed James for the loss of Berwick.

The new conspirators against the King who thus emerged were not the same as before except for Archibald Bell-the-Cat. Besides the Homes and the Hepburns they included nobles with a variety of grievances such as the Earl of Argyll and the Bishop of Glasgow. James's son and heir, James Duke of Rothesay, who had been living with his mother in Stirling castle, had reached the age of fifteen and his mother had recently died. A relative of the Homes happened to be the Keeper of the castle. That enabled the rebels to carry off the young Prince to Linlithgow where he became their figurehead. They then proceeded to blockade the King in Edinburgh castle. James managed to escape from Edinburgh to rally his supporters in the Highlands, but he was anxious to avoid making war on his son and his subjects. But the rebels' terms were stiff: in effect they demanded James III's abdication as an inept and indeed wicked King. Negotiations for a compromise broke down; civil war followed. In May 1488 James III mustered an army at Perth and led it to Stirling, where he hoped to join up with reinforcements from the Highlands. When he reached the town only part of them had arrived, while the rebel army, more numerous than his own, advanced north from Torwood. So on 11 June 1488 the armies of James and his eldest son confronted one another on or near the field of Bannockburn, the King mounted on a grey charger and armed with the sword of Robert the Bruce. The Prince gave strict orders that no one was to lay hands on his father during the course of the battle. But before the contest ended James was persuaded by his friends to leave the field so as to ensure his own safety. He galloped to the village of Bannockburn where he was thrown from his horse, seriously injured and obliged to take shelter in a local mill. There a stranger, who pretended to be a priest, was admitted to the King's bedside, where he pulled out his sword and killed him. It may well have been a premeditated act of assassination carried out because James's son had forbidden the killing of his father on the field of battle. The King was buried in Cambuskenneth abbey. A fortnight later on 24 June 1488 the reluctant victor, the young Duke of Rothesay, was crowned James IV on the historic site of Scone.

Where does the truth lie about James III's character? The Scottish historian, Professor Archibald Duncan, writing very recently, has said severely:

James III was a calamitous failure who always took the easy way out, distrustful and lazy. He was acquisitive, even ruthless, but not, as his father and grandfather, in order to live and govern well. He was a hoarder, who raised cash by demoralizing methods: the sale of pardons and debasement of the coinage. He offered neither court life and its perquisites nor war and its pickings. And he feared to govern.

Unquestionably one reason for his unpopularity was that Scotland was undergoing a difficult phase economically especially during the later part of the reign. Harvests were bad, pestilence rife, exports falling away. Yet James personally was an energetic exporter and concerned himself a good deal with commercial diplomacy, while, after all, the depreciation of the currency is a move to which governments frequently resort in times of economic stress. Rulers are always blamed for depressions, but are rarely, if ever, responsible for them.

It is of course a fact that James III had extravagant tastes. He loved beautiful things, patronized the arts, and encouraged native architecture. In fact he was a civilized and cultured monarch whose personal indulgences extended to the collection of jewelry and the purchase of attractive clothes for himself and his Queen. He was, as another modern historian has justly remarked, 'an enlightened keen-witted Renaissance prince, delighting more in the company of men as clever as himself, however lowly they might be, than in his illiterate and arrogant nobles'.

James, then, was artistic, possessing much of the delicacy and charm which is characteristic of cultured homosexuals. It is likely enough that the jealousy of his 'familiars' was enhanced because they – or some of them at any rate – were homosexual. True, it has been contended that because Bishop Lesley, writing in the sixteenth century, tells us that the King had a notorious mistress called Daisy, whom he preferred to his noble Queen, he cannot have been a homosexual. Still the future James VI was certainly homosexual and had children by a Scandanavian wife, while Oscar Wilde, most famous of English homosexuals, had children who were devoted to him. The extraordinary divergence of opinions about James III is illustrated by the chronicler, Giovanni Ferreri, who wrote of James's wife that 'to the King her husband she showed herself to be so obedient that it would . . . be difficult to find in any nation a marriage which was happier and more free from trouble'. If that was so, Margaret of Denmark must have known her place.

So far as his private conduct was concerned, if we are to trust Bishop Lesley, even towards the end of his life James was incorrigible. Leaving his son, who was to help overthrow him, in the care of his mother, 'the King lived quietly in Stirling, accompanied with some men of mean and sober estate, taking his pleasure of women, giving himself to avarice, and gathering gold and silver, whereby he became the subject of great hatred and disdain of the nobility and people'. Other chroniclers asserted that he was irreligious, 'an example to all kings that come hereafter', wrote Pitscottie, 'not to fall from God and to ground themselves upon the vain sayings and illusions of devils and sorcerers, as this feeble King did, which put him in suspicion of his nobility and [induced him to] murder and exile his own native brothers'. Yet another chronicler, Hector Boece, tells us that towards the end of his life James came under the benign influence of Bishop Elphinstone, bestowed gifts upon the churches and the poor, and burst into tears and prayer whenever he beheld an image of Christ or the Virgin Mary. That, as will be seen, was also how James VII behaved in his later years after he too had been condemned, and condemned himself, as licentious.

Is it fair to say that James III was capricious and lazy? The English chronicler, Polydore Vergil, not perhaps a good authority, thought he was impatient of criticism (aren't we all?), quick to make a foolish decision, and slow to revoke it, and the nineteenth-century historian, Patrick Fraser Tytler, blamed him for indolently neglecting his duties, particularly the administration of justice. Possibly like James VI and Charles II, James did tend to be lazy, although, like them, he could take political decisions rapidly when he was forced to do so. Except for his treatment of the Boyds when he was a young man James was a remarkably merciful ruler, as was witnessed by his behaviour towards the Lord of the Isles, his brother, Albany, and the ninth Earl of Douglas. So is it fair to call him ruthless? Certainly to enforce law and order effectively in Renaissance Scotland he would have needed to be much more ruthless than in fact he was, as ruthless as his grandfather, James I and his own son, James IV. To dismiss James III as a cruel and avaricious debauchee, who deliberately neglected his obligations as a Stewart king, is unjustifiable.

The chroniclers who discuss James III, none of whom were contemporary, are Robert Lindsay of Pitscottie, *History and Chronicles of Scotland 1547–1575* (S.T.S 1911); and John Lesley, *History of Scotland 1437–1562* (Bannatyne Club, 1830). Professor Duncan's views are in *Scotland from the Earliest Times to 1603*, a revision in 1977 of W. Croft Dickinson's book originally published in 1961, in which Professor Duncan acknowledges his obligations to a thesis on James III by Dr Norman Macdougal. See also R. L. Mackie, *King James IV of Scotland* (1958), Chapter 1, 'The Scotland of James III'.

[7]

James IV –
the Paradoxical Ruler

JAMES IV WAS fifteen years old when his father was assassinated. At first he showed no remorse for being concerned in the successful rebellion against him. His modern biographer, it is true, states that as Prince he had been 'unwilling' to become the figurehead of the insurrection and had suffered 'an uneasy conscience on the field of Stirling'. On the other hand, it was not until he was in his nineteenth year that he showed contrition by offering a reward for the discovery of his father's murderer and not until he was in his twenty-fourth year that he endowed Masses for his father's soul. Then, possibly under pressure from his confessor, he indulged in a show of masochism by wearing a heavy iron belt round his waist, which was increased in weight by a few ounces every year until his death. Nevertheless in his youth he can understandably have disliked his father's favourites and 'familiars', thought his mother had been badly treated, as she had been, and even been persuaded that his father's removal, and thus his own elevation, had been in the national interest. Certainly he soon proved himself to be no puppet monarch, though he was obliged to demonstrate his gratitude to the Homes and Hepburns who had instigated the rebellion.

James IV benefited from an excellent education. He was the only Stewart king who, like Robert Bruce, spoke Gaelic, 'the language', as a Spanish observer reported, 'of the savages who live in some parts of Scotland and on the islands'. He also spoke French, German, Flemish, Italian and Spanish; Latin, still an international language, he knew extremely well. He was, as a nineteenth-century historian wrote, 'affable in his manners, fond of magnificence and devoted to pleasure, while his Court was a perpetual scene of revelry and amusement'. Thus James IV's Court in Edinburgh foreshadowed Charles II's Whitehall, for in some ways his approach to life was similar to that of the future King of England. On the other hand, he was outwardly extremely pious, much given to his prayers and his devotions. He was abstemious in food and drink and ate no meat on Wednesdays and Fridays; he would not mount a horse on Sunday even to go to Mass; before transacting any serious business he would hear two Masses. Nothing was allowed to interfere with his annual pilgrimage to the shrines of St Ninian and St Duthac, two peculiarly Scottish saints; during Holy Week he retired regularly to the Observantine friary at Stirling, which he built and where he shared in the fasts and vigils of the friars.

At the same time James IV enjoyed exercises and sports; he shot both the long-bow and the cross-bow and became an expert in gunnery. A fearless horseman and keen huntsman, he paid up to £180 for a single hawk. Outdoors he played tennis and bowls and indoors backgammon and cards, at which he was known to lose as much as £70 in a single evening. Again like Charles II, he dabbled in science; he had a laboratory at Holyroodhouse. According to Pitscottie, he was 'well learned in the art of medicine and a good surgeon'. Whether it is right to say, as the contemporary poet, William Dunbar averred, that James strove after personal military glory is a moot point. No doubt he preferred showing off his skill in arms at tournaments and presiding over jousts by the flower of his nobility to being a general commanding in the field, a profession at which he was to prove rather inept. Finally, he was a patron of learning and literature; besides Dunbar, the poet Robert Henryson, who has been called the Scottish Chaucer, wrote during his reign as well as that of his father. The third Scottish university at Aberdeen was founded in 1495. During James's lifetime too the first printing press was set up by licence in Edinburgh to profit from producing tales of chivalry and romance as well as books of law and poetry.

The first parliament of the reign met in Edinburgh in October 1488 (James had been crowned at Scone in mid-June). Even before this the boy King constituted what may be termed his Cabinet. Naturally the victors in the rebellion were rewarded and some of the vanquished punished. Colin Campbell Earl of Argyll replaced Elphinstone, who had been loyal to James III, as Chancellor, but Elphinstone's ability was such that he was soon recalled as one of the Lords of the Council. Lord Home was made Chamberlain, Lord Hailes (created Earl of Bothwell) became Master of the Household and Keeper of Edinburgh castle, and Lord Lyle, who had been prominent in the hangings over Lauder bridge, was chief Justiciar. James Stewart Earl of Buchan, son of the Black Knight of Lorne and thus the uncle of James III, who had represented him in London, was forgiven for siding with the late King; Sir Andrew Wood, an outstanding naval captain, who earned his reputation in the previous reign, was to become in effect commander-in-chief at sea.

Broadly, the emphasis at this first parliament of the reign was placed on general conciliation – some of the previous monarch's servants were suspended from office but only for three years – and its aim was to restore law and order throughout the land. James himself sat with the Lords of the Council and went on justice ayres, accompanied by a trained justiciar, while various magnates were assigned the responsibility of maintaining justice in different parts of the kingdom until James reached the age of twenty-one. Archibald Douglas, the Red Douglas known as Bell-the-Cat, was put in charge of no fewer than five sheriffdoms, but not receiving any other agreeable favours, lost his power on the English border and was soon engaged in complicated intrigues with Henry VII of England. The victorious Homes and Hepburns were then appointed Wardens of the Marches in his place.

A parliament which assembled in January 1491 continued to cope with the consequences of the rebellion. Some statesmen were to be rewarded; some were disappointed with their rewards; others began plotting against the new régime. Archbishop Scheves of St Andrews, a close confidant of James III, was snubbed by having the bishopric of Glasgow, whose holder had approved of the rebellion, erected into a rival archbishopric, and having four sees taken from his province. Lord Home had already had the guardianship of Stirling castle added to his other duties. On the other hand, Lord Lyle, the new chief Justiciar, and John Stewart, recognized in October 1488 as Earl of Lennox, in the words of Bishop Lesley, 'notwithstanding they had been with him [James IV] at the slaughter of his father, moved by envy that the King was more governed by others of the faction rather than by them, gathered a great company and raised the late King's bloodstained shirt as their banner'. Their castles at Duchal and Dumbarton were then besieged by royal troops loyal to the new King. They resisted stubbornly and in the end were pardoned by James IV. The Earls of Buchan and Angus, though they too conspired against the Government, were also not severely punished.

This policy of moderation and conciliation paid dividends as far as the Lowlands were concerned, for Pitscottie wrote of these early years of the reign that there 'was good peace and rest in Scotland and great love between the King and his subjects'. He went on to relate how James IV

> would ride out through any part of the realm alone by himself so that no one knew that he was the king; and he would lie in poor men's houses, as if he had been an ordinary traveller through the country and would ask them, where he lodged, where the King was and what kind of a man he was and how he used himself towards his subjects and what they said about him throughout the country.

Later chroniclers all praised James for his indefatigable activity in adminis-
tering justice, describing how he agreed to requests made to him in
parliament to preside over judicial ayres wherever he could. He saw to the
enforcement of statutes aimed at procuring the swift arrest of all those who
were guilty of manslaughter or 'premeditated assaults'. Sheriffs were
instructed to keep such miscreants in custody until the King's wishes about
what to do with them were known. Bishop Lesley wrote of the period when
James had reached the age of twenty-one that he governed his kingdom 'in
great quietness, peace and justice . . . the most part of the year to the great
comfort of all his good subjects'.

James IV did all he could to secure peace in the Highlands. He followed
in his father's footsteps by using the recently created Earls of Argyll and
Huntly to offset the supremacy of the Lords of the Western Isles. Before
1499 six or seven times the King himself led expeditions to the northern
and western Highlands, where he tried by a mixture of firmness and
conciliation to gain the loyalty of the contending chieftains. John the Lord
of the Isles, who had created trouble for James III during the previous reign,
was now an old man unable to control his kinsmen and subordinate chiefs,
but his illegitimate son, Angus Og (who was assassinated in 1490), his
grandson, Donald Dubh, and his nephew, Alexander of Lochalsh, had all
continued to engage in private warfare, notably against the MacKenzies,
destroying Inverness castle and raiding the Cromarty firth.

It was natural that the parliament at Edinburgh should have been
exceedingly worried over the northern unrest; James was begged to restore
order there. In May 1493 Parliament forfeited the domains of the Lord of
the Isles, annexing them to the Crown. By way of compensation James gave
John of the Isles a pension after he submitted to the forfeiture, but other
MacDonalds and their kinsmen, particularly Donald Dubh, instigated by
Torquil McLeod of Lewis, the MacLeans, the Camerons and the Mac-
Intoshes remained obstreperous and defiant. During his various visits to the
Highlands in order to assert his authority James made good use of his small
navy, for which he established a new base at Tarbert, which was more
accessible to the sea than Dumbarton. But it was not until 1506 that
Donald Dubh was captured by Huntly, or that Torquil MacLeod's castle of
Stornaway in Lewis was subdued by gunfire. Long-term measures were
introduced. New sheriffs were set up to keep order and administer justice in
the extreme north and west of the Highlands while a new Bishop of the Isles
was appointed to bind these 'uncivilized people in their devotion to the
Church'. By the end of the reign peace had been more or less attained at least
for the time being both in the Western Isles and in the northern Highlands.

This success owed much to the Earls of Argyll and Huntly; and the Bishop of Argyll, whose castle was at Kintyre, south-east of Islay, the traditional capital of the Lords of the Isles, also played a part in the pacification. At the beginning of James's reign the need to heal divisions at home precluded any enterprising foreign policy. A truce with England had been concluded towards the end of 1488 and a seven-year truce was agreed in 1494. On the other hand, James ratified a treaty of alliance with France, whose king was Charles VIII, on 4 March 1492: this treaty was directed against England. Both Charles VIII and his successor, Louis XII aimed to extend French rule into Italy and were therefore anxious to prevent any interference from the new Tudor kings of England who still reigned over Calais and were not without hopes of regaining some of the conquests in France achieved by the Lancastrians. By relying upon the Scots to divert English attention the French were in fact pushing at an open door.

The causes of growing Anglo-Scottish enmity were threefold. First came disputes at sea. Piracy was stimulated by the development of foreign trade and therefore of merchant shipping in both kingdoms, as the centre of European commerce began to shift away from the Mediterranean. That the English were chiefly to blame is suggested by the fact that Henry VII paid compensation to some aggrieved Scottish merchants. But Sir Andrew Wood was an aggressive naval commander and gave as good as he received. From an early stage in his reign James IV interested himself in enlarging the navy. His efforts culminated in the construction of the *Great St Michael*, which consumed all the oaks and firs in Fifeshire, took five years to complete, and was said to be 'ane verrie monstruous great ship' with six-score guns and 'a thousand men of war, captains, skippers and quarter-masters'. Obviously that presented a challenge to the English which discouraged them from intruding into the Forth. But to begin with, the Scottish navy's chief purpose was to help to subdue unruly Highlanders.

Secondly, the usual unrest along the borders persisted in which both sides burned villages and stole each other's cattle, a state of affairs which particularly irritated Henry VII after he succeeded to the throne in 1509. Lastly James and his advisers hoped that because of Henry VII's uncertain tenure of the English Crown, they could profit from the Tudors' distractions to regain Berwick.

In spite of his truce with Henry VII, in November 1495 James welcomed to Scotland a good-looking young man from Tournai, who claimed to be Richard Duke of York, the younger of Edward IV's two sons, who in fact died mysteriously in the Tower of London during the reign of Richard III. This impostor, whose real name was Perkin Warbeck, had been recognized

as Edward IV's son by Edward's sister, the Duchess of Burgundy. After he
reached Scotland he was accepted as the rightful King of England by James,
who arranged his marriage to Catherine Gordon, the daughter of the Earl of
Huntly. In the autumn of the following year James, accompanied by Perkin
Warbeck, led a military expedition across the Tweed, but found to his
disgust that no Englishman was prepared to rise on behalf of the Pretender.
Thus James not only deliberately broke the truce, but invaded England.
Had it not been for the fact that Henry VII had his problems elsewhere, a
full-scale war between Scotland and England would have broken out during
1497. As it was, Henry's willingness to agree to yet another truce, again to
last for seven years, gave the impression (in the words of Professor Nicholson) that 'Scotland's military might was held in awe'. At any rate the fresh
truce paved the way for a marriage treaty which just over a century later was
to have profound consequences for the Stewarts. Even another frontier affray
did not interrupt the slow and peaceful progress of Anglo-Scottish negotiations.

James IV's ambitions for a wife soared extremely high. He sought for an
Infanta of Spain, a Holy Roman Emperor's daughter or the daughter of the
King of England who, when James sent out his roving ambassadors, was
only nine years old. Marriage was purely a political arrangement; for James
had a variety of mistresses. The first, known as Marion Boyd, in 1493 bore
him a son, Alexander Stewart; before he reached the age of eighteen the
King created him Archbishop of St Andrews, the loftiest position in the
Scottish Church. His second mistress was Margaret Drummond, whom
some thought he intended to marry, but she and her two sisters died
obscurely one day after eating breakfast and, as was customary, were
assumed to have been poisoned. His next mistress, Janet Kennedy, became
Countess of Bothwell and was generously rewarded for bearing the King
another son, James Stewart Earl of Moray. There was also an enigmatic
'L.A.' or 'M.L.A.' who figures in the royal treasurer's accounts. Finally,
according at any rate to Pitscottie, the 'wicked Lady Ford', an Englishwoman who dwelt in a castle just south of the border, had 'frequent
whoredom with the King'. He was not the first nor the last Stewart King
whose sexual objectives were versatile.

The negotiations about James's marriage were drawn out. Whether it is
true that Henry VII knew that 'the King of the Scots was a lusty bachelor of
twenty-five notorious for his gallantries', as has been suggested, and that
Henry's wife was therefore opposed to such a marriage for her innocent
daughter and that was why the settlement was delayed may be questioned.
It was rare for State marriages to be influenced by such considerations. But

questions of money were involved. To keep the kettle boiling, in September 1499 Henry VII ratified yet another truce with Scotland. Ultimately it was agreed that his daughter, Margaret Tudor, was to be given a dowry of £10,000 and her husband was to bestow on her lands and castles yielding a rent of £2,000 sterling a year. The marriage treaty was signed on 24 January 1502 together with a treaty of perpetual peace between Scotland and England and a treaty to regulate border disputes. When Henry's Ministers questioned the wisdom of the marriage on the ground that if the King's two sons died without issue the kingdom of England would fall to the King of Scotland, Henry answered that 'if that should be, Scotland would be an accession to England and not England to Scotland, for the great would draw the less'.

The child bride arrived in Scotland in the summer of 1503; the wedding was held in Holyrood abbey and the festivities celebrated in the newly built Holyroodhouse. The King bought himself two cloths of gold lined with fur for the occasion and an Edinburgh goldsmith fashioned a crown for the bride. Margaret Drummond, the King's favourite mistress, had conveniently died the year before. The poet William Dunbar wrote an epithalamium and a shorter poem to commemorate the joining of 'the Thistle and the Rose':

> *Welcome the Rose both red and white,*
> *Welcome the flower of our delight!*
> *Our secret rejoicing from the sun bien [warm]*
> *Welcome of Scotland to be Queen!*

The Rose has been described, on the evidence of one of her portraits, as lumpish and unprepossessing, but another portrait, copied by Mytens, now in Holyrood palace, does not confirm this.

During the five years that succeeded the wedding James was still occupied in pacifying the Highlands, relying on Huntly in the east, where he became the hereditary sheriff of Inverness, and Argyll in the west, with his base at the royal castle of Tarbert, to maintain order and justice; he also, as has already been noticed, employed his small fleet, carrying guns normally kept in Edinburgh castle, to subdue the outlying Western Isles. But what James failed to do was to conciliate the Highland chieftains or to fill the power vacuum created by the forfeiture of the MacDonalds. James's biographer asserts that he 'left the Highlands and Islands much as he found them, with their old feuds unappeased, with the gulf between the "Wild Scots" and the civilized Scots as wide as it had been', while another historian described the peace in the north at the end of the reign as 'illusory'.

However, the temporary pacification of the Highlands and the permanent peace with the old enemy, England (confirmed after the death of Henry VII on 1 April 1509), resulted in turning James IV's thoughts towards a grandiose project — that of leading an allied Christian army on a Crusade against the Turks. At the age of thirty-six, writes his modern biographer, James became 'a moonstruck romantic whose eyes were ever at the ends of the earth'. Unfortunately for him the Christian rulers of Europe were divided among themselves. The warrior Pope Julius II, who had succeeded the Borgia Pope Alexander VI in 1503 and was just as materialistic, had grievances against the Venetian Republic, long the bastion of Europe against the Turks, and formed with the future Maximilian I, Louis XII King of France and Ferdinand King of Aragon, the league of Cambrai to humiliate the Venetians and partition their possessions. The Venetians were duly defeated, but then the Pope regretted having invited the French into Italy, thus enabling them to take hold of both Genoa and Milan; he therefore proceeded to form another Holy League directed this time against the Most Christian King Louis XII. In August 1511 James informed the Pope that he was ready to exert his influence to prevent the shedding of more blood among Christian monarchs so that the long-hoped-for Crusade against the Infidels should not be delayed any further; as early as 1509 he had assured the Pope that he was willing himself to lead such a sacred adventure into whatever regions the Holy Father thought proper and would gladly shed the last drop of his own blood in the cause of Christendom. What he had in mind was to sail with his newly built fleet to Venice, accompanied by a sizable army, and thence take command of an allied armada and move on to Palestine. Henry VIII of England expressed his willingness to take part in so noble a scheme, which would by implication be anti-French — because Louis XII and the Pope were still at loggerheads; for the King of England was also swayed by a devouring ambition, which was to reconquer Guienne and Normandy, provinces that two generations earlier had been English dominions, relics of Henry V's complete conquest of France during the previous century.

Nothing, however, came of either of these elaborate dreams. What in fact happened in 1511 was that both the King of the Scots and the King of England found themselves absorbed in undeclared war with one another. James had given letters of marque to Sir Andrew Barton, now his favourite naval commander, since Sir Andrew Wood was getting on in years and had retired from the fray; these enabled Barton and his brothers to carry out what were in fact acts of piracy against all and sundry. Instead of negotiating over the complaints of English merchants, as he might have done under the terms of the Anglo-Scottish treaty, Henry VII dispatched his own warships to exact satisfaction from the upstart Scots: Andrew Barton was defeated and killed. Besides these quarrels at sea the usual disturbances prevailed along the borders. Both sides then concentrated on diplomatic moves to avert open hostilities. James renewed the old alliance with the French all the more willingly because Louis XII, being desperately eager for all the support he could get if the young Henry VIII were to invade his kingdom, promised James IV that once these temporary difficulties were overcome he would contribute money and arms to the Crusade for which the Scottish King was yearning.

In fact neither Henry VIII nor James IV really wanted open war, Henry because he was busy preparing to invade France, James because as long as Henry had no children, his own son, born to him and Henry's sister, Margaret Tudor on 11 April 1512, was the heir presumptive to the throne of England. All this needed to be explained tactfully to the French King; and although the treaty of alliance with France was ratified by James IV on 10 July 1512, it was not until the summer of the following year that Scottish negotiations with England for a peaceful settlement of their disputes on land and sea finally broke down.

Basically the cause of the coming war was Louis XII's unwillingness to abandon his ambitions in Italy. That was why he was so anxious for Scottish help to distract Henry VIII from landing in northern France when he himself was on his way to Italy. Furthermore Louis aimed to weaken the Papacy, his chief opponent in Italy, by calling a Council of the Church at Pisa. Henry VIII determined to hold James IV in check by persuading the Pope to excommunicate the Scottish King on the ground that his treaty of alliance with France was an immoral repudiation of his treaty of perpetual peace with England: Julius II did so on his death-bed. Henry also appointed the septuagenarian Thomas Howard first Earl of Surrey to be his lieutenant in the north instructing him to raise troops from the six northern counties so as to protect the borders from Scottish incursions. Early in June Louis XII's army in Italy was beaten at the battle of Novara, south of the Brenner pass, by Pope Leo X, who had just succeeded Julius II and had hired a Swiss professional army to drive out the French. At the end of June Henry VIII landed at Calais with a large army and laid siege to the fortified town of Thérouanne, twenty-one miles south-west of Calais on the river Scheldt. By now James IV felt compelled to burn his boats: he wrote a letter to Henry VIII dated 26 July 1513 which reached him at Thérouanne in mid-August.

In this letter James told the English King, his brother-in-law, that he had lost faith in him and required him to desist from further attacks on the Most Christian King of France, to whom James himself was bound in mutual defence. Henry was furious and refused to write a reply. Three days later he defeated the French cavalry at the battle of the Spurs whereupon Thérouanne capitulated.

Before James's ultimatum reached Henry VIII fighting had already begun on the Anglo-Scottish border. In August James had dispatched his Warden of the Marches, Lord Home, to devastate Northumberland, but he was successfully ambushed by English archers on his way back. Then on 22 August James led his main army across the Tweed and laid siege to Norham castle, which surrendered in six days. Shortly afterwards James occupied a fortnight besieging another English castle at Ford. According to Pitscottie, James dallied with the beautiful Lady Ford while his illegitimate son, the precocious Archbishop of St Andrews, dallied with her daughter. That, Pitscottie thought, was against the 'ordour of a good captane of warre to begin at Whordom and harlotterie befoir any guid succes of battell or victorie'. Be that as it may, there was something phoney about the whole campaign. James's army was of an amateur makeshift character, consisting of over 20,000 men, chiefly borderers but with a Highland brigade, which fought the best, on the right wing; a large number of soldiers had deserted after the siege of Norham. James's famous artillery amounted to seventeen brass guns, dragged from Edinburgh castle, the bigger ones requiring over thirty oxen to haul them. As they were incapable of registering satisfactorily they made a lot of noise, but only frightened the enemy. Finally James's celebrated fleet which he dispatched to help the French, contained only sixteen warships with top sails, did not reach the French coast until after September and did not fire a single shot, while 'the monstruous *Great St Michael*' ran aground and next year was sold to the French.

It has been suggested that James IV did not truly want to go to war at all; all that he aimed at was a demonstration of force on land and sea; and that he hoped such a display would induce Henry VIII to withdraw from France. This interpretation of James's strategy is possibly confirmed by the fact that rather than engage in jockeying for position he sent, on 6 September, a herald to the Earl of Surrey proposing noon on Friday 9 September as a suitable day for a battle, though it was then pouring with rain: and no site was fixed. The Scots then proceeded to encamp upon Flodden hill, 500 feet high, with their right covered by a morass and their left by the river Till, a tributary of the Tweed. James was an optimist if he imagined that the English were going to assault this formidable position at a time known in advance. Did he hope to persuade Surrey to retire rather than fight? In fact Surrey was an old campaigner; he and his son, Admiral Thomas Howard, resolved to cross the Till at two points and thus insert themselves between the Scottish army and Scotland. As they were short of both food and drink, the English wanted to settle the war as quickly as they could. Not wishing to be cut off from his supplies nor attacked from the rear James withdrew his army to a hill a mile north of Flodden known as Branxton, the first of a series of ridges in the Cheviots.

The battle began at four o'clock in the afternoon instead of twelve in the morning (which the Scots thought was cheating) with artillery fire from both sides that did little damage. Both armies fought on foot, the Scots being armed chiefly with eighteen-foot pikes, the English with eight-foot 'brown bills', that is to say spears with an axe-blade. In theory the Scottish phalanxes of pikemen, like the schiltroms at Bannockburn, should have won the battle, but the phalanxes were broken up by the enemy archers and disrupted by the slippery, uneven and sloping ground. 'Our bills', wrote the Bishop of Durham, who was there, 'disappointed the Scots of their long spears on which they relied.' The battle lasted fewer than two hours. James IV, who fought on foot at the head of the central brigade, was killed near where the rival commander stood. His body was found naked pierced with many wounds. Numerous Scottish nobility and gentry, including at least nine earls, two bishops and two abbots, also died on the field while some of the rank-and-file were drowned as they tried to cross the swollen Tweed on their way home.

The paradoxes of James IV's career relate both to his religious and foreign policies. The tribute by the contemporary Spanish ambassador to James's outward devotion, his regular attendence at Mass and so on has already been quoted. Attention has also been drawn to his eagerness to lead a Crusade against the infidel Turks. Yet one hears nothing of his penitences; he was consistently unfaithful to his Queen; and he took advantage of his patronage of the Church to distribute its wealth among his political servants and illegitimate sons rather than seeking to find posts for deserving clergy. It can of course be argued that all monarchs have to marry for reasons of State; and certainly hardly a single Stewart King (except perhaps Charles I) was without the compensation of a mistress or lover. But when it is considered that James presented his mistress, Janet Kennedy, with his lands and castle at Darnaway because they were conveniently situated on the route of his annual pilgrimage to St Duthac's shrine in Ross one is confronted with a fascinating example of the differing standards of Christian religion and Christian morality; it is known for a fact that on one occasion at least James broke his journey to the shrine at Darnaway to see Janet both on his way there and his way back. On that particular occasion he was accompanied by three falconers and four Italian minstrels.

His attitude to the filling of benefices is exemplified by his appointment after the death in 1497 of William Scheves, the first primate of the Scottish Church, of his brother, James Duke of Ross, then only eight years old, to the vacant archbishopric of St Andrews, though he could not take up the post until he reached the age of thirty; thus during the interval James was able to draw on the revenues of the see for his own purposes. After his brother, who was never consecrated, died in 1504, James replaced him with his illegitimate son by Marion Boyd, Alexander Stewart, a boy of eleven; Alexander had been Archdeacon of St Andrews when he was nine. This youthful archbishop was killed along with his father at the battle of Flodden. James Beaton, the second Archbishop of Glasgow, was a notorious nepotist and Andrew Forman Bishop of Moray was a leading diplomatist, whose interest in the welfare of the Church has been described as 'marginal'. Admittedly pluralism and absenteeism had long been commonplace; bishops were expected to be politicians or ambassadors or even military governors; but abbots were also more often than not absorbed in secular affairs on behalf of the King: for example, James gave an abbacy to a French leech because he promised to show him how to convert base metals into gold. Finally, it should not be forgotten that James was under sentence of excommunication for breach of faith when he died. The fact is that the Scottish Church was rotting during the reign of James IV. It was no wonder that the heretical Lollards took a hold during the reign or that John Knox was able to overthrow Roman Catholic supremacy fairly easily fewer than fifty years after James IV died.

In view of the trouble that James took over the building and repairing of castles, notably Inverness, Tarbert and Stirling, of his attempt to create a royal navy, including another costly ship, the *Margaret*, which more often than not was under repair, and of his concern over gunnery, though his cannon proved of little value at Flodden, where it was all lost, it might have been assumed that James had at least a well-considered foreign policy, which he could back by force. Scottish historians have stressed that his ultimate objective was to lead a Crusade against the Turks in faraway Palestine, but that, after all, was a mere daydream during the age of the Renaissance. To attain such a goal he would have needed to maintain peace not only at home but with England and other European kingdoms and also to have come to terms with the Papacy. In fact he attained none of these necessary conditions. By allying himself with France, once he had sworn to perpetual peace with England, he succeeded in alienating two Popes. By antagonizing Henry VIII, when he was married to his sister, James hazarded the chance that one day his son or grandchild would come by heredity to the English Crown. So, paradoxically, he had by his ill-conceived foreign policy endangered that union between the Thistle and the Rose which was in fact to transform the Stewarts of Scotland into the Stuarts of England.

R. L. Mackie, *King James IV of Scotland* (1958) is the best biography. Mr Mackie also edited *Letters of James IV 1505–1513* (S.H.S. 1953). For the battle of Flodden see W. Mackay Mackenzie, *The Secret of Flodden* (1931). One has the impression, however, that the part played by the English archers is underestimated. One difficulty about describing the battle is that there is no evidence from any Scots who took part in it; all the contemporary sources are English. The letters written by Thomas Ruthal Bishop of Durham to Cardinal Wolsey, printed in *Letters and Papers, Foreign and Domestic of the Reign of Henry VIII* (1920) are valuable for the period.

[8]

James V – a King
Who Died Too Young

JAMES V comes in the midst of a line of Stewart monarchs who were all minors when they inherited the throne. James I had been twelve, James II six, and James III eight. But as their majority was reached on their fourteenth birthday they did not have to wait very long before they could assume at least the mantle of authority. On the other hand, James V was but seventeen months old when he was crowned, his daughter, Mary, had only been on earth for a few days when she succeeded him, and his grandson, James VI of Scotland and later James I of England, had scarcely attained the age of thirteen months when his mother abdicated her throne and abandoned her kingdom. While the nobility quarrelled over who should exercise the realities of power during James V's minority his education was neglected; he acquired more of his personality from his heredity than he did from his environment or his books.

James V's paternal grandfather, King Henry VII of England, was a statesman of outstanding quality and his mother, Margaret Tudor, was at any rate a woman of character. On the Stewart side his father and grandfather had been not untypical Renaissance princes who used their positions to patronize the arts and crafts and to glorify their line. James IV had made Edinburgh his capital and had begun the building of the palace of Holyroodhouse there. His son was less cultured (he spoke no English and indifferent French) but he was to be the benefactor of poets, scholars and architects; he also brought over skilled craftsmen from France, Spain and the Netherlands to embellish his kingdom.

Like his father, James V loved women of his own choice, but married them for reasons of State. Inheriting his father's grey eyes and a dark complexion, he was known as 'the red tod' [wolf]. According to Bishop Lesley, he was sober, moderate, honest, affable and courteous, and he abhorred pride and arrogance. The poet Ronsard wrote of him:

La douceur et la force illustroient son visage
Si que Venus et Mars avoient fait partage.

To begin with, his mother was in effect appointed regent, though the title given her was that of her son's guardian. She was still in her early twenties when her first husband died; after she had completed her duties to him by giving birth to a posthumous son (who did not live for long) she selected Archibald Douglas sixth Earl of Angus, grandson of Bell-the-Cat, as his successor. Her choice proved unfortunate: Angus was sufficiently good-looking and graceful to be attractive to women, but was also greedy, grasping and unscrupulous. She spelt his name, appropriately enough 'Earl of Anguish'. After the marriage the Scottish Estates promptly relieved her of her guardianship; in any case they did not want a ruler who was not only a woman but English, to boot. Instead they sent for John Stewart Duke of Albany, the grandson of James II and the son of Alexander Stewart Duke of Albany, who had made such a nuisance of himself to James III and had settled in France in 1484 where he was killed in a tournament. Both of these Albanys had married wealthy French wives and were highly regarded at the Court of Paris. The second Albany, brought up in France, spoke only French and regarded France as his native land. Nevertheless he was undoubtedly heir presumptive to the Scottish throne until such a time as James V grew to manhood and fathered a child. So Albany reluctantly consented to become Governor of Scotland and was installed as such in Edinburgh on 15 July 1515.

Understandably Margaret Tudor was disinclined to relinquish her son. But Albany brought a military force, accompanied by the celebrated cannon, Mons Meg, and since she was not only pregnant again, but lacked any support from her new husband, the Red Douglas, she was obliged to yield and part with her children. She escaped to England, where in conditions of some discomfort she gave birth to a daughter, Margaret, who was to be the paternal grandmother of King James VI. Thus Albany began his regency firmly enough. Yet opinions were and are divided about his capabilities. As he interspersed his stay in Scotland with several visits to his beloved France on one excuse or another and finally left Scotland altogether when James V was only eleven, he cannot be said to have accomplished much for the Stewart kingdom except negotiating or renovating the alliance with France. Twice — in 1522 and 1523 — he attempted unsuccessfuly to invade northern England, but had been compelled ignominiously to withdraw across the Tweed even when, on the second occasion, he had been furnished with trained French troops.

During James V's boyhood the ruling factions in Scotland shifted about like coloured pieces in a kaleidoscope. His mother returned from England while Albany was spending four years in France. By then she had taken a

dislike to her second husband and was agitating for a divorce. Since Angus
had been adopted by Henry VIII as his chief agent in Scotland, she for a
time linked her fortunes with James Hamilton first Earl of Arran, who,
because he was the grandson of James II, stood next in the line of succession
to the Scottish throne after Albany. Then came another shift. Angus
disappeared into France; a parliament, which met at Edinburgh in
November 1524, then upheld a coup, carried out by James's mother and
Arran, in which they put the boy on to his throne, investing him with
crown and sceptre, and surrounding him with a guard of English archers;
then in his name they appointed new officers of State.

But this coup was effective only for a few months. Henry VIII did not
trust his sister, who was certainly unstable both in her political tastes and
matrimonial affections, as distinguished women often are. Henry, who
believed in keeping women, especially wives, under control, preferred to
place his confidence in her husband, Angus, who was soon to become her
ex-husband, as Margaret's divorce had been obtained from Rome, and she
married again a nice young man who was a Stewart. After returning to
Scotland by way of England in January 1525, Angus was restored by
Parliament to all his offices and dignities and in addition appointed
Warden of the West and East Marches.

Because of these divisions among the nobility once Albany made his final
departure for France, the Scottish Parliament that met in July 1525
resolved that four great lords should take it in turn, each for three months,
to guard the King and act in his name. The first choice was Angus. But
when in November 1525 he was called upon to hand over the King to the
next in line as Guardian, he refused to do so. On the contrary, he kept hold
of him and on 14 June 1526 announced, somewhat prematurely, that James
had become of age and could therefore govern henceforward on his own
authority. By this subterfuge Angus and the other Red Douglases engros-
sed most of the offices of State and of the royal household. Angus himself
became Chancellor after persuading James to write a letter dismissing
James Beaton Archbishop of St Andrews from that position. Thus James
became a puppet of the Red Douglases, just as James III had been a puppet
of the Boyds and James II of the Livingstons. Like his namesakes, he
resented the tutelage forced upon him and became determined to find a
rescuer. But it proved by no means easy to do this. For Angus was not only a
statesman of ambition with most of the threads of authority in his hands,
but he also showed himself to be a highly capable soldier.

James engineered his first attempt to escape from the thrall of Angus by
invoking the aid of his kinsman, John Stewart third Earl of Lennox, a

grandson of James II's daughter Mary, an amiable and likeable young nobleman. With the support of Archbishop Beaton and others he marched against Angus and a battle was fought near Linlithgow. James did his best to help by delaying Sir George Douglas, a younger brother of Angus, from joining him in the field. But is was of no avail. Lennox was killed after he had been taken a prisoner. Described with some exaggeration as 'the hardiest, stoutest and wisest man that ever Scotland bore', his dead body was covered with a scarlet cloth and the King's servants buried him on the battlefield.

Naturally James was shocked and embittered, but now he had to bide his time for revenge. In May 1528 when Angus and his brother were away from Edinburgh castle, where James was held in honourable captivity, the boy King disguised himself as a groom, managed to escape from his jailers and rode to Stirling, where Arran and other leading earls awaited him. Angus realized that the game was up. After holding out successfully against a siege of his castle of Tantallon by the King, he yielded in November 1525 and went into exile in England for the remainder of the reign, while a parliament declared the lives and lands of the Red Douglases forfeited. Thus the supremacy of the Red Douglases was broken by James V just as his great-grandfather, James II, had crushed the Black Douglases eighty years earlier. James was sixteen and a half years old when he exacted his revenge.

After all these adventures the young King, deeply suspicious of his nobility, was determined to prevent any more rebellions or disorders. Gavin Dunbar Archbishop of Glasgow, who had been James's tutor in his younger days, was appointed Chancellor; Robert Barton, his father's naval commander and a successful financier, resumed the office of Comptroller that he had held before; and the poet, Sir David Lindsay, who had been his Master Usher since his birth, ultimately received the honorific post of Lord Lyon King of Arms; his mother's third husband, Henry Stewart, was created Lord Methven and Master of the Ordnance. With the aim of pacifying the kingdom James first led two expeditions to the border country after notifying his uncle, Henry VIII, of his plans; there he caught and hanged defiant lairds and freebooters, the most famous of whom was Johnny Armstrong Laird of Gilnockie; a poem was written about his fate, which made the King say when Armstrong pleaded for his life:

> *Away, away, thou traitor strang,*
> *Out of my sight soon mayest thou be*
> *I granted never a traitor's life,*
> *And now I'll not begin with thee.*

James next turned his attention to the other historic centre of unrest, the west and northern Highlands. Here he did not exactly follow his father's policy, for he thought the Campbells were becoming far too influential. Instead he relied on the MacDonalds, previously a thorn in the side of the Stewart kings, to counterbalance the Campbells; on the other hand, he continued to trust the Gordons to maintain peace in the north. The fourth Earl of Huntly, who was about James's own age and whom the King had come to know personally when he was still subjected to Angus, was therefore allowed to retain the lieutenancy there. During this period following the fall of the Red Douglases, that is to say the early fifteen-thirties, the King sentenced several magnates including Argyll, Bothwell and Lord Home to spells of imprisonment. When a parliament met in Edinburgh in 1532 'sundry good laws', so Bishop Lesley wrote, were 'made for the common welfare of the realm, especially for the staunching of theft, strife and oppressions, which the King caused to be well kept with sharp execution all his days'. James was punctilious in going on justice ayres and in taking a personal interest in the maintenance of law and order everywhere. Even the Protestant historians, John Knox and George Buchanan, both of whom had no reason to be prejudiced in his favour since he was an undeviating Roman Catholic, and, like his father, obedient to the Papacy, wrote in praise of his assiduity in his duties. According to Buchanan, he would 'sit on horseback day and night in the coldest winter so that he might catch thieves in their harbours unaware'; Knox noted that he was called by some 'a poor man's king' and that others praised him for preventing theft and oppression. Bishop Lesley claimed that during the reign 'people lived quietly and in rest out of all oppression and molestation of the nobility and rich persons'. Indeed the inflexible way in which James V came to treat his secular nobility when they misbehaved does seem to have endeared him to the common people.

So far as foreign affairs were concerned in his time they were dominated by two considerations: first, western Europe was in the grip of three young aspiring monarchs, Henry VIII, Francis I of France and the Emperor Charles V, compared with whom the King of Scots with his poorer and less populated country could not be other than puny; secondly, ever since Martin Luther had nailed his protestant theses to the door of the castle church at Wittenberg in October 1517 the Popes had been forced on to the defensive and became anxious to secure all the allies they could find. When Albany was Regent he had negotiated a treaty with France at Rouen on 26 August 1517, which was mutually defensive against England and promised James V a French bride. Albany had also envisaged a triple alliance including the Papacy. After Henry VIII began to throw off his allegiance to Rome, Pope Clement VII became so eager to retain the obedience of the Scottish King that not only did he renew the indult which enabled James V to annex the revenues of vacant bishoprics and abbacies, but he was also willing to give James a handsome grant of funds at the expense of the Scottish Church; this concession was ratified by Clement's successor, Pope Paul III, in 1535. Complicated negotiations followed; in the end James was given £72,000, payable in instalments, nominally in order to set up a permanent Court of Session or Court of Justice, consisting mainly of ecclesiastics, who, because they were paid regular salaries, were likely to strengthen the Scottish judicial system. In fact their salaries only cost a small part of the papal grant, allowing James to spend much of it on royal grandeur.

To assist his finances further James also wanted to find himself a wealthy French wife. The treaty of Rouen had envisaged this; moreover once Henry VIII finally broke with the Papacy in 1534 an English bride, though offered, was out of the question so long as James was loyal to the Roman Church. It is also possible that the marriage of James V's father was not reckoned to have been such a success as to be worthy of repetition. At any rate after numerous diplomatic soundings James himself visited France in the autumn of 1536, but disliking the bride picked out for him by Francis I, persuaded the French King to let him marry his beautiful but frail daughter, Madeleine. The wedding was held in Notre-Dame on 1 January 1536. But the bride died some six weeks after she landed in Scotland; since no royal princesses were left available James then agreed to marry Mary of Guise-Lorraine, a widow. Thus James acquired two generous dowries and was firmly committed to the French alliance.

After James returned to Scotland he continued to keep his nobility closely in check while aiming to promote justice among ordinary people. In the autumn he ordered justice ayres to be held in the Highlands and during the winter in the Lowlands. According to Bishop Lesley, he was often present at these ayres himself, 'assisting his lords commissioners in further-ing justice and maintaining the same throughout all parts of the realm'. In some of his decisions he was motivated by suspicions of Henry VIII; he was particularly angered by the patronage bestowed by the English monarch on Angus and the remaining Red Douglases. He had twice sent the Bishop of Aberdeen, the nephew and namesake of his old tutor, Gavin Dunbar, to discuss border disputes with the English King. When he returned from his second visit Dunbar told James about Henry's behaviour towards the exiled Douglases and 'how he was given to entertaining them'; which aroused the

Scottish King's suspicions of such Douglases as remained in the country. One of them was Angus's sister, Lady Janet Douglas, reputedly a beautiful woman, who had married one of the Campbells; after being suspected of poisoning her first husband, Lord Glamis, she was accused of trying to poison the King. She was burnt to death on Edinburgh castle hill on 17 July 1537; her husband, who had witnessed her execution, was killed or committed suicide soon afterwards. John Master of Forbes, who had married another sister of Angus, was at the same time charged with planning to shoot the King with a culverin and was condemned to be hanged, drawn and quartered. A son of the beautiful lady who had been burnt was spared because 'he was young and of tender age', but sentenced to imprisonment for life. Another Douglas was ordered into exile; Patrick Hepburn Earl of Bothwell, a friend of the Douglases and pro-English, was imprisoned and then banished. Finally, Sir James Douglas of Parkhead, who had been one of the King's jailers when he was young, was summoned and accused of treason in 1540, while Sir James Hamilton of Finnart, James V's Master of Works, who had been in favour first when Angus was supreme, was put to death in August 1540 for corresponding with the Douglases and plotting the murder of the King. This veritable holocaust of James's enemies showed that he was as tough and unforgiving as his uncle, Henry VIII.

At the end of May 1540 James set out on a major expedition to the Highlands, accompanied by Cardinal David Beaton Archbishop of St Andrews, who had succeeded his uncle in 1539, by the Earl of Huntly, one of the few nobles completely trusted by the King, and by Oliver Sinclair, described as 'the most secret man living with the King of Scots', but not by the Queen who had just given birth to a son. Sinclair had received many valuable gifts and offices from James and was known as 'a minion'; Scottish historians are divided about whether his relations with James were homosexual or not. If they were, James V may have been bisexual like his father and grandson.

The voyage to the Highlands was made in twelve ships furnished with artillery; they set sail from Leith, stopped at various places along the east coast, visited the Orkneys and the Hebrides, and returned to Dumbarton in the middle of August, having circumnavigated Scotland. The natives of the Highlands and islands were overawed by the royal fleet; James carried back with him a number of chieftains as prisoners or hostages for the good behaviour of their kinsmen. According to Pitscottie, 'when the King saw that he had daunted the north parts and the isles, wherewith he greatly rejoiced when he saw his north country in subjection and in peace and at rest', he turned his attention back to the still unruly borders, imprisoning some of the lairds as a warning to others. The incarceration and banishment of Bothwell were also intended to dissuade the Wardens of the Marches from misbehaving themselves. James did not want indiscipline on the English frontier to provide an excuse for Henry VIII to interfere in Scottish affairs.

The traditional enmity between the neighbouring kingdoms was now accentuated by the Reformation. James V, as it has justly been observed, was neither a good Catholic nor a good Christian. But the Papacy felt obliged to do all it could to offset the defection of England from its allegiance by bribing the Scottish monarchy to stay loyal. Not only was James allowed to pocket the larger part of what came to be known as 'the Great Tax' on the Scottish Church, nominally levied to provide for the payment of the new Court of Justice, but in March 1535 Pope Paul III extended the period during which the Scottish King could nominate to vacant prelacies from the eight months permitted to his grandfather, James III, to a full year. In return for this concession James repudiated the Lollards and Lutherans, who stigmatized the very bases of the Roman Catholic religion, and spurned the temptations to more wealth which were provided by the example of Henry VIII's breach with Rome and his subsequent dissolution of the monasteries. Patrick Hamilton, who had advocated Luther's doctrine of justification by faith, was put to death in 1528 as one of the first Scottish martyrs. In 1530 other heretics were burnt in Edinburgh including a regular canon, two Blackfriars monks and one layman, while two priests were degraded and sentenced to perpetual imprisonment. Other heretics were tried and found guilty in Glasgow. Later another layman, Sir John Borthwick, was reprobated in his absence by the Archbishop of St Andrews and other bishops. After Sir John had been declared a heretic and was not available for execution, a waxen image of him was constructed and burnt at the market cross.

Because he was courted by the Popes James was able to find rich livings for all his illegitimate sons. Unlike Henry VIII, who believed in having wives, James is known to have enjoyed at least six mistresses, some out of the top drawer and some not. He wanted to marry Margaret, daughter of Lord Erskine, but the Pope refused him her divorce. On the other hand, his friend the poet, David Lindsay, is quoted as saying 'he was perpetually engaged upon sexual pursuit without the slightest fastidiousness'. Before his two French marriages were concluded he was able to argue that they would be useful in preventing the procreation of any bastards. But up till then he had done pretty well. Neither Clement VII nor Paul III objected to his conferring abbacies on his illegitimate sons. James explained to Clement VII in advocating the induction of a six-year-old child that while 'youth may be an obstacle to the holding of a benefice, a father's deserts and a son's promise often demand that the rigour of the law should be relaxed' or abbots-elect would 'put a restraint upon the impious'.

It has been contended that James V at least went through the motions of piety. But he was clearly not as punctilious at his devotions or in worship and pilgrimage as his would-be Crusader father. In fact he encouraged George Buchanan, the future tutor of James VI, to write anti-clerical poetry, though as it was composed in Latin it may not have penetrated very far. Sir David Lindsay, however, wrote satires in the vernacular attacking not only immoral priests but in *The Satire of the Three Estates* castigated the entire clerical order.

In view of all this it was scarcely surprising that King Henry VIII, now installed as the Supreme Head of the Church of England, should hope to win over his nephew from his pro-Catholic and pro-French propensities. Earlier he had sent James the Order of the Garter and in 1540 he dispatched one of his ablest diplomatists, Sir Ralph Sadler, to persuade the Scottish King of the marvellous benefits to be derived from confiscating Church properties. Naturally Henry feared that, instigated by the Pope, the Catholic monarchs, Charles V, whose aunt, the divorced Catherine of Aragon, had been the English King's first wife, and Francis I, who still wanted to regain Calais from its English garrison, might band together against him. If he could detach the Scots from their French alliance, that would at least be a positive advantage; furthermore he was not without hopes of uniting the two kingdoms by reviving the ancient claims of the English monarchy to suzerainty over Scotland. Which of these motives was the stronger is not entirely plain, but when Sadler paid a second visit to Scotland in 1541 he secured a promise from James V that he would meet his uncle in York that September.

The reason why Henry VIII agreed to this proposal was that he was confident that he himself could win over James to the cause of the Reformation and detach him from France, although in fact in this very year James had sent Cardinal Beaton on a diplomatic mission to France which might have resulted in the conclusion of an offensive alliance against England. When the time came, James excused himself from meeting his uncle in York on the ground that some border quarrel had first to be settled. The reason for his backing out of his commitment was because his clerical advisers (and most of James's advisers were clerics) did not want him to be tempted into becoming a Protestant; they may also have warned him that if he ventured into England he would be kidnapped. Henry, who had undertaken the long journey to his northern capital for the first time in his life and had vainly waited there for the arrival of the King of Scots, was furious. Whatever his exact reasons for breaking his engagement, James's humiliation of his uncle was the most foolish act in his life.

In the following year Henry decided upon a full-scale invasion of Scotland with the intention of extending his authority over the northern kingdom, as Edward I and Edward III had tried to do years before. Unofficial warfare had already broken out on the border and the Scots were delighted when the Earl of Huntly succeeded in defeating and capturing Sir Robert Bowes, the English Warden of the East March, near Kelso on the Tweed. Furthermore when Henry dispatched a big army under Thomas Howard third Duke of Norfolk (son of the first Earl of Surrey, victor of Flodden) it was obliged to retreat across the frontier and disintegrated after devastating a large part of Lothian. Being far from his base at York, Norfolk had difficulty over his line of communications and so lacked sufficient food and drink for his troops. James mustered a substantial army at Edinburgh, which he divided into two parts, one to feint to the east of the border, the other to attack in the west. Nearly all the great commanders in history have preached the doctrine: 'don't divide the army'; and James committed other errors. Because he had alienated so many of the secular nobility by his past ruthlessness there were many defections from his army and much reluctance about crossing the border. Moreover he quarrelled with Huntly for not following up his earlier victory and he replaced Lord Maxwell, the warden of the Scottish Marches, with his favourite, Oliver Sinclair. Finally, James himself, being taken ill, was obliged to withdraw to Lochmaben castle to await the outcome of the campaign he had launched.

Although James had scarcely reached the age of thirty, he had for a time been in poor health. He had suffered a hunting accident in Stirling, while medicines that he had purchased abroad to cure an unspecified disease had not worked or had worked badly. It is likely that the root of his troubles was mental and psychological. He dreamed bad dreams, particularly over the fate of Sir James Hamilton of Finnart, his former favourite and Master of Works, who appeared to him in his sleep, protested his innocence, and warned the King that he would remain in sorrow for a while and then would have his head struck off. The King and Queen were distressed by the sudden deaths of their two baby sons only the year before; James's mother had also just died. Now if James himself were to die, who would succeed him? The hated Earl of Angus, who was actually serving in the English army? A story has been told too that Oliver Sinclair had provided his master with a black list of secular nobles who were conspiring against him. If his armies were beaten, would he be overthrown?

Whatever the precise causes were, the Scottish army which invaded England was demoralized and divided. Possibly its officers did not want to follow Sinclair; probably they did not even know who their commander was. In any case the battle, which was fought at Solway Moss on the river Esk on 24 November 1542, quickly degenerated into a rout. Though the English were inferior in numbers, many Scottish nobles and lairds surrendered on the field; they did not even bother to escape. When James heard the news of the defeat he rode distraught to Linlithgow, thence to Edinburgh and finally to Falkland palace, 'where', according to Pitscottie, 'he remained quietly, being sore troubled both in spirit and body and no one was permitted to have access to him except his secret and familiar servants'. Here he was informed that on 8 December 1542 the Queen had been delivered of a fair daughter. One story is to the effect that he said 'the Crown came by a woman [Marjory Bruce] and will with one go [Mary Queen of Scots]; many miseries approach this poor kingdom; King Henry VIII will either make it by arms or marriage'. Yet it is rare to die of grief. One account is that James was poisoned by his own medicines. At any rate, six days after Mary's birth, he turned his face to the wall and yielded up his spirit. He was only thirty when he passed away that December.

The moral judgments pronounced by historians on James V's character and career vary, but in their essence they do not disagree. Above all, he was a Renaissance prince, who collected and spent more money on the arts and crafts than his father or any other previous Stewart king. It has been estimated that altogether he spent £50,000 on architecture during his reign. As his annual income was of about the same order and he enjoyed several windfalls such as his wives' dowries and the papal grants, that was hardly excessive. He extended the building of Holyroodhouse, Stirling castle and Falkland palace. At Linlithgow his improvements were commended by Mary of Guise as comparable with those of the finest French palaces. The new buildings at Falkland have been described as 'a Renaissance screen which hangs in front of an unaffected Gothic range', a monument to the French alliance and 'a display of Renaissance architecture without a parallel in the British isles'. The interiors of his palaces were repainted and decorated with carved medallions. James was a patron of literature, particularly of the work of such Scottish historians as Hector Boece.

It cannot be said that the historians of the sixteenth century reciprocated his patronage. Lindsay of Pitscottie, who was a Protestant, wrote that though he 'did many good acts, such as building palaces and castles and bringing great artillery to Scotland', he would not allow 'the word of God to have free passage' because it taught the need to lead a virtuous life, to renounce one's sins and especially not to commit adultery. Bishop Lesley, a Catholic, thought that the new architecture if 'very comely and beautiful' was 'superfluous and voluptuous' and cost more than the modest wealth of the kingdom could afford.

Besides being condemned for his extravagance James V was blamed for estranging the peerage. Pitscottie believed that

> this noble prince, if he had used the counsel of his wise and noble lords and kept his body clean from harlotry and the counsel of papists, bishops and courtiers, he had been one of the most noble princes that ever reigned in Scotland.

John Knox wrote that he was termed a murderer of nobility and one who decreed their whole destruction. It has always been thought to be a mistake to alienate the ruling classes unless one is prepared to sponsor revolution.

Writing today, Professor Gordon Donaldson is even more severe than Pitscottie:

> Taking into account his vindictiveness, his ruthlessness and his cruelty as well as his acquisitiveness, he must have been one of the most unpopular monarchs who ever sat on the Scottish throne.

However Professor Donaldson does not attribute James V's failings to his Stewart blood. They arose, he declares, because James was 'half Tudor . . . perhaps a Tudor rather than a Stewart in character, combining the acquisitiveness of his grandfather, Henry VII, the lust and ruthlessness of his uncle, Henry VIII, and the unrelenting cruelty of his cousin, Bloody Mary'. These are harsh words. Still it is admitted that his very severity to malefactors caused him to be admired by the law-abiding. Knox, as has already been noted, wrote that 'he was called by some a good poor man's king'. No one denied that he did his utmost to maintain his subjects in peace and quiet and free from the oppression of the rich and powerful. Lesley considered that he was a good and sure justiciar, that he protected his people from molestation, that he was severe but merciful, that he suppressed disorders and enriched his realm, and left a good store of treasure for his successor. It was no mean record.

A splendid and fair biography of James V by Caroline Bingham was published in 1971. His letters have been edited by Denys Hay (1954). The views of John Knox are in his *History of the Reformation in Scotland* (ed. W. C. Dickinson, 1949) and of George Buchanan in his *History of Scotland* (1752). The works of Sir David Lindsay have been edited by Douglas Hamer (S.T.S. 1931–6). Professor Donaldson's views are to be found in his *Scotland: James V to James VII* (1965) and *Scottish Kings* (1977). I have taken the quotation of what James V is supposed to have said on his death-bed from the seventeenth-century historian and poet, William Drummond of Hawthornden, who was born in 1585 and published his *History of Scotland 1425–1542* in 1655.

[9]

Mary Queen of Scots —
All for Love?

OF ALL THE STEWART MONARCHS Mary Queen of Scots is the only one who achieved practically nothing for her country, for its peace, welfare or culture. Yet because she is thought to have been beautiful, was married three times before she reached the age of twenty-five, and died tragically, being executed in England, as her grandson was to be, more books have been written about her than any other Stewart. Was she really beautiful? One need not be convinced of that because she had many suitors; all her marriages were arranged for political, not romantic reasons. She was over-tall for a woman; she had the long straight nose characteristic of the royal Stewarts, she had fair curly hair (when young), lovely lips and graceful white hands. She was painted by various artists who always gave her a withdrawn look which suggests she was keeping her real thoughts to herself. It is true that when she first arrived as a child at the Court of France one who was there observed that 'her beauty began to radiate from her like the sun in a noonday sky' and her future mother-in-law, Catherine of Médicis, said that 'she only had to smile in order to turn our French heads'. But none of her portraits strike one immediately as being that of an outstandingly good-looking woman, whereas that of her father-in-law's mistress, Diana of Poitiers, certainly does. What Mary possessed was charm and the attribute a later age called sex appeal. Pampered at the French Court, she found the early years of her life the happiest.

Soon after she was born and even before she was crowned at Stirling on 9 September 1543 it was agreed, under the impact of her father's defeat at Solway Moss, that she should marry by proxy Henry VIII's son, the future Edward VI, before she was ten and then should be sent to England to be brought up (treaty of Greenwich, 1 July 1543). Although the treaty promised that Scotland would not in consequence become a satellite of Tudor England, that looked likely enough to happen and was definitely not what the Scottish Establishment wanted. As Henry VIII's ambassador remarked in that year, 'in my opinion they [the Scots] would rather suffer extremities than come to subjection to England – they would have their own realm free and live within themselves after their own laws and customs'.

It was for this very reason that the second parliament of the reign revoked the treaties – one for peace, the other for marriage: the excuse was that while these had been ratified in due time by James Hamilton second Earl of Arran, who had been appointed Governor and was the heir presumptive to the throne, Henry VIII himself had failed to do so by the stipulated date: instead he acted so arrogantly towards the Scots that the anti-English and pro-French party, headed by Mary's mother, Mary of Guise, regained control. The English monarch was therefore compelled to turn to war once more in his attempt to impose his wishes on the Scottish people. But Archibald Douglas sixth Earl of Angus defeated an English army at the battle of Ancrum (near Jedburgh) on 27 February 1545 and two English incursions, generally known as 'the Rough Wooing', only succeeded in alienating the Scots further from the idea of an English alliance. In answer to appeals for help French troops landed on the east coast; though they were not very popular, judicious bribery strengthened the pro-French party, directed by the Queen Mother and the Archbishop of St Andrews, David Beaton.

After the death of Henry VIII the Lord Protector of England, the Duke of Somerset, continued trying to bring the Scots to heel with the result that the Lowlands were fought over by both English and French soldiers. On 31 July 1547 the French captured the castle of St Andrews, which was in pro-English hands, while on 10 September the Duke of Somerset defeated a Scottish army at the battle of Pinkie Cleuch and then withdrew, leaving garrisons at various places in the Lowlands, notably at Haddington west of Dunbar. The Scottish rulers, the chief of whom was Arran, now realized that in order to expel the English from Lothian they needed more French help. A close alliance was arranged. While the Scots and the French were besieging Haddington a treaty was agreed there in July 1548 providing that Mary should in due course marry the son of King Henry II of France and meanwhile should be sent there to be educated. Thus it came about that when Mary was not yet six years old, she was shipped to France under the care of Lady Fleming, the attractive illegitimate daughter of Mary's grandfather, King James IV. There the child Queen arrived in the early autumn of 1548. She was then transferred to the care of her grandmother, the Duchess Antoinette of Guise, at her palace of St Germain-en-Laye, which was to figure prominently in the story of the later Stewarts.

While Mary was being educated in France the Protestant Reformation was extended to Scotland, as Henry VIII had vainly pressed her father, James V, to do. It is fascinating to speculate what might have happened had James V, a loyal Roman Catholic and the friend of two Popes, lived longer or been succeeded by a grown-up son. As it was, although French influence was pervasive and the Earl of Arran, as Regent, was created a French Duke — of Châtelhérault — as a reward for accepting the marriage treaty, other Scottish leaders, such as Mary's half-brother, Lord James Stewart (later created Earl of Moray) and Archibald Campbell fourth Earl of Argyll were converted by the preaching of the celebrated Protestant evangelist, John Knox.

Knox had studied theology at St Andrews university and as a young man had been a disciple of the Scottish Lutheran, George Wishart, who was burnt at the stake for heresy in 1546. Possibly by way of revenge a band of Scottish Protestants or 'heretics' murdered Archbishop Beaton of St Andrews eight weeks later and seized hold of St Andrews castle. Here they were besieged by the French; Knox actually began his career as a preacher in St Andrews at that time, but by the end of July 1547 the castle was captured and Knox was punished by being made a galley slave for nineteen months. After living in England during the reign of Edward VI and two spells of study under John Calvin, the French reformer, in Geneva, Knox returned to Scotland in 1559 to become the principal architect of the reformation there.

Even before Knox was in Scotland for the third time a Congregation of Christ was formed whose members subscribed to a bond dedicated to breaking with Rome. Mary's mother had replaced Arran as Regent in April 1554, but even with the backing of French troops, proved in the long run unable to withstand rebellion by the Lords of the Congregation. Châtelhérault, who now changed sides, authorized William Maitland Laird of Lethington, one of the most capable of the Scottish Protestant leaders, to negotiate a treaty with England, then under the canny rule of Queen Elizabeth I. Even before this treaty of alliance was concluded at Berwick, as it was in February 1560, an English naval force, dispatched to the Firth of Forth ostensibly to cope with pirates, had cut the communications of the French troops, who were garrisoning Leith, with their homeland. Religion was not in fact mentioned in the treaty, but the English undertook to defend the ancient rights and liberties of Scotland against any encroachments by the French.

In the spring of 1560 Scottish and English forces united to expel the French from Leith. The Queen Mother struggled hard till the very end to defend the French cause and the Catholic religion in Scotland. But the garrison of Leith was starved into surrender. Afterwards Mary of Guise was compelled to seek shelter in Edinburgh castle where she died on 11 June. Peace was concluded at Edinburgh between Scotland, England and France during the following months; by this treaty both the French and the English forces promised to evacuate Scotland while an undertaking was given on behalf of King Francis II of France (who had succeeded his father in July of the previous year) and Mary Queen of Scots, who had married him on 24 April 1558, that they would recognize Elizabeth I as the legitimate Queen of England. But Mary refused to ratify the treaty. In order to understand her reasons for refusing it is necessary to turn back to see what had been happening to her between the time she arrived in France in August 1548 and her husband's accession to the throne in July 1559.

Mary had been spoilt and cosseted at the French Court. Henry II was fond of children as was also his Queen, the unattractive but strong-minded Catherine of Médicis. Their eldest son, Francis, was slightly younger than Mary, but they played happily enough together. Soon the Scottish Queen made friends with his sister, Elizabeth, who was her junior by a couple of years. As four young Scottish girls, all also named Mary, who had accompanied her to France, were separated from her by being placed in a convent and as her governess, Lady Fleming, was soon absorbed in a love affair with the French King that produced a son for them, Mary, more or less forgetting about the Scotland she had left as a young child, was quickly engulfed in French ways. She learned to speak French fluently, she was given a French governess and a French chaplain; her education embraced Italian, Spanish and Latin as well as the feminine pursuits of embroidery, dancing, singing and playing the lute. Her new governess extravagantly provided her with magnificent clothes, but annoyed Mary by giving some of them away without her permission. Mary also received lessons in state-craft from her uncle, Charles of Guise Cardinal of Lorraine; and she was delighted when her mother, then Regent of Scotland, came over on a long visit in 1550–1; but she was unable to return for Mary's wedding so that they never saw one another again.

Francis of Valois, to whom Mary was betrothed, has been described as 'a poor, bilious, degenerate weakling, stunted of growth and unprepossessing of face'. He was a constant invalid, but he enjoyed hunting and hawking even though they left him exhausted. Unquestionably he loved his young fiancée, who rapidly acquired maternal instincts and in effect became his nurse. After she reached the age of twelve Mary was furnished with her own household; about three years later her half-brother, James Stewart, came over to formalize the marriage treaty. When Mary was fifteen and Francis fourteen the wedding took place in the cathedral of Notre-Dame. The ceremony was magnificent. It was the first time for more than 200 years that the heir to the throne was married in Paris. Dressed in blue velvet robes and wearing a heavy golden coronet Mary, with her sickly bridegroom, was received at the door of the cathedral by the Bishop of Paris in front of an enormous crowd. Before the marriage contract had been completed three secret diplomatic instruments were signed by Mary which provided that should she predecease her husband and have no children, her rights in Scotland would be transferred to the French monarchy. Evidently she felt that it was the destiny of Scotland to be united with France. But whatever she thought, if she thought at all, the decision invited danger. Did she not know, was she not told that during her long absence from Scotland the country was in the process of becoming a Protestant realm, that the Lords of the Congregation were triumphing and anti-French sentiments growing fast?

Fifteen months after the marriage Mary's father-in-law was accidentally killed in a tournament and her young husband was crowned King at Rheims. Mary was already a crowned queen in her own right. Not long before this Queen Mary I of England, the elder daughter of Henry VIII, who had forced her country back into the Roman Catholic Church, had also died, to be succeeded by Henry VIII's second daughter, Elizabeth, the second Tudor Queen. Thereupon Mary Queen of Scots and her husband assumed the title of King and Queen of England and Ireland and adopted the English royal arms. This they did because the Catholic Church did not accept the legitimacy of Elizabeth I's succession since it had never recognized the validity of the divorce of Henry VIII from Mary I's mother.

Thus from the very outset of her public career Mary Queen of Scots deliberately provoked her cousin, Elizabeth of England. Moreover it was only after Francis II's accession to the throne that French troops had been despatched to Leith to fortify the power of Mary's mother as Regent against the Lords of the Congregation. The death of Mary of Guise was followed, as has been noticed, by the treaty of Edinburgh, negotiated between English and French commissioners in July 1560, which both put an end to the war and promised that the French Queen would no longer assume the arms of England. In August a meeting of the Scottish Estates, known as the Reformation Parliament, abolished the authority of the Papacy, forbade the celebration of the Mass, and instituted a Protestant confession of faith. Mary not only imperiously refused to ratify the treaty of Edinburgh — because it would have meant her abandoning her claim to the English throne — but she also made it clear that she could not accept the enactments of the Reformation Parliament because they would have compelled her husband to give up his own religion. As long as she was Queen Consort of Catholic France she reckoned she was in a position to defy the Scottish Protestants, who had deprived her mother, seven months before she died, of her office of Regent. But by assuming this non-possumus attitude Mary had alienated herself from the bulk of her Scottish subjects.

The reign of Francis II was abrupt. He was taken ill fourteen months after his coronation; although devotedly nursed by his wife and his mother, he died on 5 December 1560. So during her adolescence Mary suffered three losses, first her father-in-law, then her mother, and finally her husband. How much she loved the pathetic Francis is hard to say. The marriage appears to have been consummated, for at one time Mary believed that she was pregnant; she wrote a poem expressing the depth of her grief; during the forty days of official mourning she was solitary and prostrate. But then life had to go on. There was little point in her remaining in France as a new régime took over. If she returned to Scotland, not only would she be able to reign as a monarch in her own right, but she would be free to choose another husband without being hampered by French politics. After paying a round of visits to her Guise relatives and saying farewell to the new French King (a boy of eleven) and her mother-in-law, Catherine of Médicis, at St Germain, she sailed from Calais on 14 August 1561, landed safely at Leith, and was soon installed in Holyrood palace. Her future was daunting.

After she returned to Scotland Mary had three aims in mind: the first was to conciliate her subjects after her long absence; the second was to find herself a suitable husband; the last, and to her the most vital, was to secure from Queen Elizabeth I, who was nine years older than she was, the recognition of her right to succeed to the throne of England if the second Tudor Queen had no children. In order to attain her ends Mary avoided antagonizing her Protestant subjects by making a fuss over her own religion. Indeed she took as her two principal Ministers her half-brother, James Stewart, whom she later created Earl of Moray, and William Maitland Laird of Lethington, both of whom had embraced Protestantism. Seizing the bull by the horns, she sent for John Knox, who had published in 1558 his *First Blast against the Monstruous Regiment* [government] *of Women* in which he condemned the rule of Mary I in England and the regency of Mary of Guise in Scotland. Yet in a fascinating interview Mary Queen of Scots persuaded him to tolerate her authority, at any rate as long as she behaved herself according to his lights.

The fact was that Mary had no intention whatever of promoting a counter-reformation in Scotland or entering into a Catholic league; her relations with the Papacy were at best lukewarm; and when she married her third husband it was in accordance with Protestant rites. In 1567 Pope Pius V was to declare that he would have nothing to do with her 'unless, indeed, in times to come he shall see some better sign of her life and religion than he had witnessed in the past'. The most that Mary insisted upon in Scotland was her own right to receive the Mass in private. After arriving home she published a proclamation which ordered a truce or standstill in religious controversy until she reached a decision in consultation with the three Estates. Clearly, if she had in fact succeeded as Queen Mary II of England, she would have avoided the error committed by Queen Mary I of trying to compel her subjects to accept her own religion.

As to marriage, Mary favoured Don Carlos, the only son of King Philip II of Spain (though he had in turn married four wives); Don Carlos was even more of an undersized weakling than Francis II: he was an epileptic, mentally unbalanced, and liable to fits of homicidal mania. How much of that was known to Mary is not entirely clear, but maybe she was resigned to the notion of such marriages. The idea of it was originally adumbrated before she left France, but as the French and Spaniards were habitual enemies, it was easier to pursue such a negotiation from Scotland. In the end Carlos went completely insane and was put to death at his father's order. Another possible candidate was Archduke Charles of Styria, a younger son of the Holy Roman Emperor, Ferdinand I, who was reputedly courteous and affable and apparently neither misshapen nor mentally disturbed. He was also put on offer to Queen Elizabeth of England. But he possessed two disadvantages: he had no kingdom and no money. A Catholic husband needed other attributes. Finally the new French boy King, Charles IX, was said to have a penchant for his charming sister-in-law; but as he was only twelve years old, she would have had to wait some time before he became useful to her.

Queen Elizabeth made it perfectly clear that she did not want her cousin to marry a Catholic prince; both Don Carlos and Archduke Charles were therefore taboo; and as Mary's aspiration was to be recognized by Elizabeth as her heiress presumptive and was therefore anxious to please her, this ruled them both out of the matrimonial stakes.

In 1563 Mary dispatched Maitland of Lethington to London – he had already visited Queen Elizabeth in 1561 – partly to pursue her claim to succeed to the English throne and partly to reopen the question of her marrying Don Carlos by private negotiations with the Spanish ambassador to the English Court. In the following year Mary sent Sir James Melville to England for the same purposes, but it was now finally learnt that the

Spanish match was out of the question while Queen Elizabeth, always a shrewd diplomatist, insisted that Mary must marry an English nobleman. Pressed harder, she made the astonishing suggestion in the spring of 1564 that Mary should marry a widower, Robert Dudley, her Master of the Horse, whom she later created Earl of Leicester: it was astonishing because it was notorious that Dudley was Elizabeth's own acknowledged male favourite and that she had even played with the thought of marrying him herself, at least until he came under suspicion of killing his wife. Later the English Queen sent an embassy to Scotland to suggest that if Mary married Dudley, they might come and live with her at her own expense and that she would then recognize Mary's title to succeed to her throne. That would indeed have been a unique *ménage à trois*. Mary did not take offence. It was, however, a fantasy. Elizabeth's chief Minister, Sir William Cecil, only advocated the idea in the hope of shunting Dudley off to Scotland, while Dudley himself much preferred to remain in England; after all, it was still on the cards that Elizabeth might change her mind, as she often did, and marry him herself.

While these marriage negotiations were in progress Mary had been coping with members of her nobility who were as obstreperous as usual. The third Earl of Arran, son and heir of the Duke of Châtelhérault, who had, like the Archduke Charles, been a suitor both to Elizabeth and to Mary, revealed or invented a plot to kidnap the Scottish Queen. Among others he accused James Hepburn Earl of Bothwell of conspiring against Mary and her Government. It turned out that Arran was mentally unhinged so he was shut up in Edinburgh castle for his own safety; nevertheless it was on his testimony that Bothwell was arrested and imprisoned without trial. Châtelhérault's castle at Dumbarton was forfeited on the ground that he was implicated in the plot.

Turning her attentions from the Lowlands to the Highlands, Mary resolved to deal with the fourth Earl of Huntly and his son, Sir John Gordon, who were also believed to have designs against her and her Ministers. She herself went to Inverness where Alexander Gordon, another of Huntly's sons, refused to admit her into the castle, an act of disobedience for which he was promptly put to death. Because of the Gordons' intransigence Huntly was outlawed in October 1562; he retorted by defying the Queen, who had returned from Inverness to Aberdeen, but the royalists defeated the Gordons at the battle of Corrichie. There Huntly fell from his horse to meet a natural death. His son, Sir John, was executed. It has justly been pointed out that Mary's decision personally to fight and punish the Gordons, the most Catholic clan in the entire country, underlines her lack of religious enthusiasm. Professor Donaldson writes that 'Mary's equivocal policy was a conspicuous success, for she was able to engineer a unity among the Scottish magnates which had hardly been paralleled since 1513'.

Once the negotiations over Don Carlos collapsed a new candidate for Mary's marriage came under scrutiny: this was Henry Lord Darnley, the son of Mathew Stuart Earl of Lennox and his wife, by birth Margaret Douglas. The Countess of Lennox was the daughter of Margaret Tudor by her second husband and therefore the granddaughter of Henry VII of England. By the rules of heredity Darnley stood next after Mary in the line of succession to the English Crown. Were Mary to marry him not only would her own claim to this succession be fortified, but he would furnish an answer to Elizabeth's demand that Mary should marry an English nobleman. Lennox had been exiled from Scotland during the reign of James V, had been attainted, and had his estates forfeited, but had acquired estates in England. Darnley had been born in England. So both were Elizabeth's subjects. Ever since the death of Francis II the Countess of Lennox, a lady of ambition, had been intriguing to obtain this very marriage for her son. In 1563 Queen Elizabeth had been persuaded to write a letter to Mary on behalf of the Lennoxes asking for the repeal of the attainder and the restoration of their lands in Scotland. So she could hardly refuse permission for Lennox to visit Scotland in order to settle his affairs there; and although she tried to stop him, Darnley followed his father to Edinburgh where he arrived in February 1565.

Darnley was nineteen years old, a little taller than Mary and not bad-looking; he had been carefully coached by his mother and made an excellent impression on the Queen of Scots. According to Sir James Melville, Mary at once 'took very well with him' and said that he was 'the properest and best proportioned long man that ever she had seen', though Melville himself had earlier told Queen Elizabeth that 'no woman of spirit would choose such a man, who more resembled a woman than a man'. Later when Darnley caught the measles and was put to bed in Stirling castle Mary exhibited her expertise as a nurse, as she had done with her first husband. It was then, according to her latest biographer, that Mary fell 'violently, recklessly and totally in love' with her young cousin. Maybe that was so, but she had now learnt that the negotiations for marriage with Dudley in return for the formal recognition by Queen Elizabeth of her right to succeed to the English throne had broken down completely. Moreover she had been widowed for five years and had no urge to follow Elizabeth along the virgin path. Though Moray and her other Protestant advisers did not favour the match – Darnley was a Catholic of a very mild sort, though he attended

Knox's sermons — Mary's secretary, an Italian musician named David
Rizzio, was all for the marriage. Permission was sought from the Pope
(because of their consanguinity) and on 29 July 1565 the wedding was
celebrated in Holyrood palace. Queen Elizabeth was furious with Mary for
marrying in haste without consulting her; she sent a special envoy to stop it,
but he arrived too late.

The marriage put Mary's brother Moray's nose out of joint; he disapproved of her defying Elizabeth; he therefore tried to arouse the Protestant
Lords of the Congregation against his Catholic sister, though in fact he had
a very poor case for invoking religious prejudices. Darnley had actually
professed the Protestant religion while he lived in England; he had gone to
Calvinist services in Scotland; and although the marriage had been con-
ducted with Catholic rites, he had not even taken the nuptial Mass. So he
had already shown himself to be no papist fanatic. Mary gave reassurances to
the Church reformers, promising that she would not change her policy of
toleration. Only Archibald Campbell fifth Earl of Argyll, first of a long line
of rigid Calvinists, and James Hamilton Duke of Châtelhérault joined
Moray in open rebellion and Queen Elizabeth refused to give them any help;
she could scarcely approve of insurgence against another queen. Though the
rebels managed to enter Edinburgh on 31 August, they won no support. By
6 October Moray was obliged to escape across the frontier to seek asylum in
England. Mary's victorious harassing of the Protestant rebels is commonly
known as the Chaseabout raid.

Once more Mary had shown herself brave and astute in handling her
discontented nobility. To counterbalance Moray and the Campbells
she forgave the Gordons, freed John Hamilton Archbishop of St Andrews,
who had been imprisoned for saying the Mass, permitted Châtelhérault
to go into banishment, and allowed James Hepburn Earl of Bothwell
to return from exile. In February 1566 Bothwell married Huntly's
sister, Jean Gordon, thus uniting two of Mary's strongest groups of
adherents.

Momentarily Mary's position looked secure. Not only had she suppressed
the rebellion easily enough and reinforced her Council, but she had pacified
the Reformers and by her marriage enhanced her claim to succeed in due
course to the throne of England. But she had one grave disappointment: her
marriage was a failure. Darnley, four years younger than herself, proved
arrogant, greedy, lazy, stupid, gullible and unfaithful. He demanded the
Crown Matrimonial, which meant that he would continue as King if Mary
predeceased him and had no children. His demand was refused; and in no
time at all his worthlessness and Mary's recognition of it became general

knowledge. He had, however, achieved something, for before the end of 1565 Mary knew that she was pregnant.

But Mary's feeling of safety was soon to be undermined when Moray, Argyll and others, who had been defeated in the recent rebellion and were due to be put on trial for treason, linked up with a second group of dissatisfied noblemen, including James Douglas fourth Earl of Morton and Maitland of Lethington, who had not been involved in the Chaseabout raid. A bond was drawn up, signed by the rebel lords, by Moray and other exiles in England and by Darnley himself. This bond provided for securing the Crown Matrimonial for Darnley, for upholding the Protestant religion, for the reinstatement of the rebels and for sparing neither life nor limb in advancing Darnley's honour. These conspirators were able to adopt Darnley as their figurehead because he was angered by the Queen's contemptuous treatment of him and was even persuaded that she was unfaithful to him, preferring her secretary Rizzio, 'a merry fellow and a good musician', to whom she entrusted much of her business and with whom she played music and cards in her spare time.

On 9 March, three days before the rebels were due to stand trial before Parliament, one of the signatories of the bond, Patrick Lord Ruthven, a bloodthirsty ruffian, leading a gang of armed men, who included Lord Morton and his half-brother, George, burst into Mary's apartments at Holyrood, where she was having supper with Rizzio and some of her ladies and had been joined by Darnley. Rizzio was accused of dishonouring the Queen; he was then dragged away from her into the next room where he was stabbed fifty or sixty times, the first blow, said to have been struck by George Douglas, being deliberately made with Darnley's own dagger. The violence was such that Mary and her unborn child might easily have been injured or killed. So well armoured and armed were the conspirators that the Queen's guards and servants were powerless: both Bothwell and Huntly, who were in the palace and may also have been intended victims of the plotters, managed to escape. Ruthven, Morton and the rest, having carried out the assassination withdrew from the Queen's apartments, leaving her alone with her ladies and servants. Once she had been told of Rizzio's awful death, she calmed herself and said, 'No more tears now; I will think upon revenge.'

Darnley, in whose name the murderers had cynically acted, was the weak link in their chain, as Mary realized. She persuaded him that neither of them was any longer safe in Edinburgh and so two days later they rode away to the castle at Dunbar, where they were joined by Bothwell, its owner, Huntly and other loyal noblemen. Less than a week afterwards Mary returned to Edinburgh at the head of eight thousand armed men, half of them borderers raised by Bothwell. Finding themselves incapable of resisting, the conspirators fled to England or elsewhere. Mary, though she had employed all her charm and acting skill to detach Darnley from them – and they were infuriated at his treachery – had now come to detest him, all the more so when the conspirators sent her the bond which he had signed to proved his complicity in the plot against her and therefore indirectly in the murder of Rizzio (though he may have thought the intention was only to seize and try the unpopular favourite). Just under a year later Darnley was to pay the penalty for his part in the plot. Meanwhile he was virtually separated from the Queen and ostracized; he reverted to his licentious habits.

The future James VI was born in Edinburgh castle on 19 June. When Darnley came to see him Mary publicly announced: 'God has given you and me a son, begotten by none but you.' But when the child was baptized on 17 December, Darnley did not put in an appearance. After her safe delivery, as a delayed reaction to the terrifying ordeals she had been through, Mary was taken ill and was often nervous and hysterical. She came more and more to rely on Bothwell. He was a nobleman seven years older than the Queen; he had been greatly trusted by her mother who had made him Lieutenant of the Border and Admiral of Scotland. A cultivated man, popular with ladies, he was adventurous and irreligious. Although Mary had forgiven her brother, Moray, for his open rebellion against her (she did not then know that he had been involved in the conspiracy against Rizzio, as he was out of the country at the time) she naturally ceased to trust him in the way she had done when she first came back from France. She depended, above all, on the vigour of Bothwell.

The dramatic events that occurred in Scotland during 1567 and the first half of 1568 have been the subject of deep controversy among historians and Mary's numerous biographers. One thing at any rate is clear: that is that she had come to hate Darnley, who had not only proved a broken reed but a traitor as well. In November 1566 she paid a visit to Craigmillar castle near Edinburgh where members of her Council met. Here she made it plain to them that she wanted to be rid of Darnley, but was anxious to avoid divorce since that might invalidate the claims of her newly born son to inherit the thrones of Scotland and England. She was assured that a way would be found. In January 1567 a conference took place at Whittingham, a castle belonging to the Douglases, in which Bothwell, Morton, who had just returned from England, his cousin, Archibald Douglas, and Maitland took part. Whether there or at Craigmillar a bond was signed, similar to that drawn up against Rizzio in March of the previous year, but this time against Darnley who, after his behaviour in Holyrood, had no friends left. According to the Queen's servant, known as French 'Paris' (who had previously been a servant of Bothwell), Argyll, Huntly, Maitland, Morton and Lindsay, who had married a Douglas, were all involved in the new plot, but not Moray. At about the same time Mary, who had released Archbishop Hamilton of St Andrews from imprisonment and had restored his consistorial jurisdiction during the previous December, revoked it once again. This has been interpreted to show that she had, after all, been contemplating a divorce, which the Archbishop could have arranged, but by January 1567 had abandoned the idea. Ten days later Mary went to Glasgow, where Darnley was lying ill with syphilis, and after nursing him, persuaded him to come with her to a house near Edinburgh, where he could convalesce, as the air was supposedly better than at Holyrood. Who exactly chose the house, which belonged to a certain Robert Balfour, is not clear; apparently Mary had first suggested Craigmillar castle, belonging to the Douglases, but Darnley refused to go there because he distrusted the Douglases. However a town house of the Douglases lay near the house chosen which was known as Kirk o'Field.

Darnley's apartment was on the first floor of the house; the Queen's was underneath. Darnley stayed there for the first ten days of February; Mary remained there with her husband and promised him that on their return to Holyrood on 10 February she would resume conjugal relations with him, which had been suspended ever since the murder of Rizzio. Kirk o'Field was only three-quarters of a mile from Holyroodhouse and on Sunday 9 February Mary left to be present at the wedding of two of her servants and to attend a State dinner, but she returned to Kirk o'Field in the early evening. About ten o'clock that night she left Kirk o'Field once again so as to appear at a masque which she had undertaken to patronize. It is not certain whether the Queen suddenly recollected her commitment or not; a report exists that affirms positively that she was wearing a mask when she was with her husband in the early evening. At any rate her presence at this masque furnished her with an explanation or at any rate an excuse why she did not again return to Kirk o'Field that night, which was the last night when Darnley would be sleeping there.

After Mary had been to the masque she spent a long time in conversation with Bothwell, though what they were talking about is a matter for speculation. Then she herself stayed the night at Holyrood while Bothwell (according to subsequent testimony) went to Kirk o'Field with the intention of supervising the destruction of the King. At two in the morning of 10

February a terrific explosion, heard throughout most of Edinburgh, blew up the house at Kirk o'Field. Darnley with one of his servants, according to his father's belief, hearing suspicious noises, had jumped from the first floor and escaped in their night-gowns. They were both found strangled in the grounds. Women who lived nearby swore that they had heard Darnley exclaim: 'pity me, kinsmen, for the sake of Jesus Christ, who pitied the world'. The word 'kinsmen' suggested that the actual murderer was a Douglas, the most likely one being Morton's cousin, Archibald Douglas, who had signed the Craigmillar bond.

The circumstantial evidence that Mary connived at her husband's murder is strong. It was she who had persuaded him to leave Glasgow, where his father had many friends; it was she who nursed him for ten days, although she had made known that she hated him, and had tempted him with the promise that when he recovered he might return to their marriage bed; it was on the only night when she was not sleeping at Kirk o'Field that Darnley was killed; and she is known to have been in long and earnest conversation with Bothwell, who, according to the evidence of his servants, left Holyrood after this conversation with the intention of blowing up the house at Kirk o'Field with gunpowder. If Darnley had not managed to escape from the house before the explosion took place, all that might have happened was that people would have believed that it was a political crime aimed at both the King and the Queen, who just by chance was not there, while the perpetrators could not have been traced. Mary herself underlined this explanation when directly afterwards she wrote two letters in which, though her concern over her husband's death was perfunctory, she laid stress on her own narrow shave.

It has sometimes been argued that no fewer than three parties were milling about in the quadrangle which surrounded Kirk o'Field on the night of the crime. That is surely improbable except in a detective story. All the evidence that was subsequently collected in one way or another indicated that Bothwell was in league with the Douglases, headed by Lord Morton, who fourteen years afterwards was to be put to death for his acknowledged part in the crime. Hardly anyone has ever seriously doubted that Bothwell was the conspirator in chief. Sir James Melville wrote that immediately after the murder was known 'everybody suspected the Earl of Bothwell and those who durst speak freely to others said plainly that it was he'. A week afterwards murder placards were set up in the streets of Edinburgh accusing him. The evidence of the part he played, given later by his servants, though procured by torture, is sufficiently plausible to be creditable. Mary herself was known as a daring young woman, as she had recently demonstrated by the Chaseabout raid. When later she was a prisoner in England she occupied herself in all sorts of plots aimed at the overthrow of Queen Elizabeth, finally welcoming plans for her assassination. Nothing in her character precludes the likelihood that she connived at Darnley's murder. But the most telling argument against Mary is that after all sorts of hurried arrangements, including the trial and acquittal of Bothwell in Edinburgh, which was a put-up job, and a quickly planned divorce for his wife, only three months after Darnley died, Mary married the man who was still generally believed to have been responsible for his predecessor's murder.

Whether she actually fell in love with Bothwell — who had first shown his resourcefulness and loyalty at the time of Rizzio's murder — is difficult to ascertain. Certainly no definite proof exists that they were lovers before Darnley's murder. But in two letters that she wrote from Glasgow before she brought Darnley to Kirk o'Field — one to Bothwell, the other to Moray, she not only gave details of her unhappy relationship but also related how she had 'to feign something to him . . . to make him trust me'. Like her great-grandson, Charles II, she was a first-class liar. In the letter to Bothwell she wrote: 'I remit myself solely to your will and send me word what I shall do, and whatever happens to me, I will obey you. Think also if you will not find some invention by physic, for he is to take physic at Craigmillar' and in her letter to Moray she said of Darnley 'you never heard one speak better nor more humbly, and if I had not proof of his heart to be as wax and that mine were not as diamond, no stroke but coming from your hand could make me but to have pity of him'. Mary's admirers have had the utmost difficulty in explaining away these letters, which they admit are for the most part genuine.

Whatever Mary's feelings were towards Bothwell — and after her two disastrous previous marriages to weaklings she must surely have turned eagerly to a supposedly strong man on whom she could depend, Bothwell was certainly not in love with her. His ambition was to become the King of the Scots. A week after being acquitted at his trial because his accuser, Darnley's father, dared not enter Edinburgh, he gave a supper party at which he persuaded a number of earls, bishops and barons to sign a long document — yet another 'bond' — pledging themselves to promote his marriage to the Queen. Five days later he abducted Mary on her way back from Stirling, where she had been visiting her son, to Edinburgh and carried her off to his castle at Dunbar where he seduced or raped her. The consequence was that three months later she had stillborn twins, but the object of the exercise, in which it has been agreed that Mary acquiesced, was to make the marriage urgent. The wedding took place in the great hall at Holyrood on 15 May.

Nothing in Mary's whole unhappy life was more foolish than this rushed marriage. Bothwell bullied her, reducing her to tears, while many of her subjects dubbed her a whore. A rebellion against the newly-weds was swiftly organized, for the lords who signed the bond submitted to them by Bothwell were no more loyal to him than they had been to Darnley. Morton and Maitland were to the fore. Both sides raised armies, but the Gordons and Hamiltons, who might have turned the scale in Mary's favour, did not reach Carberry hill, eight miles south-east of Edinburgh, where the confrontation took place on 15 June, in time to save her. The confederate lords demanded that the Queen abandon Bothwell. However badly he had been behaving towards her, she firmly refused. Bothwell advised her to retire to Dunbar castle, but she thought she would be fairly treated by her opponents, so her husband galloped away alone. They never met again. After a variety of adventures Bothwell died a prisoner in Denmark at the age of forty-three. Mary was placed in custody in a castle, once again belonging to the Douglases, on an island in Loch Leven. Here she was browbeaten into signing a deed of abdication. On 29 July her son, thirteen months old, was crowned King James VI and her half-brother Moray was appointed Regent. Though she was not to die until twenty years later, her reign as a Stewart monarch was at an end.

By far the best book on Mary is *The Enigma of Mary Stuart*, compiled and edited by Ian B. Cowan (1971) in which the various contradictory interpretations of her actions are set out. The best biography is by Antonia Fraser, *Mary Queen of Scots* (1969) which has a full bibliography; it supersedes T. F. Henderson's two-volume biography published in 1905. Two of the sources produced to blacken Mary's conduct after she reached England, the 'Casket letters' and the 'Book of the Articles', have been elaborately examined: the first by M. H. Armstrong Davison (1965), the second by Gordon Donaldson, in *The First Trial of Mary, Queen of Scots* (1969). Mary's letters to Bothwell and Moray, referred to in the text, were spatchcocked in the second Casket letter: that was the opinion of Mr Davison.

[10]

James VI and His Mother

JAMES VI WAS THE MOST precocious and best educated of the Stewart
kings of Scotland and thoroughly deserved his title of 'the wisest fool in
Christendom'. Like other monarchs who succeeded to the throne as minors,
his principal difficulties arose when he was young. His mother revoked her
deed of abdication after she escaped from Lochleven castle in May 1568, and
all she would concede to her only child was that she would 'associate' him
with her if she were restored to authority. In fact she might easily have
resumed power not long after James's coronation. For she managed to
gather a larger army than that collected by her brother Moray, who had
been appointed Regent for James in May 1567, but her generals, particularly the fifth Earl of Argyll, proved incompetent and they were defeated at
the battle of Langside near Glasgow. Mary fled south and was then taken
with a score of loyal followers in a fishing boat to England; a day or two after
she arrived there she was installed in Carlisle castle; thence she threw herself
on the mercy of Queen Elizabeth I. She knew that she still had devoted
supporters in Scotland, that at twenty-five she was still a marriageable asset
(once a divorce from Bothwell had been secured), and she was confident that
her sister Queen would be bound to aid her against her rebellious subjects.
In fact, as events turned out, she would have been wiser to have escaped to
France.

Elizabeth adopted a policy of extreme caution. She invited Moray as
Regent to come to England and explain his side of the case. When he
arrived at York in October it was he and his colleagues who – in theory at
any rate – were put on trial, though the word 'trial' is imprecise as it was
more an investigation of the situation in Scotland by three commissioners
appointed by the English Queen; it was styled a conference. At first
everything went pretty well for Mary. She was accorded honourable hospitality while the chief English commissioner, the Duke of Norfolk, who had
recently lost his wife, actually contemplated marrying her. Moray's retort
was to throw as much mud as he could at his sister to blacken her

reputation. He instructed George Buchanan, a distinguished classical scholar and avid Calvinist theologian, to write a 'Book of the Articles' outlining the case against Mary. Furthermore when he was at York Moray showed the English commissioners privately a number of letters that were purported to have been written by Mary to Bothwell before and after Darnley's death, which had been discovered by one of Bothwell's servants in a silver casket. During the year or more that had elapsed between the time of their discovery and their display at York these letters had been doctored with some degree of cleverness. Scholarly research has proved that one of them was not addressed to Bothwell at all and that some of them were written by another woman who had been desperately in love with him. It has been suggested that one of Mary's former ladies in waiting, Mary Fleming, whose handwriting was like that of the Queen, might have copied them out as a service to her husband, William Maitland of Lethington, one of the Protestant lairds who had sided with Moray against his sister. As, however, the original letters have disappeared and only copies translated into English (or French) have survived, this is simply speculation. In any case the English commissioners at York were not particularly impressed by the letters; nor was Queen Elizabeth, who may or may not have read them.

As little progress had been achieved in the investigation, Elizabeth ordered that the conference be moved from York to Westminster. But she would not allow Mary to come south; she was held in Bolton castle in the West Riding of Yorkshire. At Westminster Sir William Cecil and the Earl of Leicester, two of Elizabeth's closest advisers, were added to the commission. The 'Casket letters' and some poetry, which Mary was alleged to have written in French, were then publicly submitted to the commissioners and Mary, still at Bolton, was invited to answer the accusations against her. She refused to comment on the 'Casket letters' (which were not then shown to her); instead she drew up her own counter-charges against Moray, such as his part in the murder of Rizzio, which were put before the conference on Christmas day. Queen Elizabeth wound up the proceedings on 11 January 1569, after her commissioners had announced that nothing criminal had been established against the Queen of Scots, but at the same time asserted that she had not proved that Moray and the rest of the ruling nobility had been in rebellion against her. The Earl of Moray, his colleagues and Mary's own commissioners were then allowed to return to Scotland at the end of the month. But Mary herself was removed from Bolton, which was thought to be too near the Scottish border to ensure her safe captivity, to the castle of Tutbury in Staffordshire where George Talbot Earl of Shrewsbury, who owned the castle, was appointed her guardian, in fact her jailer.

While his mother remained closely guarded in the English midlands, James was being educated at Stirling. He took a liking to his governor, Sir Alexander Erskine (though not to Erskine's sister-in-law the formidable Countess of Mar, who looked after his 'physical wants'), and his junior tutor, Peter Young. His senior tutor, George Buchanan, the very scholar whom Moray had selected to denigrate the King's mother, was a Stoic philosopher, who did not believe in sparing the rod. 'My Lady Mar', Sir James Melville recorded in his memoirs, 'was wise and sharp and held the King in great awe', as did Buchanan. Peter Young, he added, 'was more gentle and loath to offend the King at any time'. James also took a liking to two abbots, both Erskines, of Cambuskenneth and Dryburgh respectively, whose task it was to teach the boy outdoor sports, starting with hunting and hawking and extending to archery and golf. He came to adore riding and hunting with hounds after stags. Although he was not grudged good food, he suffered from rickets; it has been suggested that 'perhaps hunting, his favourite sport, freed him from the restrictions of the body; on horseback the ungainly youth became a fleet-footed centaur'; but he often fell off.

His learning was prodigious. Latin before breakfast, Greek afterwards, and lots of theology and morality all the time. He also mastered French. When he became a young man, he first wrote poetry (don't we all?) then prose. But the teaching of Buchanan was counter-productive. James was never persuaded that his mother was a murderess, as Buchanan maintained in his *Detectio*. He also came to dislike Puritans with their 'preposterous humility'; and he soon refused to be lectured by ministers on how he ought to behave. In later life he was to insist that a monarch was the head of the Church as well as of the State.

Before he really assumed authority himself James saw four Regents come and go. Moray was murdered by the Hamiltons, who were pro-Mary, in 1570; he was succeeded after a few months by James's paternal grandfather, the Earl of Lennox. One of Mary's partisans, Kirkcaldy, Laird of Grange, who was Provost of Edinburgh and dominated the capital from the castle, organized a raid on Stirling castle by night with the aim of seizing some of the lords who supported the King: in the confused fighting that followed the Regent was shot in the entrails and had to be carried back into the castle where he 'made a blessed end'. The five-year-old boy saw his grandfather being brought in mortally wounded, his first sight of a brutal death. It was no wonder that for most of his life James was pacific. Lennox was followed as Regent by the first Earl of Mar, who was rather ineffective and died a natural death soon after his appointment. Finally, James Douglas fourth Earl of Morton, who had been a recognized leader of the anti-Marian party ever since the Queen's enforced abdication, a tough, bold, unscrupulous man, like so many of the Douglases, became Regent in November 1572 when James was only six. Earlier in that same year James's mother had been getting herself involved in a crackpot scheme to marry the Duke of Norfolk and head a rising against Queen Elizabeth with Catholic assistance and the promise of ultimate aid from the King of Spain and the Governor-General of the Netherlands, the Duke of Alva. The plot was unearthed; Norfolk was condemned to death and the English Parliament demanded Mary's execution, which Elizabeth refused.

Where Mary had gone wrong from the very beginning, after her defeat at Langside, in promoting her own cause both in Scotland and in England, was in not seeking French assistance, on which she had a claim as a dowager Queen. But now suddenly an opportunity opened when Esmé Stewart sixth Lord of Aubigny, a nephew of James's grandfather, the late Earl of Lennox, and therefore a distant cousin of the King, arrived in Scotland with the original intention of restoring Mary to her throne and re-establishing the Roman Catholic religion in Scotland. It did not work out that way at all: what happened was that after D'Aubigny, a strikingly handsome and cultivated courtier, thirty-seven years old, reached Edinburgh on 17 October 1579 with 'many new fashions and toys' he quickly won the complete devotion of James, now thirteen, and by doing so, contributed to the overthrow and execution of Morton, whom James feared and hated. To strengthen his position D'Aubigny even publicly announced his conversion to the Protestant faith and gave up any idea of bringing Mary back to Scotland.

Morton had earlier first lost and then regained full authority. James, who was considered to be of age when he was twelve, knew that he was simply a figurehead for Morton since, though he had given up his Regency, he still effectively governed the kingdom as first Lord of the Privy Council. It was Morton's foes who sent for D'Aubigny. Queen Elizabeth, relying upon Morton as an ally, was alarmed when she learned of D'Aubigny's presence in Scotland lest it presaged a reaction of the Stewart Government towards an alliance with France. She sent an ambassador to Edinburgh (now at last cleared of Mary's partisans, who long held the castle on her behalf) to sustain Morton's crumbling power and to warn James against D'Aubigny whom in March 1580 he had created Earl of Lennox, the title that had been held by his grandfather. Elizabeth's intervention was in vain. In December 1580, acting upon the instructions of Lennox, James took Morton hunting, treating him with every friendliness. But on the following day James Stewart, the second son of Lord Ochiltree, who had been appointed by

Lennox the Captain of the King's Guard, appeared before the Privy Council
to accuse Morton of plotting the death of James's father fourteen years
earlier. Morton confessed that he had indeed known in advance about the
plan to murder Darnley, though he had not carried it out. Tried before an
assize court, consisting of his enemies, he was condemned to be executed.
On 2 June 1581 he was beheaded and his skull set upon the tollbooth or
town hall in Edinburgh. James rewarded Lennox and Captain Stewart for
ridding him of Morton; Lennox was created duke and given Morton's castle
of Dalkeith, while Stewart was made Earl of Arran. But Lennox's supremacy as the young King's favourite did not maintain him in power for long.
In August 1582 William Ruthven the fourth Baron Gowrie, son of the man
who had brutally murdered Rizzio, kidnapped the King while he was
hunting near Perth and then compelled him to issue a proclamation against
Lennox and Arran. Lennox, after failing abysmally to rescue his young
master, returned to France where he soon died. James, who was now
seventeen, never forgot his humiliation. He determined to escape. By June
1583 he did so. Less than a year later Gowrie confessed to treason and was
executed.

It is necessary to appreciate how tortured was the boyhood of James VI.
He never saw his mother, for whom the Countess of Mar was a poor
substitute. Buchanan had tried to turn him against Mary and had bullied
him mercilessly. He therefore sought among such nobles as he was allowed
to meet for comfort and support. 'Nurtured in fear,' wrote one who met him
at this time in his life, 'he had the one deficiency that he does not often dare
to contradict the great lords, though none the less he loves to be thought
bold and resolute.' He looked to a variety of men, who he felt he could trust,
the first Earl of Mar, Mar's young son, Peter Young, Esmé d'Aubigny,
James Stewart and the Earl of Atholl. It is pretty clear that his relationship
with D'Aubigny was homosexual. (David Moysie, a contemporary, wrote,
'at this time his majesty, having conceived an innate affection to the said
lord d'Aubigny entered into great familiarities and quiet purposes with
him'.) That was why the blow was so crushing for James when D'Aubigny
was compelled to return to France soon to die there. About him James wrote
one of his earliest poems on the Phoenix, 'the object sweet whereon my
heart is set'. But these adventures and tribulations made James all the more
determined to become his own master; it was no mere pose. Too late his
mother offered to 'associate' him with her in the government of the
kingdom, thus renouncing her claim to be restored to full authority if her
release from captivity in England could be procured. After enjoying the
love of Lennox, James could not be moved emotionally by the plight of the

mother he never knew, who had dwelt a prisoner in England for over fifteen years, as he passed from childhood to manhood. When she sent a messenger to him James never asked about her health nor her happiness. She was simply another political problem. As Antonia Fraser has written, he 'played Mary along, until it became obvious that he had more to gain from the goodwill — and the coffers — of Queen Elizabeth than from the "Association" with his mother'. In March 1585 it was decided by him and his Council that such an association should neither be granted nor spoken of any more. James emerged from his checkered childhood as a young prince filled with ambition and pride, restless and aggressive, who, like several of his predecessors as Kings of the Scots, did not scruple over how he favoured his friends or foiled his enemies. Mary's messenger, the brother of her French secretary, thought that James had 'a marvellous mind, filled with virtuous grandeur and a good opinion of himself', but added that he did not realize the poverty of his kingdom and tended to be idle, spending too much time in hunting, and leaving his business to others.

In the autumn of 1583 after James's escape from the Ruthven lords, Arran, according to Sir James Melville, 'insinuated himself so far upon his Majesty that he took upon him the whole management of affairs and caused sundry noblemen to be banished'. Nevertheless there is no reason to suppose that the King, now advanced in adolescence, had not approved and may indeed have initiated the policy that Arran as Chancellor put through. That policy was to assert the authority of the Crown, to press for a closer alliance with England and, if that were not forthcoming, to intrigue with the Catholic Powers, France, Spain and even the Papacy to bring Queen Elizabeth to her senses. In May 1584 James held a parliament which declared that the King was the head of the Church, that general assemblies were not to meet without his permission, and that the institution of bishops was to be maintained. The Presbyterians called these the 'Black Acts' and certainly for a time they halted the pretensions of the Kirk to dictate to the Crown. As to relations with England, at first negotiations went slowly, since both the Queen and her principal Secretary of State, Sir Francis Walsingham, whom she sent to interview James, were under the impression that they could order him about much as they wished, which was astonishingly poor psychology.

In fact an exchange of special ambassadors passing to and fro between England and Scotland improved matters entirely. Elizabeth let it be known that she would welcome an alliance guaranteeing mutual assistance in the event of an invasion from overseas, for she did not want the armed forces of Spain, with which for various reasons her relations were bad, to land in

Scotland, and she sent James a gift of £4,000 and a promise of a regular
pension of £4,000 a year to sweeten his temper. For his part, James made it
clear to Elizabeth that he did not want his Catholic mother to return to
Scotland and associate him with her in the government and that he
preferred a Protestant to a Catholic alliance. This agreeable progress in
negotiations was temporarily interrupted when Elizabeth was angered over
a border affray in which a son of the Earl of Bedford was killed, a mishap
which James blamed on Arran. James was upset, but vacillated, first
imprisoning Arran and then releasing him. Elizabeth, however, reacted
strongly. She 'let slip' the exiled Scottish lords, who had fled to England
after James's escape from Ruthven castle. They rapidly collected an army,
allied themselves with other discontented nobles in Scotland, and marched
upon Stirling. Arran, who was universally detested, fled; the various
contending groups of nobles balanced one another out; thus James, nearing
the age of twenty, unexpectedly discovered himself, as he wished to be,
master of events. The negotiations with England were resumed and a formal
agreement was reached in July 1586. Not only did James receive his
pension, but Queen Elizabeth in a typically convoluted sentence implied
that she did not deny the King's right to succeed her on the throne of
England.

James refused to allow this harmony to be disturbed by the trial and
execution of his mother (8 February 1587) for engaging herself in plotting
the overthrow of Queen Elizabeth during the later part of 1586. James has
been condemned as callous because he placed his own political future above
any attempt to save his mother's life. But the evidence about how he
behaved is conflicting. Though he had corresponded with his mother, he
had never sympathized with her or understood her. She had upset him by
refusing to acquiesce in his tenure of the throne of Scotland. Moreover it has
not been denied, even by Mary's admirers, that she had constantly plotted
against Elizabeth. Naturally James was under pressure from many of his
subjects to save the life of a former Scottish monarch. But what could he do?
Neither by threat nor promises could he have prevented her execution after
she had been put on trial, found guilty of treason, and the death warrant had
been signed. The story that he was 'gleeful' when he received the news of his
mother's death is incredible in a man who was nothing if not emotional.
Finally, he could scarcely have cast the blame on Elizabeth, who was careful
to refrain from ordering the execution herself and even had her principal
Secretary of State, Davison (one of Walsingham's successors), imprisoned
and dismissed for making use of the warrant that she had in fact signed.

In the decade that followed the execution of Mary Queen of Scots the history of James's kingship mingles the realistic with the fantastic. He was fortunate in discovering a Chancellor of outstanding quality in Sir John Maitland, brother of the William Maitland who had loomed so largely in James's mother's life. James liked him not only because his policies were sensible and moderate, but because in common with the King himself Sir John wrote poetry and had a facetious sense of humour. He also stood outside the warring clans of the nobility whose permutations and combinations had for so long disconcerted Scottish history. Indeed it was unusual for a Chancellor to be neither a peer nor a cleric belonging to a noble family.

James took Maitland with him when in October 1589 he embarked at Leith on a voyage to Scandinavia to consummate his marriage. This was one of the many fantastic episodes in James's life. For unquestionably he was a homosexual, his first and greatest love having been Esmé d'Aubigny, whose sons he adopted after their father's early death; he was attracted by a number of handsome young men, ranging from the Master of Gray, whom he employed as an ambassador, to the young Earl of Huntly, who married D'Aubigny's daughter. An English intelligencer wrote at this time that the King 'never regards the company of any woman, not so much as in any dalliance' while later in his life the nature of his attachments to the relatively worthless but good-looking Robert Carr and George Villiers was notorious. He postponed the negotiation of marriage as long as he decently could and then defended himself by announcing that his reasons were that he had been alone 'without father or mother, brother or sister, king of this realm and heir apparent of England': thus, he added, 'my nakedness made me weak and my enemies strong, for one man is no man, as they say'. The marriage had its political overtones. For it was obvious that the choice of a Protestant princess was desirable; his selection of Anne, a younger daughter of the King of Denmark with a fair-sized dowry, was welcomed in the Scottish burghs, for considerable trade was done with the Baltic countries. Anne was fifteen and her husband twenty-three. When storms delayed her arrival in Scotland James romantically sailed as a knight errant to fetch her: the marriage was celebrated in Oslo. The newly wedded pair reached Scotland in May 1590. At first all went swimmingly. Anne bore James seven children including the future Charles I. A dumb blonde, she had neither the brains nor the education to satisfy the Scottish Solomon, while she annoyed him by becoming a Roman Catholic. Fairly swiftly he resumed his homosexual habits.

This quixotic trip abroad was one fantasia; another was the fear that was engendered in James by the persecution he suffered from Francis fifth Earl of Bothwell, a nephew of Queen Mary's third husband and grandson of

King James IV
(1488–1513) by an
unknown artist.

Margaret Tudor, whose
marriage to James IV in
1503 led to the
Stewarts becoming
kings of England.

Above. King James V (1513–42) and his second wife, Mary of Lorraine.

Below. The 'Stirling Head', believed to be James V of Scots, originally a wooden medallion, part of the ceiling of the king's presence chamber in Stirling castle.

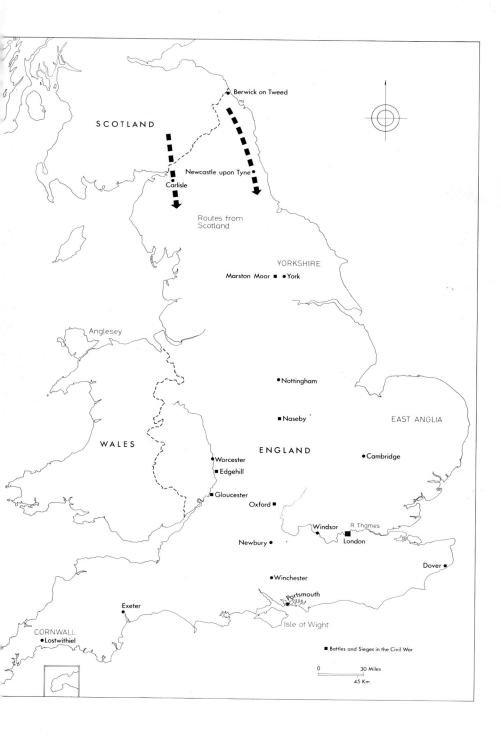

SCOTLAND

Berwick on Tweed

Newcastle upon Tyne
Carlisle

Routes from
Scotland

YORKSHIRE

Marston Moor ■ ● York

Anglesey

Nottingham

Naseby ■

EAST ANGLIA

WALES

ENGLAND

● Cambridge

Worcester
Edgehill ■

Gloucester ■

Oxford ■

Windsor   R. Thames

Newbury ●   London ■

Dover ●

Winchester ●

Portsmouth

CORNWALL
● Lostwithiel

Exeter ●

Isle of Wight

■ Battles and Sieges in the Civil War

0   30 Miles

45 Km

Stuart England.

The execution of
Charles I
(1625–49): a
woodcut from a
tract published in
1649.

James V, whom James VI himself had made an earl in 1587. This Bothwell was an unstable and lawless character, but handsome and entertaining and at one time a royal favourite. 'James', we are told, 'hung about his neck and embraced him tenderly.' His strength was derived from the fact that he had much influence on the English border and symbolized the dislike of the nobility for the upstart Chancellor Maitland.

When James was away from Scotland getting married, Bothwell was supposed to have recruited the help of wizards and witches, especially a midwife named Amy Simson. She affirmed that

> in company with nine other witches, being covened in the night by Preston-pans, the Devil their master being present, standing in the midst of them, a body of wax, shapen and made by her, wrapped within a linen cloth, was first delivered to the Devil; who, after he had pronounced his verdict, delivered the said picture to her and she to her next neighbour, and so every one about, saying: 'This is King James VI ordered to be consumed at the instance of a nobleman, Francis Earl Bothwell.'

James had Bothwell imprisoned in Edinburgh castle, but he managed to escape to the border country where he played games of hide-and-seek. In June 1592 he besieged the King in Falkland palace, trying to batter his way in; in July 1593 he again invaded Holyroodhouse and again terrified James, who was obliged to promise him a pardon. Finally, in April 1594 Bothwell appeared at Leith where he menaced the King with an escort of cavalry, thus compelling James to gallop back to Edinburgh in search of safety.

Bothwell's antics had their serious side because he actually received support from the Catholic lords in the north such as Huntly and even on one occasion from Queen Elizabeth. Thus he vitiated the policy that James and Maitland were pursuing, that of enforcing law and order and subjecting recalcitrant nobility to discipline. In the end their combination of conciliation with firmness was effective. To begin with, in 1589 before James went to Scandinavia, the King had ridden north to Aberdeen, which he entered without having to fight a battle. The Catholic lords in the northern Highlands then surrendered to mercy; though found guilty of treason, they were only imprisoned for a few months. In February 1593 when these same Catholic lords were again obstreperous James travelled north once more and drove them into hiding in Caithness. Lastly, in the autumn of 1594 James sent the young Earl of Argyll forward to cope with the third rising by Huntly and the Catholic lords, but when he was defeated, James had to take action himself. The rebels again vanished into Caithness, but later with the King's permission they departed into exile abroad. Thus by the time John

Maitland died in the following year James had virtually imposed his authority throughout the land.

But one final fantastic episode occurred in August 1600 when James had matured as King. He went out hunting near Perth where he was persuaded to visit Gowrie house, the property of the Ruthvens. The third Earl of Gowrie, who was his host, was the grandson of the Ruthven who had murdered Rizzio and the son of the Ruthven who had led the Ruthven raid of 1582. James afterwards asserted that he had been enticed there to investigate a story about a mysterious pot of gold. But he was locked into a room in a turret whence he cried 'treason!' and had to be rescued by his attendants. The most likely explanation of his presence there unarmed is that he was attracted by the young Earl, who was twenty-two, and his brother, who was twenty, while they for their part planned to avenge themselves on him for the execution of their father. Possibly they had some coup in mind for which ample precedents existed in the history of the Stewart kings. As it turned out, it was the two Ruthvens who were killed when James was rescued and their estates were forfeited for treason.

This extraordinary adventure, which has been variously interpreted by Scottish historians, in fact symbolized the King's success in curbing the restlessness of the nobility during his last years as the active ruler of Scotland. Had James Stewart not become King of England, as he did in 1603, he might have proved himself even more effective than his ancestors in securing law and order both in the Lowlands and Highlands. He had been able to impose his will on the Presbyterian ministers whose claim to override the monarchy so far as religious affairs were concerned had been frustrated. As Professor Donaldson has pointed out, since 1596, the year in which Knox's successor as leading Presbyterian minister, Andrew Melville, addressed James as 'God's silly vassal', 'although his problems within Scotland were not yet solved, the way was clear for him to pass from defence to a policy of aggression which from that point onwards he steadily pursued'. Once he became a man he was never a mayor of the palace or a mikado.

During tnese years James had evolved and publicized his own political philosophy, in three books, *The Trew Law of Free Monarchies*, the *Basilikon Doron*, which he wrote for the benefit of his eldest son, Prince Henry, and *Daemonologie*, in which he discussed witchcraft, having discovered that it was exploited by Bothwell to frighten him and undermine his authority. In arguing the case for monarchy based on patriarchy James denied that subjects could depose a ruler who broke his 'original compact' with them: there was no such compact. A monarch derived his power from God. The

Basilikon Doron is essentially a practical exposition of the duties of a king, based on his own experiences. Some of its moral teaching is odd, as in it he warns his son not only against excessive eating and drinking but also the practice of sodomy, all weaknesses of his own. In later life James scarcely practised all he preached, while his opinions as expressed in *Daemonologie* underwent a radical revision.

In the Victorian past James, as the first Stuart King of England, was castigated by Whig historians for upholding the 'divine right' of monarchy as against the incipient parliamentary democracy, advocated first by the Levellers in mid-seventeenth century England twenty years after James himself was dead. But the fact is that nearly everyone in the sixteenth and early seventeenth centuries believed in divine right of one sort or another. Once the authority of the Papacy was repudiated Protestant monarchs had necessarily to claim that they were responsible for the government both of Church and State directly to God alone. Similarly the Scottish ministers contended that since the spiritual life of the country was more important than its secular life, so they, in their general assemblies, were supreme over the monarchy as the sun is over the moon. Andrew Melville insisted that there were two kings and two kingdoms in Scotland: one was that of Christ Jesus the king: His kingdom was the Kirk of which James VI was a mere subject. Again, fathers believed that they were divinely appointed to rule over their wives, their children and servants. Thus James's teaching was by no means eccentric or outrageous in his own time. Patriarchy was a reality. Yet James recognized from his own misadventures in Scotland how genuine were the limitations upon the exercise of his authority; so he was usually ready to conciliate his opponents and critics. This ultimate understanding of the facts of political life was what made him a much wiser ruler than his successor, Charles I.

For James VI of Scotland see Caroline Bingham, *The Making of a King* (1968) which describes his life up to the age of seventeen and *James VI of Scotland* (1979); D. H. Willson, *King James VI and I* (1965); Antonia Fraser, *King James VI of Scotland and I of England* (1974), a perceptive illustrated essay; and Gordon Donaldson, *James V – James VII*, already cited. *James's Political Works* were edited by C. H. McIlwain in 1918. Among the original sources the *Memoirs of Sir James Melville* (ed. A. Francis Stuart, 1929) are outstanding. For Mary's last years see Conyers Read, *Mr Secretary Walsingham and the Policy of Queen Elizabeth* (1925).

[11]

The Scottish Stewarts
in Retrospect

THE AVERAGE ENGLISHMAN knows little enough about Scottish history except for the legend of Bruce and the spider. The impression he receives about the position of the Stewart monarchs derives backwards from King James I of England, who as James VI of Scotland, was twice kidnapped and treated with little deference by his leading Presbyterian subjects. Delving into medieval history, one finds that it seems to consist of a meaningless struggle between these monarchs and their nobles, who were always restless, defiant and ambitious, regarding the Stewart kings at best as the first among equals.

Yet the Stewart dynasty continued uninterrupted for a period of nearly 250 years; whereas during that time both Richard II and Richard III were overthrown and England was governed in turn by the Plantagenets, the Yorkists, the Lancastrians and the Tudors. While it is true that the Scottish nobility were often recalcitrant, it was not nearly as impressively powerful as were the English peers who fought against each other in the so-called Wars of the Roses; nor was there any alignment of Scots magnates as constitutionally effective in ordering their monarch about as the Lords Ordainers in the reign of Edward II or the Lords Appellant in the reign of Richard II. Admittedly the Black Douglases and the Red Douglases at times challenged the Crown, but never, except during the reign of Mary Queen of Scots, were the Douglases able to subjugate or force abdication upon the hereditary rulers of their land.

One reason for the Stewarts' longevity was that they realized, on the whole, that they governed a poor kingdom with a small population. For that reason most of them tried to keep out of wars and adopted a pacific rather than a martial attitude towards foreign policy. At times they had to enter into alliances with the French in order to protect themselves against domination by the English. In consequence of that they suffered several defeats, as at the battles of Flodden and Solway Moss. In the Middle Ages it was customary to admire warrior kings: that is why Robert Bruce is better known and respected than any of his Stewart successors. The first two Stewart kings are generally dismissed as nonentities, but the fact is that Scotland stood in need of a rest after the war of independence and was more prosperous under the two Roberts than it was under Robert Bruce and his son, David. James I and James III equally avoided war as much as they could. James I's aim was to give his kingdom quiet and a firm government. James III worked for peace at home and abroad; though not neglecting the defence of his country, he preferred to patronize the arts and learning and to stimulate native architecture. The King who did allow himself to be dragged into war — though, like his grandfather, James III, he was a Renaissance prince knowledgeable about art and architecture — was James V, whose ill-conceived foreign and domestic policies ended in the rout of his army at Solway Moss. But James V, it can be argued, was not a typical Stewart king; he was more like his uncle, the aggressive Henry VIII, whom he foolishly antagonized.

Scottish relations with England before 1603 were invariably unhappy. Even though James IV, by marrying the daughter of Henry VII, paved the way for the union between the two kingdoms, it was not until James VI grew to manhood and came to terms with Queen Elizabeth I, that the traditional enmity of the Scots towards the English, comprehensible enough in the light of the history of the two kingdoms, was assuaged. Nevertheless the anglicization of Berwick on Tweed was a reminder that the English kings possessed the military might to cross the border whenever they wished to do so and were thus able to seize Scottish burghs and castles in the Lowlands. Yet the Scots of Stewart times were warlike enough and made fine soldiers, but it was not until the reign of Charles I that they were able to demonstrate that they could defeat the English again in a national cause.

If the Stewarts never managed to extend their authority south of the Tweed, they enlarged their kingdom by acquiring the Orkneys and Shetlands. The realization, though it was slow in coming, that the Scottish Government needed naval strength rather than a host of spearmen to maintain order in the north and the neighbouring islands and to defy the Baltic kingdoms, was an important step forward. A navy was needed too for the protection of commerce against pirates and privateers. None of the Stewarts was indifferent to the development of trade and industry, although it was not until fairly recent times that the invention of whisky, the fashionableness of tweed cloth and the discovery of oil in the North Sea gave what was a country basically poor in natural resources (except for coal) the air of growing prosperity.

Again, meditating upon the early history of Scotland, one has to recognize that the Stewart kings were far from unique in finding it difficult to hold in check border warriors, ambitious earls and Highland chieftains and thus promote law and order throughout their country. All European kingdoms from Spain to Russia were disturbed by intestinal feuds during the later Middle Ages. The Stewart kings had in turn to resist the pretensions of the Black Douglases, the Red Douglases, the Homes and the Hepburns, the Hamiltons, the Campbells and the Gordons. It was because the border earls, like the Highland chieftains, were able from time to time to boast a semi-independent jurisdiction that some Scottish historians have argued recently that in spite of linguistic and economic differences there was no real distinction in the political and constitutional character of the Lowlands and Highlands.

In fact surprisingly little is known about the early history of the Highlands. The Highlanders themselves left hardly any written evidence, while, as the King's officers and officials rarely penetrated the glens, ministerial records only touch lightly upon what went on there. It is not until the sixteenth century that scholarship about the Highlands becomes richer. For this reason it is difficult to sit in judgment on the Stewart rulers for their inability to establish order in the northern part of their kingdom. Writing about the fourteenth century, the chronicler, John Fordun, states that 'though given to rapine, the Highlanders were faithful and obedient to their king and country and were easily made to submit if properly governed'. Again, a twentieth-century historian has contended that if the Stewart kings had paid as much attention to the Highlanders as Robert Bruce 'and gone frequently among them instead of trusting to the intervention of scheming rivals, there is distinct evidence . . . that they would have had little reason to complain of the loyalty of the men of the Highlands'.

This is no doubt arguable, but it was a long and arduous journey into the Highlands and because of the nature of the geography the clans found it easy to defy the kings who ruled from the Lowlands. What more could the Stewarts have done than they in fact did? Place their capital in Perth perhaps, as James I had intended? The defiance of the monarchy began with the first MacDonald Lord of the Isles, who created trouble for David II. But he married a daughter of Robert II, by whom he had several children, so that this tie of kinship promised the hope of conciliation between the Highlands and Lowlands. However, the MacDonalds acquired such supremacy in the Western Isles and the northern Highlands that the two parts of the kingdom more and more drifted apart. During the period when James I was a prisoner in England the MacDonalds aspired to be kings of Scotland. It has been seen how Edward IV of England entered into negotiations with the MacDonalds with a view to establishing a Scottish kingdom confined to the Highlands while the Lowlands were to be acquired by England. Indeed the Lord of the Isles, a modern Scottish historian has observed, 'stood in exactly the same relationship to the heads of the important kindred within his spheres of influence as did the King of the Scots to the rulers of provinces in this part of Scotland'. He had his own Council and Ministers and appointed commissioners to treat with the English monarchs.

Thus it was not until the time of James IV who, following 'in the firm footsteps of James I and James II' (to quote another Scottish historian) 'tackled the problem of the Highlands and islands' by personally leading military expeditions northwards and dispatching naval squadrons to the Hebrides as well as invoking the support of the Mackenzies, Campbells and Gordons, that the Stewart monarchy overthrew the MacDonalds by forfeiting their lands. Even after that the gulf between the Lowlanders and the Highlanders was not bridged. Henry VIII was to be informed, not unfairly, that 'the Wyld Isles of Scotland . . . have always been enemies of the realm of Scotland'. It was through a patient policy of conciliation, mixed with firmness, that the Stewart kings managed with difficulty to establish some measure of peace throughout the whole of their kingdom. It was left to James VI to introduce a scheme of colonizing parts of the Highlands and islands (such as Lewis) with Lowlanders, to insist that Highland landholders should produce their title deeds at his Exchequer court, and to require the Highland chieftains to be personally responsible for the behaviour of their clansmen. These chieftains were even expected to appear regularly before the royal Council to report on their success in maintaining law and order by punishing criminals and other malefactors. By instituting these arrangements James VI had a fair degree of success in pacifying the Highlands. Yet that this pacification was neither complete nor permanent was to be shown by the rebellions in the seventeenth and eighteenth centuries. Still, the part played by the Stewarts in civilizing the wild Highlands should not be underestimated.

By and large the Stewart rulers of Scotland were not cruel nor unscrupulous. They did not try to govern their subjects by terror or threats. For the most part they were 'poor men's kings' and reserved their ferocity for unruly nobility. Even there in general they avoided the wholesale forfeiture of lives and estates. What they did was at times to allow their tempers to get the better of them, as in the case of James I's treatment of Murdoch Duke of Albany and his two sons, James II's knifing of the eighth Earl of Douglas,

James III's revenge upon Sir Alexander Boyd, James V's mercilessness to Johnny Armstrong, Queen Mary's request for the elimination of Darnley, James VI's disposal of the third Earl of Gowrie and his brother.

It is one of the terrible facts of political history that men at the top have few friends and many enemies. In England, as will be seen, the descendants of the Scottish Stewart monarchs were not noted for their gratitude even to their best servants, as was witnessed by James I's treatment of the Earl of Middlesex, Charles I's sacrifice of the Earl of Strafford and Charles II's indifference to the fate of his sister-in-law's secretary, and so on. Kings, who in early British history were the ultimate source of authority, had no choice but to harden their hearts on occasion. Yet none of the Stewart kings of the Scots were tyrants; they were human beings who, whatever their faults, were aware of their duty to their subjects and their dynasty.

For the poverty of evidence about the history of the Highlands see Bruce Webster, *Scotland from the Eleventh Century to 1603* (1975). The first twentieth-century historian quoted is Dugald Mitchell, *A Popular History of the Highlands and Gaelic Scotland* (1900). A different view, to which Professor Gordon Donaldson kindly drew my attention is expressed in *Scottish Society in the Fifteenth Century* (ed. Joseph M. Brown, 1978) from which I took the quotations on 'the Wyld Isles' and the Lord of the Isles.

12

James I and
'the Promised Land'

AFTER JAMES STEWART King of the Scots also became King of England – he was to be crowned at Westminster on 25 July 1603 – he found pleasure in travelling around a country richer and more populous than that in which he had been born. In opening a conference on religion, held at Hampton Court palace during the second year of his new reign, he took off his hat and thanked Almighty God for his goodness in bringing him into 'the Promised Land'.

The population of England was over five times that of Scotland – it had increased by some 40 per cent during the sixteenth century – while the most fertile areas, which provided rye for bread, barley for ale, and hops for beer, were more extensive than in Scotland, although they may have been relatively overpopulated. The country was divided between 'woodland', that is to say forests and pastoral land, where pigs and cattle grazed, and 'champion' – open fields devoted to mixed farming. As in Scotland, the south, particularly the home counties surrounding London, was far more prosperous than the north. The east coast also contained many cornfields. Much of the north (excluding Yorkshire) was poor and backward. There travellers had to be provided with guides because of the bad roads and guards to protect them from highway robbery. In the reign of Queen Elizabeth I northern England was, in the words of Dr Rowse, 'a country of great spaces and difficult communications, a world of its own looking towards Scotland and its hereditary enemies across the border. Its society was still feudal, with an admixture of moss-trooping and cattle-raiding.'

As James, after leaving Scotland, made his leisurely way south from Berwick he may not have noticed much about this, for he was far too intent on the miraculous change in his own fortunes. By the time he arrived at York he was supplied with all the trappings of royalty, money, jewels, coaches and trumpeters. As soon as he arrived in London, which was then stricken with plague and pestilence, he hastened to inspect the Crown jewels and the sprawling palace of Whitehall, but he never came to care much for his new capital and afterwards resided there only for business reasons.

London was the heart of England even more than it is today. The population numbered a quarter of a million, completely outstripping any other town, while its commerce, because it was the principal port in the kingdom, dealt with about two-thirds of the export and import trade, though many other ports, of which Bristol was the largest, were pretty active. While trade and manufacture were expanding, most of the people derived their livelihood directly or indirectly from agriculture and fishing. The two main industries – woollen cloth and linen – were based on products of the countryside and were widely dispersed. Sheep farming was as extensive as in Scotland, for it yielded meat as well as wool. Cattle were to be found everywhere; fruit farming varied the diet of the well-to-do. James appreciated it, for he was greedy with strawberries, melons and cherries.

Agricultural productivity was relatively low. Although manure was plentiful, sheep's dung being chiefly used, the land was left fallow every two, three or four years. Little technical progress had been achieved, the only fertilizer commonly applied being marl. But the enclosure of land to eliminate the uneconomic strip system of cultivation or to change it over from arable to pasturage was making great headway. Because of the rapid growth of population in the sixteenth century and the inflation of prices throughout Europe real wages were at their lowest point during the early years of James I's reign. For rural workers housing was poor and inadequate; firewood was hard to come by; their ordinary diet consisted of bread and cheese. There was much unemployment. Vagabonds were severely treated, being pushed from parish to parish in accordance with the Elizabethan poor law; the genuinely unemployed and the aged were largely dependent on charity, which was generously supplied by the rising merchant class. The gulf between the poor and the rich was wide, exemplified by the over-crowded and insanitary slums of Westminster, which nestled beside the House of Lords.

The cloth industry was then at the peak of its opulence and contributed the bulk of the exports to Europe and the Middle East. After the cloth industry, in which the 'new draperies', particularly serges, largely woven out of imported wool, were beginning to challenge the 'old draperies', such as kerseys (a coarse narrow cloth) – this development was to hit sheep farmers later in the seventeenth century – the extractive industries, especially tin, iron, lead, copper and coal were of the next importance. Because of the scarity of timber, coal was brought to London, chiefly from New-castle upon Tyne, carried there by coastal shipping, to warm houses and cook food, but it was also supplied to manufactures of different sorts ranging from soap boiling to glass-making.

Contemporaries believed rightly that James had taken charge of an affluent kingdom. 'England', declared Thomas Wilson patriotically in 1600, 'for the commodities it yields is known to be inferior to no other country saving that it wanteth wine and spicery.' It cannot be doubted that, at any rate for the nobility, the gentry and the yeomanry, the merchants and the professional classes, including the servants of the King, it was a much wealthier country than Scotland had ever been. Moreover it had thrown off many medieval customs and habits. Subsistence husbandry was on the decline, the influence of the hereditary aristocracy was lessening, the power of the Church had been undermined, and social mobility was increasing. For example, the apprentices of merchants could hope to become rich and then marry into the landed classes. The purchase of offices was another way in which parvenus might rise up the social scale. Many jobs were to be found in Whitehall, as they still are: 'the Court being', according to Arthur Wilson, 'a kind of lottery where Men that venture may draw a Blank and such as have little may get a Prize'.

The differences which marked off the new reign from the old derived partly at least from the character of the rulers. Elizabeth had been a popular Queen, admired by all her subjects, who had reigned gloriously for forty-five years, the date of her accession being celebrated as a public holiday. She had defied the Spaniards and succoured the Dutch. Her progresses around the country had made her accessible, many houses being remembered by the fact that 'Queen Elizabeth slept here': her peripatetic Court was the centre of national life. James I, on the other hand, when he was not addressing parliaments, spent his time hunting from a variety of country houses and was by no means easily approachable and was rarely affable. In fact he despised the middle classes and certainly did not exert himself to caress his subjects as Elizabeth had done. The other difference was that the two-chamber parliament, including a House of Commons which had steadily grown in influence since the time of Henry VIII, was much more powerful and independent-minded than any Scottish parliament. This was largely owing to the rise of the gentry, who constituted the bulk of the membership, and of merchants representing the ports in the Commons. In Scotland hardly any middle class existed. In England a feudal hierarchical society was dissolving into a commercial state with a medieval jurisprudence. James was a highly intelligent man, but it was hard for him to grasp this changing situation or the fact that the English parliaments needed to be conciliated rather than browbeaten.

Although the House of Commons contained neither parties nor formed opposition, it soon showed the new monarch, a foreigner, that it was perfectly ready to teach him how he should run his business. When James tried to take decisions about disputed election results out of the hands of the Commons at the beginning of his reign, he was compelled to back down. Although he assumed the title of King of Great Britain in 1604, his plan to unite the two kingdoms by statute was rejected. Finally, a proposal known as the Great Contract, put forward by his chief Minister, the Earl of Salisbury, to abandon the feudal dues belonging to the Crown in return for an annual income of £200,000 to be voted by the Commons, was rebuffed. When he first addressed the Commons James had told them that he was sure that they did not mean to be seditious, but that he considered himself to be the fount of all laws and claimed that they needed either his initiation or approval; he also insisted that parliament was merely his advisory council and that he did not require to be instructed how he ought to govern. He explained that he was a very experienced king, chosen by God to be a mortal God himself and that he disliked rash and hair-brained fellows or babblers with an itch for talking. Though his first parliament sat for several sessions, his second parliament, called in 1610, rose without passing a single act and was therefore known as 'the Addled Parliament'. Thus James and his parliaments were divided.

What sort of a man would the members of parliament and those of his English subjects who were in a position to study him closely have found James I to be? He was of middle height, had large eyes and a tongue too big for his mouth, which tended to make him slobber. His health at first was good, as it should have been when he spent so much of his time in the open air hunting. But he ate and drank indiscriminately; he took roast beef without bread or vegetables and too much of it since his hunting made him hungry. He liked his drinks to be strong, particularly sweet wines and Scotch ale, but was said to have drunk 'out of custom rather than any delight'. When his brother-in-law, King Christian of Denmark, visited England in 1606 they drank each other under the table. After he reached the age of fifty James suffered from gout and arthritis. He could not bear pain – who can? – and for that reason he drank more than before, no doubt in the hope that it was a soporific. This accelerated the decline of his health. Towards the end of his life he became prematurely senile.

Unlike most of the Stewart Scottish kings, he was grossly extravagant. Money meant little to him: after all, England was a rich country. What he failed to appreciate was that the Crown estates were not an infinite source of capital. His predecessor, Queen Elizabeth I, won the reputation of being parsimonious, but even she had to sell off estates worth over £813,000; during the first six years of his reign James disposed of royal properties valued at £425,000. By that time he had accumulated a debt of a million pounds. Elizabeth's annual expenditure had been about £300.000 a year; James's amounted to about £500,000, but it has to be remembered that he was a married man. Francis Osborne, a sceptical country gentleman, who did not admire the King, wrote that 'all kings cast away money the day of their enthronement, but James did it all his life'.

One of the main reasons assigned for James's prodigality and indebtedness was that after he came to England he splashed money on his Scottish favourites who had accompanied him to the Promised Land. It was complained that the various devices he employed to raise money such as 'impositions' (import duties additional to the Customs, levied by prerogative) and 'monopolies' or patents were 'a cheat' on his English subjects raised for the benefit of the Scots, 'the nation being rooted up by these Caledonian bores'; and it was said that one of his most notorious Scottish favourites, Robert Carr, afterwards Earl of Somerset, was able to exploit the King's patronage 'before he had either wife or beard'.

It was because of the hostility felt towards such favourites that James was unable to procure a legislative union between his two kingdoms; it was alleged that Scotland had nothing to offer but eggs, geese and 'such drugs for the cure of jaundice as might be found in our own hedges'. James had personally exerted himself to obtain a divorce, agreed to by a commission of bishops, so that Carr could marry another peer's wife. But Somerset overreached himself. In 1616 he and his Countess were found guilty of contriving the murder of a prisoner in the Tower of London and were disgraced. Before that James lit upon another favourite, this time a strikingly handsome Englishman, in George Villiers, whom he rapidly promoted to become Duke of Buckingham. Neither Somerset nor Buckingham had an iota of the ability of Robert Cecil Earl of Salisbury, whom James had inherited as his Secretary of State and later appointed Lord Treasurer. Yet when Cecil died, largely of overwork, in 1612 James expressed small gratitude or condolences and announced that he would carry on personally all the duties performed by Salisbury, which in fact he was too lazy to do.

James's Ministers recognized that he was an outstandingly acute statesman. His bishops were impressed by his grasp of theology and in the early part of his reign he acquired prestige abroad as a peace-maker. But he had his limitations. He was an intellectual, who promoted learning in the universities, but was indifferent to aesthetics and science. A vain man, who enjoyed adulation, he was neither a pedant nor a buffoon, He had his prejudices – commendable ones, it can be argued – since he condemned both duelling and smoking. One of his defects as a king was that because he was so quick-witted and could make up his mind rapidly, he became increasingly indolent and content to leave day-to-day administration to be supervised by men favourites, who had not a tenth of his own capabilities.

James's chief interests as a statesman lay in religion and foreign affairs. The Puritan movement, aiming at more sermons, more direct prayers by the faithful and the abolition of all ritual, including surplices and the ring in marriage, was beginning to grow in strength at the outset of his reign in England, having survived an onslaught from Elizabeth's Archbishop Whitgift, who was soon to die. Leading Puritans presented James I with a petition, said to have been signed by a thousand clergymen, seeking the reform or, more accurately, the purification of the Church of England, which, they thought, had in its present practices violated the teaching of the Apostles. James called a conference, as has been noticed, at Hampton Court between Puritan representatives and bishops, headed by Richard Bancroft, about to become Archbishop of Canterbury in place of Whitgift, to discuss what ought to be done to unite all Christians under one Anglican umbrella. James was by no means unsympathetic to the Puritans, at least to start with. He agreed to certain changes in the prayer book, accepted the need for more preaching, and consented to a reduction in the authority of the bishops over the clergy. He also favoured a new English translation of the Bible, as he disliked the existing Geneva version. But what he would not stomach was the introduction of a Presbyterian system, which would have allowed general assemblies, including laymen, to determine ecclesiastical legislation and nullify the power of the bishops, as it had done in Scotland. James asserted that Scottish presbytery did as well agree with monarchy 'as God with the Devil'; it meant that any Jack and Will, Tom and Dick could censure him; his supremacy would then be undermined: he coined the apothegm 'no bishop, no king'. Thus the conference was a partial but not a complete failure.

It has to be remembered that James himself was a convinced Calvinist, as were most of the English clergy; he did not accept what was deemed the revolutionary tenet of free will, advocated by the Dutch theologian, Jacobus Arminius; in fact later in his reign James approved of the punishment of the Arminians in Holland and he was reluctant to make William Laud, an able administrator who sympathized with the Arminian views, into a bishop. When Bancroft died in 1610 he appointed the Bishop of London, George Abbot, who favoured the Puritans, to succeed him as archbishop. The King also agreed to limit the playing of games on Sundays, which was distasteful to Puritans and has been right down to modern times; he laid down only that 'lawful sports' might be played after Sunday church services: these excluded football and golf. The idea that James was anti-Puritan is erroneous. What he disliked was extremism. 'I mean not to compel men's consciences,' he told one of his parliaments, 'for that I ever protested against.'

With regard to his other Christian subjects, the Roman Catholics, James's attitude was to change greatly. Before he left Scotland he had looked for every kind of influence that he could possibly find to bring pressure on Queen Elizabeth to acknowledge him as her heir. To secure the support of rulers of Catholic kingdoms he had assured them that he would grant toleration to their fellow religionists if they, for their part, would recognize him as the rightful successor to the throne of England. He actually made an approach to the Pope. James's agents had undoubtedly exaggerated the concessions that the future English King was ready to grant, even conveying the impression that he might change his own religion as Henry IV of France had recently done. But what James really had in mind was simply leniency towards the Catholic laity who disobeyed the penal laws.

Because Elizabeth I had been excommunicated by the Papacy and threatened with assassination, laws passed during her reign against Roman Catholics had been numerous and horrific. Catholic priests, who proselytized or refused to leave the country when they were ordered to do so, were liable to the death penalty for treason; Catholics over the age of sixteen could be heavily fined if they travelled more than five miles from their homes; those who failed to go to church on Sundays were fined £20 a month. So English Catholics breathed a sigh of relief when Elizabeth died: for James was known to have promised toleration, his wife became a Catholic, and he had treated Scottish Catholics with moderation even when they rebelled against him. James's chief concern after his enthronement was to ensure that English Catholics would be loyal to him. He feared the Jesuits and favoured the exile of all Catholic priests. But he was tolerant towards the laity and suspended for a time the enforcement of fines for not attending Anglican services. He had a daydream of presiding over an international conference aiming to reconcile the Protestants and the Catholics in Europe as long as the Pope was willing to stop intervention in secular affairs. As a result of what one of James's biographers calls with some exaggeration his 'excessive clemency' the English Catholics became optimistic about their future, but they had in fact been misled by promises attributed to the King before he left Scotland.

The result of their disappointment was the Gunpowder Plot. Headed by a Catholic country gentleman, Robert Catesby, a plan was adumbrated to dig underneath the House of Lords, fill a cellar with piles of gunpowder and blow up parliament, King, peers and all, when it met in November 1605. One of the conspirators wrote a letter to a Catholic nobleman, Lord Monteagle, warning him not to attend Parliament as all in it would receive 'a terrible blow . . . though they shall not see who hurts them'. Monteagle took this letter to the Earl of Salisbury, who guessed it might refer to a gunpowder explosion, though James afterwards claimed that this interpretation of the letter was his alone, as was the giving of orders for a thorough search of the cellars under the House of Parliament. On 4 November Guy Fawkes, a soldier of fortune born in York, who had been hired to guard the gunpowder in a cellar, was arrested. The conspirators were rounded up and put to death. Although James sensibly assured Parliament that the plot was devised by a few fanatics, not by the English Catholics as a whole, he had always dreaded assassination, was reminded of the dangers he had faced when he was King of the Scots alone, and insisted that all Catholics must from then on take an oath of allegiance, and all Catholic priests and Jesuits be banished from England. But the laws against the laity were only enforced sporadically during the reign. It was left to the Puritan movement, which waxed hot in Charles I's reign, to show their virulence against the Catholics, condemning them as the servants of anti-Christ or the Whore of Babylon and threatening their extinction.

James's comparative moderation towards the Catholics formed a background to his foreign policy. Soon after he became King of England he concluded peace with Spain, though he later reluctantly agreed to a proposal to join France in guaranteeing a truce concluded between the Spanish and the Dutch, who had rebelled against Philip of Spain and had been fighting for their independence since 1568. From then on James was most anxious to be friendly with Spain, whose wide empire and military might deeply impressed the rest of Europe. He sought a Spanish wife for his eldest son, Prince Henry, who was unenthusiastic and died of typhoid in November 1612. The marriage treaty which James did in fact negotiate in the same year was that of his only daughter, Elizabeth, to the Protestant Elector Palatine, Frederick V. As events turned out, this marriage, which was celebrated in February 1613, was to vitiate James's policy of peace both at home and abroad.

In spite of marrying his daughter to one of the leading Lutheran rulers in Germany and himself entering into an alliance with the German princes who belonged to a Protestant Union, James continued to hanker after an alliance with Spain. It is generally assumed that the arrival at James's Court in 1613 of the wealthy and cultivated ambassador, Sarmiento de Acuña, later Count of Gondomar, who was a master of flattery and soon on intimate terms with the King, affords the principal explanation of James's sanguine pro-Spanish policy. Gondomar certainly pressed for a marriage alliance, but, as James's second son was only thirteen at the time when he came to England, he did not rush his fences. The reason why Gondomar wanted the marriage was that he was aware of England's potential naval strength, exemplified in the past by the defeat of the Armada and the successful naval raids on Spain and its empire, directed by Francis Drake and the second Earl of Essex, and was eager to avoid the repetition of such attacks on his country. Secondly, a decade after the death of Philip II, who had left his kingdom exhausted and involved in long wars with the Dutch and Portuguese, his successor, Philip III or, more precisely, his favourite Minister, Lerma, was obliged to accept a period of peace.

On James's side it is perfectly true that after the death of his eldest son and the long illness of his wife (she died in 1619) and the demise of his ablest Minister, Salisbury, he felt increasingly lonely and ready to welcome the agreeable company of the persuasive Spanish Grandee. Yet James had specific reasons for wanting Spanish friendship. First, he hoped for an access of wealth, especially since the House of Commons had rejected Salisbury's plan for a Great Contract. The Spanish empire boasted vast gold and silver mines so that a marriage treaty seemed to promise a generous dowry. Secondly, James was anxious about his own personal security, understandably so after the exposure of the Gunpowder Plot. An agreement with Spain would, he thought, guarantee the loyalty of English Catholics. Finally, James was not without hope that he would then be invited to become a diplomatic mediator capable of obtaining peace throughout the whole of Europe, reconciling the most fanatical Protestants with the most reactionary Catholics. In 1619 the Venetian envoy in London reported that James believed that he could not keep the peace nor even remain alive without union with Spain.

But his daughter's marriage to Fredrick V in fact proved the prelude to an event that brought war not peace to Europe. Her young husband (he was twenty-two at the time) accepted the offer of the throne of Bohemia made to him by the Bohemian Protestants, who rejected the claim of the Habsburg dynasty that the kingship, though nominally elective, was theirs by right since they had ruled it for a hundred years. The King they rejected was Archduke Ferdinand of Styria, a devout Catholic and pupil of the Jesuits, who soon after he claimed the throne was also elected Holy Roman Emperor

(Frederick V being one of the Electors who voted for him). The new Habsburg Emperor was utterly determined to retain Bohemia and he invoked the assistance of the Spanish Habsburgs, who proceeded to invade Frederick's patrimony of the Rhenish or Lower Palatinate, which they occupied in August 1620. The leading Protestants were vociferous in James's third parliament, that met at the beginning of 1621, demanding that the King should take action to restore his son-in-law to his lost throne.

What could James do? He had no army and his navy was less than half the strength it had attained under Elizabeth. To start with, James attempted to conciliate his new parliament by confirming the privileges of the Commons, by accepting the punishment of his Chancellor, Francis Bacon, who was impeached for corruption, and by revoking certain unpopular patents, in return asking the Commons to grant him generous supplies.

But the King soon discovered that he could only obtain money to hire soldiers if he gave way to requests by the Commons, who wanted a revival of war against Spain, the enforcement of the penal laws against Catholics, and a Protestant marriage for Prince Charles. James was furious at what he regarded as the usurpation of his prerogative right to determine foreign policy. The Commons, however, protested that foreign relations were a proper subject for counsel and debate in parliament. The King retorted by tearing out the page in the Commons journals which recorded this protest and in December 1621 by adjourning and then dissolving Parliament; he also had some of its members arrested. Instead of relying on support by Parliament he fed himself on the illusion that in return for a marriage treaty between Prince Charles and Philip III's young daughter the Spaniards would at least restore Frederick V to the throne of the Palatinate. But a Spanish army occupied Frederick's capital of Heidelberg on 22 September 1620 and Frederick himself, after having been decisively defeated at Prague in November 1620, was compelled to flee with his English wife and their children for safety first to Brandenburg and then to Holland.

James I agreed to one last effort to procure the marriage treaty with Spain in return for Spanish withdrawal from the Lower Palatinate. His favourite, the first Duke of Buckingham, who was both his Lord High Admiral and his Master of the Horse, had become on close terms of friendship with Prince Charles, then in his early twenties. Charles asked the King to allow them to travel to Madrid incognito to finalize the marriage treaty. James himself was only in his early fifties, but his health had seriously deteriorated. His devotion to his 'two sweet boys' overcame his better judgment and he let them go. But whatever Gondomar might have thought, neither

Philip IV (a youthful Prince who had succeeded his father, Philip III, in 1621) nor his able Minister, Olivares, nor, above all, the youthful Spanish Infanta, who loathed the idea of marrying a heretic, was ready to consent to the treaty unless Prince Charles would allow the children of the marriage to be brought up as Catholics and preferably declared himself to be a Catholic. They also demanded that James should issue a proclamation suspending the penal laws against English Catholics and obtain the approval of the proclamation from an English parliament. Although a marriage contract was actually signed in the summer of 1623, the negotiations finally collapsed. Buckingham and Charles returned home bent on revenge for their humiliation in Madrid. When a new parliament was called in February 1624 Buckingham informed it that the Spaniards had never had any genuine intention of helping Frederick V to regain the Lower Palatinate. Thereupon the two Houses petitioned James to end all treaties with Spain and offered him their assistance if war followed.

Thus in the very last year of the King's life England was pushed into war. James I allowed Count Ernst Mansfeld, a German mercenary general, who had first been hired by Frederick V, but had been defeated by the Duke of Bavaria, to recruit an army of 12,000 Englishmen by impressment. They were sent to the United Netherlands with a view to regaining the Lower Palatinate, but after spending the winter of 1625 without pay or adequate food, they deserted or disintegrated. So James's foreign policy lay in ruins. Instead of becoming a glorious peace-maker, who united Christian Europe, he had lived to witness the outbreak of the Thirty Years War in Germany, which tore it apart, a war that had been provoked by the foolishness and incompetence of his own son-in-law.

The King's final days on earth were sad. He quarrelled with his last parliament and was even temporarily alienated from Buckingham. He was unable to save his Lord Treasurer, the Earl of Middlesex, who had mended his finances, from impeachment, though he warned his son that this impeachment, promoted by Buckingham, would prove to be a dangerous constitutional precedent, a warning that proved absolutely right. In the autumn of 1624 James visited his estates in the southern midlands where he had found so much happiness, but he was too crippled with arthritis even to go hunting. At Theobalds, his favourite palace, he was struck down by fever and there he died after convulsions on 27 March 1625. His ascent into heaven was to be depicted by Rubens on the ceiling of the banqueting chamber of Whitehall, where it may still be seen.

By contrast with his triumphs in Scotland James's reign in England had been almost an unrelieved failure. When he left Scotland he had promised to return there every three years. In fact he only went there once and then because he so prized his authority as Supreme Governor of the Church of England that he aimed to impose Anglican rituals on the Presbyterian Kirk. Five Articles that he persuaded a General Assembly in Perth to pass by a majority dealt with conversion, baptism, confirmation and the Christian year: this Assembly also approved of the drawing up of canons and a new prayer book. By pushing through these Articles against the real wishes of the Scottish clergy he was adopting a policy that was to be followed by his son with fatal consequences. Apart from this visit, as James observed, 'I sit and govern Scotland with my pen.'

In England it would be wrong to say that James I's government was unintelligent or unconstructive. The trouble was that, unlike Queen Elizabeth I, he was unable to manage his parliaments, at any rate after the Gunpowder Plot had for a time introduced harmony. This shortcoming was not entirely his fault, since it was hard for him to recognize how significant the rise of the English gentry was and how it had transmuted the House of Commons into an independent-minded political body that it was necessary to conciliate. That was the main reason why his domestic policy proved ineffective.

Furthermore James I, wrapped up in the affections of his men favourites, particularly those of Buckingham, failed to appreciate the genius of his leading English subjects, including his Lord Chief Justice, Sir Edward Coke and his Lord Chancellor, Francis Bacon and his Lord Treasurer, the Earl of Middlesex. He sacrificed the clever and versatile Walter Ralegh, whom he allowed to be put to death on the request of Gondomar, on what was probably a trumped up charge. The breakdown of James's foreign policy, however, should not blind one to the fact that it was honourably intended, though James's obsession with the inviolability of kingship made him unsympathetic both to the Dutch and to the Bohemian Protestants on the ground that they were rebels against divinely instituted authority. It is ironical that one of his earliest critics, Sir Anthony Weldon, who felt resentment because he had been denied an office at Court, while condemning him for being extravagant, cunning and blasphemous and for preferring 'mean men in great places' nevertheless ended his appraisal of his character by writing:

In a word he was (take him altogether and not in pieces) such a king I wish this kingdom had never any worse, on the condition, not any better; for he lived in peace, died in peace and left all his kingdoms in a peaceable condition, with his own motto: *Beati pacifici*.

D. H. Willson, *King James VI and I* (1965) is the best complete biography to date. *James I* (1967) by the late Archbishop David Mathew was written in his usual elusive style. A collection of quotations about the King will be found in Robert Ashton, *James I by his Contemporaries* (1969).

13

Charles I and the
English Civil War

THE FUTURE CHARLES I, born at Dunfermline palace on 19 November 1600, had been promptly baptized because he was not expected to live. In fact he survived the hazards of babyhood but grew up to be a small man, though this has been obscured from posterity through the flattering portraits painted of him by Anthony van Dyck. As a child it took time for him to learn to walk and speak; that was why he was not brought down from Scotland to join his father and mother in England until 1604. Charles grew up to be reserved and always stuttered, but he accepted his father's belief that monarchy was a divine institution and that he was responsible for his actions to God alone: hence he never lost his dignity. While his elder brother, Henry, was an extrovert, a keen athlete, who enjoyed swimming, walking, playing tennis and golf, Charles was an introvert and an aesthete, early developing a refinement in taste which was to make him a connoisseur of the arts. This was partly owing to the influence of his mother, a generous benefactor to the versatile Inigo Jones, the Royal Surveyor, who not only produced a series of masques for her benefit (mostly written by Ben Jonson) but designed her country house at Greenwich. Charles must also have inherited the excellent taste of his great-grandfather, James V of Scotland, who had spent so much money on embellishing his palaces. Long before he became King, Charles was inviting Dutch artists to enter his service and was bidding for paintings by Dürer and Titian. When he went to Madrid with the Duke of Buckingham on their unfortunate mission to acquire a Spanish bride for him, he arranged to buy Raphael's Cartoons and met the talented young painter, Velazquez.

After his father's death Charles retained Buckingham as his principal adviser, a rather remarkable fact because the favourites of royalty have rarely been hereditary. Charles called him 'Steenie', and wrote to him once (in August 1627) to say, 'Upon all occasions I am glad to remember you, and that no distance of place, nor length of time, can make me slacken, much less diminish my love to you'. Because of his anti-Spanish sentiments

Buckingham for a while became popular in the kingdom, but the war against Spain was generally thought to have been mismanaged by him. Thus when at the outset of his reign Charles addressed his first parliament in the belief that it would vote him generous supplies to pay for another campaign, he was disappointed. Only two subsidies were granted (worth about £127,000) and tonnage and poundage (Customs duties) were voted for one year only. In fact, however, the King's Treasurer continued to levy tonnage and poundage, for without them the war could hardly have been fought at all. As it was, an attempt by an amphibious force to capture the port of Cadiz in the autumn of 1625 was a fiasco. From then on the House of Commons laid the blame for the failure of the war squarely on Buckingham and urged his impeachment. To protect the Duke, Charles dissolved both of his first two parliaments and prorogued the third. In August 1628 Buckingham was assassinated by an aggrieved army lieutenant. This meant that as Charles had no other close advisers, he was left on his own to govern the country as best he could.

Before Buckingham died Charles was embroiled not only in the war with Spain, but involved in an attack on France as well. Charles had married Henrietta Maria the sister of Louis XIII King of France, in the first year of his reign and had hoped for an alliance with France against Spain. That was not realized. Instead war against France began in 1627, arising chiefly out of squabbles at sea and over commerce. For this new conflict Buckingham was also regarded as responsible. As Lord High Admiral he had believed that the royal navy could easily defeat the French at sea, while by lending military support to the French Protestants or Huguenots, who were holding out against Louis XIII's chief Minister, Cardinal Richelieu, in La Rochelle, he thought the French King would soon be compelled to come to terms. In fact two attempts to relieve La Rochelle proved disastrous and the refusal of the House of Commons to vote Charles money for war until their many criticisms of Buckingham's conduct of affairs had been met, left Charles without a war chest. The various schemes in which he then indulged to raise money by reviving obsolete feudal rights merely annoyed the Commons more. That was one of the factors which contributed in due course to the outbreak of the first civil war.

It has sometimes been stressed that Charles had been disappointed with the behaviour of his young and inexperienced French wife, largely because she had, in accordance with the marriage treaty, brought over many servants and priests in her entourage who, he was persuaded, were blighting his happiness. He had therefore ordered Buckingham to drive them away by fair means or foul. But this was not an important reason for the breach with France since a compromise was reached. In August 1627 Charles was able to write to Steenie: 'I cannot omit to tell you that my wife and I were never better together; she upon this action of yours [the attack on La Rochelle] showing herself so loving upon all occasions, that it makes us all wonder and esteem her more'; after Buckingham's death Henrietta Maria gradually took his place as Charles's confidante.

Two months after the Duke's assassination a crisis arose in the relations between Charles I and his third House of Commons: this was because of Charles's continuing need for money to pay the costs of the wars against Spain and France. Apart from the income derived from estates belonging to the Crown, which had been greatly reduced by Elizabeth I's and James I's sales, the King had at his disposal the receipts from the Customs (that is to say, both tonnage and poundage and the 'impositions' – or additional rates – first raised by prerogative powers in the previous reign) and loans which the King was able to extract from his wealthier subjects and the City of London. When a request for the voluntary payment of subsidies was rejected, he introduced forced loans and imprisoned over seventy gentlemen who refused to provide them. To diminish the expense of the armies poor men were compelled to serve under martial law as soldiers or had soldiers billeted on them, receiving only promissory notes in return. So it was natural that when Charles summoned his third parliament and invited it to help, protests were indignant. For though military attacks on papist countries were not unwelcome to the majority in the Commons they declined to vote any fresh taxes or acquiesce in the unauthorized levying of tonnage and poundage until their immediate grievances had been remedied.

After much manoeuvring Parliament agreed in May 1628 to draw up a 'petition of right' as a public protest against what were regarded as arbitrary methods of government. This petition, passed as if it were a public Bill through both Houses, quoted ancient statutes to show that forced loans, billeting and martial law, together with the imprisonment of subjects without cause shown, were all unconstitutional. The Commons implied that they would vote five subsidies once the King accepted their petition. He was not anxious to do so because he firmly maintained that all the precedents were on his side: he had done nothing which his predecessors had not done before him. But the Commons were adamant. At first Charles compromised by saying that he would see that 'right be done according to the laws and customs of the realm', but they were dissatisfied with such generalities; so in the end the King gave his answer in the usual form: 'Let it be done as is desired.'

The Petition of Right, which, like Magna Carta before it and the Declaration of Rights after it, has always been precious to constitutional historians, was a landmark in Charles I's reign. But, curiously enough, it did not specifically mention the King's levying of tonnage and poundage without the consent of Parliament as being a grievance. However, eighteen days after Charles had assented to the Petition of Right, the Commons passed a resolution on the subject 'humbly declaring' that his receiving these unauthorized dues was a breach of 'the fundamental laws' of the kingdom. Charles could stand no more from his faithful Commons. He insisted that the levying of tonnage and poundage had always been an accepted part of the royal prerogative since the days of King Edward IV 200 years earlier. He was of course fully aware that he could not maintain a royal navy without the money obtained from the Customs. Therefore he informed Parliament on 26 June 1628 that he owed an account of his actions to God only; he also asserted that it was the responsibility of the judges – whom his father had regarded as lions under the throne – and not of the House of Commons to interpret the laws of the land. Thus even before Buckingham died the lines of battle, wrapped up in medieval politenesses, were being drawn.

Charles recalled the Commons in January 1629, but they were still in an angry mood. Through their instigation merchants had been refusing to pay Customs duties and some of them (including one member of parliament) had found their goods seized in consequence. Furthermore the Commons, consisting, as they did, largely of Puritans or puritanically-minded members, turned their attention to questions of religion as well as of taxation. It has to be recalled that Queen Elizabeth I had always maintained that foreign policy and religion were the sole concerns of the Crown. Following in her footsteps rather than those of his father, Charles, who himself was a deeply religious man as well as having meticulous good taste, did not care for churches being treated as shopping centres or debating societies. He reminded the Commons that he was Defender of the Faith and Supreme Governor of the Church and that his desire was that 'curious search be laid aside' and no one should interpret the holy scriptures or thirty-nine articles of the Church of England except 'in the literal and grammatic sense'. But many members, including young Oliver Cromwell, who represented Huntingdon, his birthplace, in the House, asserted emphatically that the bishops and other clergy favoured by the King were teaching 'flat popery'. In March 1629 Charles ordered the adjournment of the House to allow tempers to cool, but when the Speaker tried to do so, he was held down in the chair while resolutions condemning 'innovations in religion' (that is to say the introducing of 'popery' and 'Arminianism') and forbidding the collection and payment of tonnage and poundage without the consent of Parliament were passed unanimously. This provocative action exhausted Charles's patience: he decided that he would henceforward govern his kingdom as best he could without calling another parliament.

Once this parliament was dissolved Charles published a lengthy declaration to all his subjects, telling them of how happy the nation was where every man was free from oppression and sure of impartial justice; he added that in his opinion 'envenomed spirits' had deliberately contrived to destroy 'the blessed harmony' between them. After he had produced this justification for his conduct Sir John Eliot and nine other members of parliament were singled out as envenomed spirits, accused of sedition and thrust into prisons; but they were told by the Court of King's Bench that they would at once be released on bail if they promised good behaviour in the future. Eventually all were released except Eliot, to whom the King was implacably hostile because he believed that he had inspired the fanatic who murdered his beloved Steenie.

Charles was convinced that the House of Commons had been trying to extend its authority and interfere in matters which had always been the King's sole prerogative, such as religion, the administration of justice and the management of trade, while 'in former times the Knights and Burgesses', he explained, 'were wont to communicate to the House such business as they brought from their counties'. That was why he was determined in future to govern without calling another parliament – and no one else, he stressed, could call one – if this could possibly be avoided. But how was he to find the money to pay for his wars? Unquestionably the Crown was heavily in debt in 1629. Consequently he had no alternative but to conclude peace with Spain and France. The Spanish treaty was effectively negotiated and indirectly conferred economic advantages on the kingdom by bringing bullion to London. The main author of the treaty, Sir Francis Cottington, though he had few bargaining weapons at his disposal, nevertheless succeeded in gaining much the same terms as had been obtained by James I in 1604 when Spain was still smarting from naval defeats it had suffered under Queen Elizabeth.

How far Charles himself really ruled his kingdom during the eleven years that followed the dissolution of his third parliament has been much debated. Some specialists in the history of this period consider that Charles was lazy, being more concerned with his own personal interests than with day-to-day administration. Others maintain that he was in fact highly conscientious. What does appear certain is that he divided and ruled.

Undoubtedly groups of his advisers busily intrigued against one another. Lord Portland, who was Treasurer from 1620 to 1635, and his friend, Cottington, who was both Chancellor of the Exchequer and Master of the Court of Wards, worked hard enough in his service and were probably not corrupt in any meaningful sense of the word in the seventeenth century. On the other side, William Laud, whom Charles appointed Archbishop of Canterbury in 1633, and Sir Thomas Wentworth, a former member of parliament and protagonist of the Petition of Right, whom Charles had created Viscount Strafford and was President of the North until 1633 when he became Lord Deputy of Ireland, both asserted that Portland and Cottington were 'Lady Mora' or 'Mistress Delay' and her maid servant When Portland died Laud tried hard to persuade Charles to appoint Strafford as his successor. Strafford himself was unenthusiastic about the idea because his tough administration in Ireland earned him twice as much as Portland had obtained from the office of Treasurer. As for Charles, he was evidently not sure that he would have been comfortable with such a strong man always at his side; he preferred less tiresome characters around him. So he first created a Treasury Commission with Laud at its head and later made William Juxon Bishop of London Lord Treasurer, thus enlisting a combination of ecclesiastical and secular talents not known since the days of Cardinal Wolsey. Charles also refused Strafford an earldom when he asked for it. Like his father, Charles was not particularly loyal or grateful to his best Ministers. When he did bestow favours on them, he often did so ungraciously.

For some time the King's Government functioned smoothly enough. After 1629 there were what have been called 'seven fat years'. The ending of the wars meant a growth of commerce and industry and an expansion of Customs revenue. Various expedients, such as the revival of fines on gentlemen who spurned knighthoods, and the sale of patents, opprobriously called monopolies, increased the royal revenues. By 1639 the annual income of the Crown was about £850,000 and as Charles was less extravagant than his father had been, that proved sufficient to meet his needs in peace-time. But whereas the revival of these feudal dues were mere pinpricks upon the gentry, and merchants acquiesced reluctantly in the levy on the conduct of foreign trade, the revival in 1634–6 of ship money, raised for the upkeep and improvement of the royal navy, affected directly or indirectly almost the whole of the King's subjects and produced widespread discontent.

Ship money was not a new tax; it had been imposed on ports and coastal counties in the reign of Queen Elizabeth to enlarge the fleet. In Charles's reign piracy and privateering had been intensified in the English Channel and elsewhere: to deal with it new warships were needed. What was different than before was that from 1634 this tax was collected annually and was extended to all counties and boroughs. As to the collection, it was in the hands of the justices of the peace, who assessed on property as well as land, and was paid by the sheriffs directly to the Treasurer of the Navy; so it was a highly efficient tax, hard to evade. Moreover in 1636 a new book of rates for additional Customs was issued. Thus Charles's subjects believed that they were being grossly over-taxed without of course the consent of Parliament. The Earl of Warwick, himself a seaman of note, told the King he would not raise a finger to make his tenants pay ship money against their consciences and in the summer of 1637 John Hampden, a wealthy Buckinghamshire landowner, brought a test case about the tax in the Court of Exchequer. Although he lost the case, some of the judges ruled in his favour. The publicity arising from the case brought about widespread refusals to pay the tax. Modern experience has taught us that high or unjustifiable taxation invariably creates political unrest.

Before the unpopularity of the royal Government, owing largely to taxes of various kinds, had risen to its peak in the later 1630s, Charles I had manufactured another set of problems for himself in Scotland, which he visited in 1633 to be crowned. Educated in the religion of the Church of England, like his father, he staunchly supported the bishops in both his kingdoms; he also approved 'the beauty of holiness' sought after by Archbishop Laud. His stay in Edinburgh cost his Scottish subjects, who also complained that they were far too heavily taxed, the sum of £40,000. His coronation in the abbey church at Holyrood was performed with the ritual and ornaments distasteful to the Presbyterians; and when Charles took steps to procure conformity between the Kirk and the Church of England he aroused further opposition.

Up till then the Presbyterians had not been too restless, for James I's Five Articles, though not repealed, had been largely ignored, while the Scottish bishops were moderate men without the authority wielded by their opposite numbers in England. Charles took up a commitment made by his father to introduce a new set of canons and a new prayer book. The canons, which were published in January 1636, embodied the Five Articles, discouraged extempore prayer, and did not refer to general assemblies or presbyteries. They also required the acceptance of a new prayer book even before it had been published. This prayer book, framed by Scottish bishops but taking the English book for its model, granted concessions to Scottish Presbyterian opinion, for example in the form of the communion service, but in several respects lent colour to the notion that ritual and ornaments were to be permitted, thus inserting a flavour of popery. In July 1637 organized opposition manifested itself in a demonstration in St Giles church (which James I had converted into a cathedral) and was followed by a sheaf of petitions demanding the withdrawal of the new book. The bishops were condemned and riots followed. On 28 February a National Covenant, drawn up by leading Scottish clergy and laymen, was widely subscribed to. It was no mere manifesto against 'popery', but in the words of Professor Donaldson, 'an appeal to the rule of law against the royal prerogative and the King's arbitrary courses, an appeal to history and precedent'. The signatories were neither disloyal nor subversive, but swore to defend 'the true reformed religion . . . to the utmost of that power that God hath put into our hands, all the days of our life'.

Under such pressure Charles gave way for the time being. The prayer book, canons and Five Articles were suspended and permission was given for a general assembly of the Kirk to meet in Glasgow. This Assembly not only annulled the new ecclesiastical measures, but deposed the bishops and defied the royal commissioner, the third Marquis of Hamilton, when he ordered it to dissolve. Charles was infuriated. Both sides prepared for war.

The army that Charles raised to fight the Scottish Covenanters was a scratch army. His difficulty was that he had insufficient money to pay for its arms, supplies and equipment. He was reduced to calling on the militia or 'trained bands', which in fact were untrained, ordering his nobility, as if they were still living in the Middle Ages, to contribute funds or services, and enlisting professional officers who were out of work such as Lieutenant-Colonel George Monck. He placed main reliance, however, on his ship-money fleet, aiming to outflank the Scots by capturing Aberdeen, which was effectively defended by James Graham Earl of Montrose, a keen Covenanter. The Scots were much better organized and their morale was high. Though the English land forces succeeded in crossing the Tweed, they were soon compelled to withdraw because they could not be maintained so far forward from their bases in England. So a truce was patched up at Berwick in June 1639. The King promised to call a parliament and another general assembly in Scotland and to accept the abolition of the bishops. In fact he was only playing for time. In April 1640 he summoned a parliament in London, the first to meet for eleven years, in the hope that it would vote him supplies to defeat the hereditary enemies across the border. When it refused to do so, Charles dissolved it in May and three months later invited Thomas Wentworth, who had at last been created Earl of Strafford and taken his place in the House of Lords, to direct a second campaign.

This time Charles recruited a fair-sized army, which he himself joined early in York. But the Covenanters invaded England; after firing cannon across the river Tyne, they routed the English cavalry and demoralized the English infantry. Once again Charles was left with only one resource if he wished to repel the Scottish rebels: that was to call another parliament at Westminster. This was to become famous as 'the Long Parliament', which contained many Puritans who openly sympathized with the Scots so far as religion was concerned. Moreover it used the opportunity to reiterate the need for Charles to assuage the grievances, which had already been outlined by the acknowledged leader of the House of Commons and Charles's principal critic, John Pym, in the previous parliament. The King now therefore had not only to battle with his Scottish subjects but his English subjects as well. He was in a particularly weak position because the two Scottish campaigns, known as the Bishops Wars, had revealed three facts: first, that he was a poor military organizer, incapable of finding good generals; secondly, that he was not to be trusted because he gave promises to gain time which he did not intend to honour; lastly, that he was easily intimidated because in the first campaign no fighting had taken place at all and in the second he succumbed to a whiff of grapeshot.

The House of Commons, which foregathered on 3 November 1640, at once showed itself to be intensely censorious of Charles's Government. Little evidence has been found to show that it had been packed by an 'opposition party'. Estimates by specialist historians that out of a total of 507 members some 200 were future royalists are beside the point. For unquestionably over nine-tenths of those who sat during the early months of the first session complained of injustices which had accumulated during the past eleven years and had petitions of one sort or another from their electors to put forward and support. To give one example, George Digby, a member for Dorset, who in 1643 was to be appointed by Charles I as his Secretary of State, was among the first to advocate the drawing up of a remonstrance against all the King's Ministers and has even been called by a modern historian a member of 'the opposition'. But the acknowledged leader of the House, John Pym, soon realized that the best way to acquire a position of political strength was to attack specific Ministers of the Crown. Within a week of its first meeting the impeachment of the Earl of Strafford by the Commons before the Lords was moved.

How far could Charles himself be blamed for this state of affairs? The introduction of ship money as a regular tax, though justifiable, was unwise: after all, emergencies are rarely continuous. Equally provocative was the revival of other pernickety forms of taxation, based purely on the exercise of the royal prerogative, which had long fallen into disuse. The futile war against the Covenanters resulted in a Scots army being encamped on English soil, which strengthened the hands of all those in Parliament who sympathized with the Calvinist position about Church government. But it has to be recognized that it was taxation without the consent of the Commons, not the so-called innovations in religion that was the most far-reaching complaint in England. John Pym himself was not an extreme Puritan, if he was a Puritan at all; and a distinguished lawyer, John Selden, also a member of parliament, admitted that 'we charged the prelatical clergy of popery to make them odious, though we know they are guilty of no such thing'. It was easy for determined politicians to allege that Archbishop Laud and those who thought like him were aiming at reunion with Rome since the Queen, who was known to influence her husband, was a devoted daughter of the papacy, while one or two of Charles's Ministers, like Portland and the Secretary of State, Thomas Windebank, were believed to be practising Catholics.

The basic reason for the discontent expressed in Parliament was therefore resentment at what was generally regarded as illegal taxation. It was not, however, a time of economic depression. During most of the 1630s land rents were rising, Customs receipts growing and merchants doing pretty well. Taxation was no higher than, if as high as, elsewhere in Europe. So naturally enough Charles found it hard to understand what all the grumbling was about. Studying the authoritarian position of other kings at the time and remembering what his father had taught him about the historical place of the monarchy in the English constitution, Charles had adopted a policy – though it may have been incoherent – of securing uniformity of religious practices, the building up of an independent financial situation for the Crown, and suppressing dissidents, if necessary, by force. Professor Lawrence Stone has suggested that it was just possible that 'a personally more charismatic king with an irreproachably Protestant reputation and more cautious and far-sighted advisers' might have paved the way towards enlightened despotism. But Charles had no standing army, no efficient bureaucracy, no large sources of income, and no Ministers to whom he gave his full confidence. He found himself incapable of protecting Strafford; when the attempt to impeach him virtually failed, the King signed away his life on 9 May 1641 by agreeing to an act of attainder which enabled the majority in Parliament to condemn him to death without trial by statute law. Charles was then the victim of organized intimidation showing a weakness of character almost incredible in a ruler who had aimed at absolutism.

After the execution of Strafford on 12 May the King gave way all along the line, yielding to pressure from the House of Commons. The whole fabric of the prerogative, enjoyed by his predecessors ever since early Tudor times, was quickly dismantled. Laud, like Strafford, was to be put to death by act of attainder. Parliament, the King agreed, could not be dissolved without its own consent; future parliaments were to meet every three years. But Charles still obstinately hoped that he could regain his lost powers. Once more he visited Scotland, this time intending to grant concessions as the price of enlisting an army to fight for him in England. Such a mission in the light of what happened before verged on the fantastic.

When Charles came back to London in November 1641 he was confronted by a Grand Remonstrance condemning all his previous policies in over 200 clauses; he then realized that he was being asked to become a puppet King, a thought he could not abide. And when he discovered that 148 members of parliament had voted against the Remonstrance, he saw the possibility of forming a royalist party. Rather foolishly he tried to arrest five leading members of parliament for treason, but they escaped and hid in the City. In desperation after this setback Charles left his capital for the north of England. Eight months later he managed to scrape together an army there, aiming to use it to overthrow the opposition leaders, as they had now become, and fight his way back to power by civil war.

It was on 22 August 1642 that Charles by raising his standard at Nottingham formally called upon his subjects to restore him to full authority. When, to avert war, negotiations had taken place between the two sides it soon emerged that a workable compromise was impossible. Charles might have consented to a mixed monarchy, that is to say a form of government in which the rights of the king and parliament were each clearly defined, but Pym and his colleagues distrusted him so much that they refused to agree to a peaceful settlement unless Parliament was awarded the right to nominate all the royal Ministers, officers and officials, control the education of the King's children, and have at its command both the militia and the navy. The King had already conceded much; but he refused to be merely a ceremonial figure in the State. So the war began and went on until, beaten in the field, Charles was obliged to surrender himself to Parliament as an honourable prisoner in February 1647.

To discuss in any detail the long-term and the short-term causes of the English civil war or its military course is unnecessary. But one needs to assess how far the character, policies and abilities of Charles I affected them. Ultimately, it is pretty generally agreed, the rise of the gentry as reflected in the growing strength, influence and independence of the House of

Commons was the most important long-term cause of the conflict between Parliament and the Stuart monarchy. Neither James I nor Charles I, both born in Scotland, where class divisions were different, had actually grasped this fact. Yet James, at least towards the end of his life, had been conciliatory towards Parliament and even acquiesced in the impeachment of two of his Ministers. Charles handled all of his parliaments badly. He was an aloof aesthete, who simply assumed that the Commons were bound to help him in his war with the Scots, the traditional foes of Englishmen throughout the Middle Ages.

The short-term cause of the struggle was, above all, Charles's financial problems. Because of the sale of Crown properties, the cost of the ill-conceived foreign wars, the antagonism aroused by the collection of ship money as well as the employment of such expedients as forced loans and the billeting of soldiers, he was left with no choice but to throw himself on the generosity of his wealthier subjects, who naturally required their grievances to be met before they voted him supplies. By denying him help and frightening him with the aid of London mobs, they quickly drove him to the wall after he had signed away the life of Strafford. Yet though he conceded almost everything he was asked, he finally felt obliged to fight or betray the Stuart monarchy.

With regard to the war itself, Charles did not show himself to be a bad general, at any rate so far as tactics were concerned. He accepted good advice in fighting the first battle of the war at Edgehill in Warwickshire in 1642; he was victorious on several fronts in 1643; during 1644 he defeated one of the best Parliamentarian commanders at a battle near Oxford; later he outmanoeuvred his rival commander-in-chief, the third Earl of Essex, after chasing him into Cornwall; finally, he came pretty well out of the second battle of Newbury, where he was surrounded and outnumbered, but got back safely to his headquarters in Oxford. Yet he had two glaring defects, especially as a strategist. The first was that he was always hesitant about choosing between alternatives, the second was that he behaved ineptly towards his subordinate commanders. If he had led his army on London directly after his moral victory at Edgehill, he might conceivably have ended the war at a blow. If in 1643 he had really planned converging movements on the capital (a strategy with which he has often been wrongly credited) he might have compelled Parliament to surrender. Again, had he not written a foolishly worded letter to his nephew, Prince Rupert, in 1644, Rupert might never have fought a superior army at the battle of Marston Moor where his defeat had the consequence of losing most of the north of England to his enemy. Finally, if the King, instead of delaying in the midlands in 1645 and being trapped at Naseby in Northamptonshire, had marched to the Scottish border to join his brilliant commander, the Marquis of Montrose, who had virtually conquered Scotland on his behalf, he might still have won the victory that would have enabled him to conclude peace on terms favourable to his dynasty.

As to his commanders, on several occasions he neglected the advice of Prince Rupert, although to start with he had alienated his first commander-in-chief by giving Rupert independent control of the cavalry, his best arm in the war. Not only did Charles reject Rupert's request to advance on London after Edgehill, but he refused to assault Gloucester in 1643, instead trying vainly to starve it out and thus allowing it to be relieved. At Naseby he permitted himself to be deflected from a counter-attack and in the end he dismissed Rupert, whom he had promoted to be his Captain General, because in 1645 he was obliged to surrender Bristol, which was already known to be indefensible except by a large army. Charles also gave contradictory orders to General George Goring, a boisterous character but an able officer had he been carefully handled. If Charles had not allowed Goring to fight in the west of England in 1645 instead of staying with the main Royalist army, he might not have lost the battle of Naseby. Of course it can be argued that the King's feelings did him credit. During the early stages of the war he optimistically believed that he could easily bring the Parliamentarians to their knees. That was why he recoiled from assaulting London at the cost of many innocent lives. It was for the same reason that he would not give the order to storm Gloucester in 1643. But wars cannot be fought in kid gloves. If Charles had not wanted ordinary people to suffer through the fighting, he should not have embarked on the war in the first place, but have acceded to the demands of the Parliamentarians in the hope that he would profit later from a loyal reaction to his humiliation.

As it was, Charles lost the first civil war and later lost a second civil war and his life as well. It is often said that Charles I, like his second son, the future James II of England, was an obstinate, tenacious and inflexible man. In support of this claim he is quoted as having said when he was still Prince of Wales: 'I cannot defend a bad nor yield in a good cause.' But this epigram did not really harmonize with his actions at all. He did in fact yield to the Parliamentarians over many questions. Towards the close of the first civil war he offered to allow Presbyterianism to be introduced into the Church of England for three years pending an agreed ecclesiastical settlement. As his Queen not unnaturally wrote to him at the time, if he were prepared to go as far as that, why not accept Presbyterianism altogether, provided that was the price he had to pay to regain his throne? He gave way to the majority in Parliament over the execution of Strafford, though he had promised the Earl that he would not allow him to suffer in life, honour or estate. After standing up for all his prerogatives in 1629, he was willing to accept the principle of 'mixed monarchy' in 1642. After in the end giving his assent to the Petition of Right, which condemned the levying of taxation without parliamentary consent, he announced that it did not apply to the collection of tonnage and poundage, though this had in fact required the assent of the Commons for a hundred years. Finally, after being made an honourable captive in Hampton Court palace in 1647 and having given his word that he would not try to escape, Charles fled from there to the Isle of Wight where despite the comprehensive Royalist capitulation at the end of the first civil war, he planned with the aid of some of his Scottish subjects, to be known as the Engagers, led by the first Duke of Hamilton, to launch a second civil war against Parliament.

Ever since he had become a prisoner Charles I had tried to play off his various opponents against one another before finally committing himself to the Engagers. For his obvious duplicity at this stage of his life, which he no doubt believed necessary on the ground that the means justified the end, he came to be increasingly distrusted. So after the Scots and English Royalists, who had risen again on his behalf, were crushed by the end of 1648, it was scarcely surprising that he was brought to trial as a war-monger or a Man of Blood.

Now at last Charles did prove himself to be inflexible. For he refused on any account to acknowledge the authority of the court set up with commissioners who were to act both as his judges and his jury. His refusal was justifiable enough because the court had been established merely by a House of Commons which could not have contained more than seventy and probably fewer than fifty members where once there had been over five hundred. Furthermore the ordinance had been rejected by a House of Lords reduced to sixteen peers. Thus what had been created was a revolutionary tribunal.

When the trial opened on 20 January 1649 in Westminster hall Charles was accused of

a wicked design totally to subject the ancient and fundamental laws and liberties of this nation, and in their place to introduce an arbitrary and tyrannical government . . . and to bring this design to pass he hath prosecuted it with fire and sword, levied a cruel war in the land against Parliament and the Kingdom . . .

Arguably he had declared war on Parliament when he raised his standard at Nottingham, but history certainly does not show that he had any fixed design to introduce arbitrary government: rather he claimed that he ruled by law and sound precedents. On the first day when he met his judges he insisted that though he was a lawful king, this was not a lawful court and he could not submit to it. He therefore put forward no defence; though he spoke hesitantly he never lost his dignity except once when he dropped his stick. Few lawyers of any standing served as commissioners, let alone the Chief Justices of the realm. He was pronounced guilty, but it was with some difficulty that fifty-nine out of the original 135 commissioners were persuaded to sign his death warrant.

It was not until the afternoon of 30 January 1649 when he stood upon the scaffold erected outside Whitehall palace that Charles attempted to clear himself 'both as an honest man, a good King and a good Christian'. He blamed the war on 'ill instruments' by which presumably he meant Lieutenant-General Oliver Cromwell and others in the Parliamentarian army. He also said that 'an unjust sentence that I suffered to take effect is punished now by an unjust sentence on me': he referred of course to the execution of Strafford five-and-a-half years earlier. That indeed was the turning point in Charles I's tragic life. Yet the resolution that he showed at the very end of it and the statement that he made that he desired the liberty and freedom of his people, guaranteed by the laws of the land, created the legend of a virtuous Christian king who endured martyrdom without flinching. That legend, above all, was what saved the Stuart dynasty from destruction in the middle of the seventeenth century. Just over eleven years later his eldest son, Charles II, was to be rapturously restored to the thrones of his ancestors.

There is as yet no standard full-scale biography of Charles I. John Bowle's biography, published in 1975, is good on Charles's culture but perfunctory on his politics and military skill. Dame Veronica Wedgwood's books, *The King's Peace* (1954), *The King's War* (1958) and *The Trial of Charles I* (1960) offer by far the most convincing psychological analysis of his character. An excellent highly illustrated book is D. R. Watson, *The Life and Times of Charles I* (1972). *The Letters of King Charles I*, a selection edited by Sir Charles Petrie, appeared in 1935. My own account of the causes and course of the civil wars is in *A Concise History of the English Civil War* (1974).

14

Charles II and
His Family Devotion

CHARLES PRINCE OF WALES and Earl of Chester was not yet nineteen when his father was executed. The shock given by the news of it, which he received in Holland was not unexpected but severe. During his early youth he had been a member of an exceptionally happy family. But though he loved and was loyal to his father, he had begun to realize that he had been a misguided king. In the last letter he received from his father, written from the Isle of Wight just before Charles I was brought to Westminster for his trial, the young Prince had been told how he ought to behave when he became king himself:

> Show the greatness of your mind, rather to conquer your enemies by pardoning them than by punishing . . . Censure us not for having parted with too much of our own right; the price was great; the commodity was security to us, peace to our people. And we are confident that another Parliament would remember how useful a King's power is to a people's liberty . . . Give belief to our experience, never to effect more greatness or prerogative than what is really and intrinsically for the good of our subjects (not satisfaction of favourites) . . . The English nation are a sober people; however at present under some infatuation . . . To conclude, if God give you success, use it humbly and far from revenge. If He restore you to your right upon hard conditions, whatever you promise, keep.

This letter fascinates, for it shows by implication what Charles I had learnt from life. He accepted the idea of a 'mixed' or what may be called a semi-constitutional monarchy, with prerogative rights employed only for what was conceived to be the public good. He regretted his early enslavement by Buckingham; he appreciated that he himself had unwisely made promises that he did not really intend to keep; and he knew that this had contributed to his downfall.

But the future Charles II, however devoted he was to his father, had already acquired a mind of his own. For over three years of his adolescence from 1646 to 1649, after he had left Oxford, he had been away from Charles

I's direct influence. In the autumn of 1646 he had been sent to the west of England to be in nominal command of the armed forces protecting the last bastion of Royalist England. There he had seen how some Cavaliers found enjoyment while others had adhered to their duty. Then on his father's orders he had left England to seek safety in France. In 1648 during the second civil war, launched by his father, he had taken command — and not merely nominally — of a number of warships that had revolted against the Parliamentary régime and come over to Holland, where he met them. But the second civil war was swiftly lost. It is doubtful if Charles was impressed by what his father told him about keeping his promises. He was to receive completely different advice about how he should behave from his mother, who since 1644 had been in exile in Paris. She was to write to him in 1650: 'You must not think it necessary to keep any treaties further than they may serve your ends.'

In fact during his formative years Charles learned from events rather than from parental counsel or from books. His first governor when he was a child, the immensely wealthy and cultured Earl of Newcastle, not only advised him to avoid bookishness, but had instilled in him the belief that he must be 'brave, noble and just' and be 'courteous and civil to all', especially to ladies. Newcastle's teaching evidently impressed him more than that of his parents, whose conduct had been shaped largely by their different religions. Had it not been for his passion for conformity Charles I might not have needed to fight his unsuccessful Bishops Wars against the Scots, which led him into disputes with his English parliaments, while had Henrietta Maria not been so openly a proselytizing Roman Catholic, the Puritan movement might not have suspected her of a Catholicizing policy. Thus the future Charles II came to realize that a monarch should keep his own religion to himself and try to avoid provoking his subjects into rebellion over religion. The key factor, which he had first to take into account after his father's execution, was that in the three Stuart kingdoms different religions prevailed: in England the Protestant compromises known as Anglicanism, fashioned by Henry VIII and Elizabeth I, in Scotland the Presbyterian Kirk, chiefly created by John Knox, and in Ireland the Roman Catholicism both of the native Irish and the Anglo-Irish. It became obvious to him that religious questions must be submerged and royal authority employed as far as possible to promote liberty for Christian consciences. If, as seems likely, he imbibed such lessons in his youth, they were to be reinforced when after his father's death he was acclaimed King by all dedicated Royalists wherever they were and whatever their faith.

Charles II's first aim was to regain the three Stuart kingdoms which his father had lost, but his resources were extremely limited. England was under the firm control of the New Model Army, first raised by Parliament in 1645, which had speedily won the second civil war. In Ireland the first Marquis of Ormonde, a large landowner, a Protestant and a faithful Royalist, had succeeded in obtaining a treaty between the Irish Royalists and the Irish Catholics, who agreed to fight for the Stuart monarchy so long as their religious freedom was respected. But Oliver Cromwell, who had already proved himself to be an outstanding commander, led an expeditionary force to Dublin and inflicted a series of defeats on the Irish. Charles then looked for help from Scotland.

The Scots had not approved of the execution of a king who belonged to a dynasty that had ruled them not ineffectively for over 250 years. The demands of their emissaries, who met Charles at Breda in the United Netherlands early in 1650, were stringent. They asked him to sign the two Covenants, that is the National Covenant, which upheld the Presbyterian ecclesiastical system in Scotland, and the Solemn League and Covenant (originally drawn up in 1643 as the basis of an alliance with the English Parliamentarians) providing not only for the reformation and defence of the Church in all three kingdoms but specifically for uniformity of religion throughout all of them. Thus Charles was being asked not only to impose a Presbyterian system upon England (to which his father had temporarily agreed) but also in Ireland, where the Catholics were in a majority outside Ulster. Charles hesitated about accepting these terms, which he saw were bound to alienate the Irish and the English Anglicans, who had fought for his father. Moreover he had hopes that the Marquis of Montrose, who although a Covenanter, had served his father and proved to be a soldier of genius, might manage to conquer Scotland on his own behalf. But Montrose had been unable to enlist an adequate army and failed to achieve much progress in the Highlands. Therefore Charles very reluctantly resolved to conclude a treaty with the strict Covenanters and sent orders to Montrose to lay down his arms. His messages and promises never reached the Marquis, who was defeated and captured by an army of Lowlanders under the command of General David Leslie. Condemned for high treason, Montrose was hung, drawn and quartered and held up to obloquy as a traitor to his country.

Charles's behaviour to Montrose did not differ materially from his father's treatment of the Earl of Strafford. Both of them were assured that their life, honour and property would at all costs be protected. In Charles II's case, however, he honestly intended to save Montrose's life, believing that if the Marquis once laid down his arms, he would be allowed by the

Covenanters to go into exile and be ready later to fight for him in England. Montrose died nobly, telling the ministers who attended him on the scaffold that he acknowledged no sin, 'but feared God and honoured the King'. When eventually Charles capitulated to the hard terms imposed upon him and entered Edinburgh as the puppet of the Marquis of Argyll, an extreme Presbyterian, who spent most of his life praying and intriguing, he was compelled to gaze upon Montrose's skull, placed on the tollbooth and the limbs displayed on the town gates. It was a hideous experience that Charles never forgot nor forgave. He hated his Scottish hosts, but concealed his emotions in the hope that if he acquiesced in their wishes, they would restore him to his throne.

In fact Argyll and the junto who now governed Scotland had no intention whatsoever of invading England on their King's behalf. They were fully aware of the strength of the New Model Army, and had a shame-faced desire not to ignore but only to humiliate this Scottish Stewart monarch. The English republicans, now with Oliver Cromwell as their Captain-General, decided against risking another invasion from Scotland, similar to that carried out by the Engagers under the first Duke of Hamilton in 1648. They therefore resolved upon a preventive war; an army was dispatched across the Tweed which soon threatened Edinburgh. The Scots, whose Covenanter army, which was much larger than that under Cromwell's command, but not nearly so well trained, was overwhelmingly beaten at the battle of Dunbar on 3 September 1650. Charles soon recognized the opportunity afforded by this setback. On the very day of the battle he wrote a letter complaining of the Covenanters' 'villainy' and 'hypocrisy'. Up till then he had indeed been a Presbyterian puppet, swearing oaths and giving promises galore. Now if he could unite the Scottish Covenanters, the former Engagers, and the Royalists (mostly Highlanders) under his own flag, he felt sure that with such help he could regain his authority in England, as his father had vainly attempted to do. Argyll was obliged to acquiesce in Charles's rehabilitation and actually took a leading part in his coronation as King of the Scots at the historic site of Scone; but he refused to have anything to do with Charles's attempt to overthrow Cromwell and invade England.

In August 1651 Cromwell, whose further advance into Scotland after his victory at Dunbar had been held up along the line of the river Forth, succeeded in outflanking Stirling, the fortress protecting the route to Perth, the temporary Scottish capital. Charles, who once he had been crowned, had been accepted as the Scottish commander-in-chief, slipped past the English army and made for Lancashire and the Welsh border, where he hoped to swell his forces with Royalist recruits. He was accompanied by David Leslie on his march into England, leaving behind the sulky Argyll. Leslie, however, was a defeatist, the Royalist reinforcements scarcely materialized, and although Charles penetrated as far south as Worcester, an undoubtedly loyal city, he was there cut off and surrounded by Cromwell in charge of three republican armies. Charles fought courageously, skilfully and daringly, but, after a battle lasting five hours, was conclusively defeated. Though the bulk of his army was taken prisoner, he himself managed to escape from England; on 18 October 1651 he was welcomed by his mother and two brothers, Prince James and Prince Henry, upon the hospitable soil of France.

For the next nine years of his life Charles and his fugitive Court tried desperately to enlist foreign assistance to procure his restoration. He looked first to the French, then to the Dutch (who were at war with the English Commonwealth from 1652 to 1654) and lastly to the Spanish. So long as Oliver Cromwell survived (he was appointed Lord Protector of the Commonwealth in December 1653) and controlled a substantial army and navy all the efforts of Charles and his Ministers were vain. But after Oliver's death in 1658 his son was overthrown by the leaders of the republican army, who then proceeded to quarrel among themselves. In the end, during the spring of 1660 General George Monck, the military governor of Scotland, who had overthrown Argyll and established effective rule by an English garrison not only over the Lowlands but also the recalcitrant Highlands, himself tired of the anarchy in England; he led part of his army into England resolved to reinstate the Stuart monarchy. Believing, as he did, that he was accurately interpreting the wishes of the English people, Monck insisted upon the election of a free Parliament. When it met in Westminster in April 1660 this convention, as it became known, invited Charles II to return to London.

Charles's handling of the opportunity provided for him was clever. Though he had earlier been promised help by the Spanish Government, which since 1657 had been at war with the Commonwealth Government in alliance with France, the King realized that it would be tactful for him to leave Catholic territory (his Court was established in Brussels) and make ready for his return home in the United Netherlands where the Dutchmen in authority were impeccable Protestants. He astutely promised General Monck and the English Covention that the republican army would be generously treated, that 'liberty of conscience' for all Christians would be assured, and that the delicate questions of a land settlement and the punishment of his father's murderers would be referred to the decisions of a parliament. Thus he had mastered the lesson, never learnt by Charles I and only partly appreciated by James I, that Parliament as an institution had become a fundamental part of the English way of life. It might be packed with royal adherents, it might be bribed or cajoled, summoned or adjourned, but it must henceforward be accepted and consulted. A year after Charles set up his government in Whitehall palace a new parliament replaced the Convention which had invited him back to England. What was in effect his second parliament, meeting first in May 1661, was overwhelmingly Royalist and Anglican. It became known as the long Cavalier Parliament, for it met on and off for eighteen years.

It has already been noticed how the character of Charles II had been influenced by the environment of the civil war away from his parents during his adolescence. Both during his last years in England and his exile in France and later in the Spanish Netherlands he found he had two enemies to avoid – boredom and lack of money. When in the south-west of England he had not been allowed to fight in battle, while his wishes were frequently disregarded by his Council. In France he had come to envy the life of his brother, James, who enlisted as a volunteer in the army of the Queen Regent, where he rapidly acquired the rank of lieutenant-general. Though Charles had shown himself eager to invade England whenever a Royalist rising was in prospect and even contemplated returning to Scotland to join his friends among the Highlanders, he was restrained by his Ministers, who naturally did not want him to risk his life again, as he had done at Worcester.

As to money, Charles was nearly always in want because his mother kept a tight hold on funds received from the French Court even after her son was recognized as King; and when he finally left Paris, the Spaniards delayed in providing a pension they had promised him. Moreover the years he spent at or near the French Court with all its glitter and extravagances made him wistful over his income that was at times so low that he could not even afford to buy himself a decent meal. But he took it cheerfully. 'We pass our time as people can do that have no more money,' he told a friend, 'for we dance and play as if we had taken the Plate Fleet.' His financial difficulties were scarcely his own fault, for he felt it his duty not only to care for his meagre staff, but also to sustain a rudimentary diplomatic service.

So it was hardly surprising that impatience was the keynote of Charles's character. Twelve years in exile from England was a long time. He clutched at any straw: unwisely he encouraged the Royalists in England to rise on his behalf too soon. To offset his frustration he indulged in many love affairs, of which the most notorious was that with a Welsh girl, Lucy Walter, who bore him a son, later to become famous as James Scott Duke of Monmouth. The young King does not appear to have spent much money on these mistresses, even when he had it to spare, for few of them were particularly genteel and could not have expected much from him. How many mistresses he had before his return to England is not known (he himself complained that the number was exaggerated), but it did his reputation little good among his staider subjects. John Evelyn, a cultivated stalwart of the Church of England, who first met Charles when he was eleven years old and corresponded with him in exile, recorded in his memoirs when the King died that he would have been 'an excellent prince doubtless had he been less addicted to women'.

Mixing, as he had to, with all sorts and conditions of men and women, Charles soon realized that it was pointless and tiresome to follow the advice given him by the Earl of Newcastle to be aloof, polite and ceremonious; he preferred to be affable, debonair and easy of access. During his exile he fascinated everyone who had any dealings with him including the stiff Spaniards. Whether, as has been claimed, he was genuinely light-hearted is a different matter, for surely what he always wanted was to regain his Crown in England by hook or by crook and then to keep it without having to go on his travels again. Like his grandfather, he showed himself to be extremely quick-witted. In exile he rarely hesitated over a decision, for he tended to rush at any chance which he believed would bring him nearer his goal.

His principal Ministers were for the most part considerably older than himself; although he trusted them implicitly and would hear nothing against them, he preferred the company of men about his own age, such as the second Duke of Buckingham. His advisers, including Hyde, his Chancellor of the Exchequer, Ormonde, his Lord Lieutenant of Ireland, and Edward Nicholas, his senior Secretary of State, deplored his insouciance and what they called his laziness. After his humiliating experiences on his first arrival in Scotland, where the Covenanters insisted upon his making promises that they knew he was unlikely to keep, it was scarcely surprising that he grew cynical. He inherited from his parents the feeling that any commitment was justifiable if it was likely to contribute to his ultimate victory over his enemies.

It has to be remembered that he was still a young man when he returned to France in 1652 and though he was conscious of his duties as a king in exile he could hardly be serious all the time. His cousin, Louis XIV, who, unlike him, was rarely to lower his dignity, also sowed wild oats. Charles was criticized because after he was forced to leave France he enjoyed himself in Cologne and Aachen with his widowed sister, Mary. He was condemned for travelling in a too leisurely way to Spain in 1659 and contrasted unfavourably with his brother, James, though it was admitted that he earned respect from the Spanish and French diplomatists who were then negotiating a treaty of peace. His most trusted servant, the Marquis of Ormonde, was of the opinion that he took 'immediate delight in empty, effeminate and vulgar conversation' and Edward Hyde considered that he was indolent because he disliked having to write letters in his own hand. But the fact was that, like James I, he was highly intelligent and always ready to exert himself when he thought it necessary, but he abhorred routine duties that he thought he could leave to his conscientious Ministers. And although they were liable to grumble among themselves about his behaviour, he was such a fascinating young man that they forgave him easily. As Hyde once wrote sympathetically, 'if you knew what a miserable life the King leads, and how he is used, you would believe that he acts not his part amiss; nor is it enough to say it is his own fault'.

After the Restoration settlement had been completed and Charles had been voted an annual income by Parliament, he had to determine his foreign policy. Although the Spanish had helped him more than the French during his years of exile, he so much admired the grandeur of the French Court and was so impressed by the autocratic power of the young King Louis XIV, that he wanted a French alliance. On 21 May 1662 he married a Portuguese princess, Catherine of Braganza, with the full approval of the French because although they were no longer at war with Spain, they were anxious to make things as difficult as possible for the Spanish Habsburgs and therefore aimed to give indirect assistance to the Portuguese, who had been in revolt against the Spanish monarchy for twenty years.

The French had also concluded a defensive treaty with the Dutch, who were long at war with Spain, but the new King of England found it less easy to be on good terms with them as they had deprived his sister Mary's son, William, of the position previously held by the House of Orange. Moreover, as Charles soon discovered, the Dutch and his English subjects were constantly quarrelling over naval and commercial questions. The House of Commons, which in September 1660 had passed a stringent Navigation Act directed at injuring the Dutch carrying trade, in fact showed itself eager for war against the Dutch. Neither Charles nor his principal Minister, Edward Hyde Earl of Clarendon, who had become Lord Chancellor in 1658, wanted to be involved in such a war. The King had no army apart from a few palace guards and one or two regiments retained for the purposes of internal security and the navy, though very effective under Cromwell, was worse equipped than the Dutch navy, which was employed to protect their wide-flung mercantile marine against pirates and privateers. War at sea between these two maritime powers broke out almost spontaneously in 1665. In the end the Dutch were victorious so that Charles, despite the fact that he had been voted substantial sums of money by Parliament to wage the war, was compelled to accept peace on terms inferior to those obtained by Cromwell after the previous war between the two nations had been concluded in 1654.

The Earl of Clarendon was the scapegoat for the failure of this war with the Dutch; he was menaced with impeachment for high treason and forced into exile. Charles's chief adviser on foreign affairs, Henry Bennet, now created Viscount Arlington, had a Dutch wife and was antipathetic to the French. The Dutch had withdrawn from the war with England partly because they were exceedingly nervous about French foreign policy which was directed towards partitioning the Spanish empire. In the spring of 1667 Louis XIV had sent in a large army, ably commanded, to attack the Spanish Netherlands (modern Belgium). Out of fear of French aggression the Dutch concluded in 1668 a defensive alliance with England, which was joined by the Swedes, and became known as the Triple Alliance. This treaty was mainly the work of Arlington, but Charles, who insisted that he was his own Foreign Minister, favoured it because he believed, rightly as it proved, that it would have the result of making Louis XIV seek a treaty with England. If that were arranged satisfactorily, then revenge could be exacted upon the upstart Dutch and, once crushed, their country could be divided between France, England and the youthful William III of Orange, Charles II's nephew.

Prolonged and complicated negotiations, in which Charles's sister, Henriette Anne, a Catholic princess, married to Louis XIV's brother, was directly concerned, culminated in a secret Anglo-French treaty, both offensive and defensive, that was signed at Dover in May 1672. Charles loved his young sister devotedly and had Catholic sympathies himself: 'We shall never have any quarrel,' he once told her, 'but as to which of us love the other most . . .' This was a personal factor in Charles's foreign policy. The treaty included a clause whereby Charles promised before the war against the Dutch, envisaged in the treaty, began, to declare himself a Catholic and aim by his example to lead his English subjects back into the Roman fold. Historians have debated how far Charles was sincere in giving this promise; the most likely explanation is that he wanted to convince Louis that his intention to destroy the Dutch Protestant Government was genuine.

The House of Commons proved far less enthusiastic about the new war against the Dutch than they had been over the earlier war. Charles therefore had the utmost difficulty in scraping together the funds needed to supply his navy; furthermore the Dutch succeeded in preventing the English navy from fighting them off their own coasts. Consequently a plan to land an amphibious force in the Dutch rear, while they were being attacked by the French army frontally from the west, broke down. In 1674 Charles was forced out of the war and had to be content with offering his services as a mediator; but naturally the Dutch did not trust him. They demanded that he proved his desire for peace was genuine by a military demonstration against the French. So anti-French had English public opinion become by the late 1670s that Charles was indeed driven to contemplate intervention on the Dutch side and one or two regiments were actually raised and dispatched to the Netherlands. However, by 1678 both the French and the Dutch were tired of an exhausting and expensive war: so they concluded peace without taking much notice of the would-be English mediation.

For the remainder of his reign Charles II kept out of war. He made one or two secret agreements with Louis XIV by which in return for French subsidies he undertook to connive at French aggression, which thenceforward was directed chiefly against Germany and ultimately against Spain. Louis managed to seize both Strasbourg and Luxembourg; then he keenly awaited the demise of the ailing and childless King of Spain, known as Carlos the Sufferer, in the grandiose hope of swallowing up most of the Spanish empire.

The reason why Charles II lent his support to French ambitions was because for a number of reasons he feared that an English republican movement might be revived and compel him once more to go into exile. As he had no army — for the Commons obliged him to demobilize the new regiments that he enlisted towards the end of the Franco-Dutch war — he felt doubtful whether he was capable of resisting a rebellion were it to take place. His once enthusiastically loyal Parliament, stiff with Anglicans, had by 1678 turned against him and his Ministers, partly because it had become violently anti-French and partly because it suspected that Charles was pro-Catholic, more especially as it was generally known that his brother, James, had already been received into the Catholic Church. So in the last resort Charles had to depend on French help if he were to retain his throne and if his brother (since Charles had only illegitimate children himself) were to be allowed to succeed him peaceably. That was the chief reason why Charles continued to be pro-French. Nevertheless he did try rather ineffectually to exert such influence as he had with Louis XIV to limit French aggression, notably in the Spanish Netherlands, since its occupation by French troops might be a threat to the independence of Great Britain.

Charles's domestic policy was largely fashioned by his determination that his brother should succeed him on the throne. Unlike his father, Charles did not resent Parliament's initiation and passing of Bills without his prior approval. The Cavalier Parliament was pretty reactionary. It carried through a series of measures designed to prevent nonconformists (that is to say the clergy and their congregations who refused to accept the Act of Uniformity or to use the Common Prayer Book) from worshipping as they wished. It also pressed for the enforcement of anti-Catholic measures comprising a penal code that had been on the statute book since the reign of Elizabeth I. Because of commercial and naval rivalry with the Dutch this Parliament passed a group of Bills known collectively as the Navigation Acts. Charles with his Catholic sympathies and his realization that the English Presbyterians had contributed markedly towards his Restoration had vainly tried to set up a comprehensive Church, which would have embraced Presbyterians as well as episcopalians, and then in 1662 published a Declaration of Indulgence, which would have allowed him to dispense with the Act of Uniformity by using his royal prerogative. The House of Commons objected to this so vehemently that Charles took the easy course of abandoning it.

As the Cavalier Parliament sat for eighteen years its membership was substantially altered by by-elections which changed its complexion. By 1675 when Charles appointed Thomas Osborne Earl of Danby, who had earlier distinguished himself as Treasurer of the Navy, to be his chief Minister, the Commons had become emphatically anti-French and anti-papist, being provoked in particular by the known Catholicism of James Duke of York. Not only did it compel Charles to withdraw a second Declaration of Indulgence, which he had issued the year before by virtue of his prerogative, thus suspending the entire penal code, but also obliged him to give his consent to a Test Act excluding Roman Catholics from all public offices.

This second Declaration of Indulgence was really published by the King so as to meet, in part at least, the promises given by him in the secret treaty of Dover. After Charles entered the Dutch war on the side of France it was generally realized that he was at heart pro-French. So an unpopular foreign policy impinged on domestic affairs, for because of Danby's involvement in the King's secret negotiations with France an attempt was made by the Commons in 1679 to impeach him. To save his Minister Charles then dissolved his Cavalier Parliament, but a new House of Commons pushed through a Bill of attainder condemning Danby for high treason, similar to the Bill that was passed forty years earlier against Strafford.

The King recoiled in the face of parliamentary pressure: Danby was dismissed and confined to the Tower of London. Charles had earlier acquiesced in the impeachment of his first leading Minister, the Earl of Clarendon, and had dismissed his friend, the second Duke of Buckingham from the lucrative office of Master of the Horse, which he bestowed on his illegitimate son, the Duke of Monmouth. In 1682 Monmouth was involved in discussing a scheme of rebellion against his father aiming to force Charles to renounce the claim of his Catholic uncle to succeed to the throne. By a mixture of conciliation and firmness Charles protected all his Ministers and relatives; he had to dispense with no fewer than three Houses of Commons which passed Bills to exclude James from the succession. Neither Clarendon nor Danby was put to death; Monmouth escaped any punishment for his plotting; James duly followed his brother as King in 1685. None of the previous English Stuarts had been particularly loyal to their servants: thus it is fair to say that Charles behaved better than his two predecessors, for he actually managed to secure Danby's release from imprisonment before he himself died.

One cannot underestimate the tremendous pressures to which Charles was subjected during the last decade of his life following his withdrawal from the third Dutch war. He learned from experience that it was wiser to give way over what he regarded as non-essentials, such as the two Test Acts preventing Roman Catholics from holding offices and commissions of any kind and from taking their seats in Parliament. But he fought hard and tenaciously to defeat Bills excluding his brother from the hereditary succession. The idea that, like his paternal grandfather, Charles was exceptionally lazy has been exaggerated. For example, he attended meetings of his Council three times a week as well as the Committee of Foreign Affairs, the precursor of future Cabinets; he concerned himself personally with foreign policy, sometimes playing off his Ministers against one another. He refused to be intimidated by the opposition in the House of Commons, which came to be known as Whig, and had gained strength because of the frenzy engendered by an imaginary Popish Plot 'revealed' by an unscrupulous clergyman, Titus Oates, in 1678. The King took care that he himself received adequate military protection, notably when he summoned his last parliament to meet at Oxford in 1681. Then he drove his principal political antagonist, the first Earl of Shaftesbury, into hiding and exile after he had been acquitted of treason by a London Grand Jury.

Shaftesbury, known to history as the founder of the Whig party, had been utterly determined that no Roman Catholic should again become an English monarch as 'Bloody Mary' had been over a hundred years earlier.

But Charles, himself a Catholic at heart, outmanoeuvred him, managed to turn the government of London against Whiggism, and when informers came forward to reveal plans to assassinate both himself and his brother (an episode described as 'the Rye House Plot' because it was near a house of that name that the alleged murder had been planned) was able to turn the tables on his critics. If anyone can be called the founder of the Tory party, it was Charles II himself. When he died, the Whig party had been decimated and James Duke of York, an avowed Roman Catholic prince, was enthusiastically welcomed to the thrones of his ancestors both in England and in Scotland.

Of all the Stuart rulers of England Charles II was the cleverest, if not the wisest: he worked hard as well as playing hard. He learned two things from his father's behaviour if not from his advice: the first was that to tell lies was necessary, at any rate in times of crisis. Deliberately therefore he made promises which he had no intention whatsoever of fulfilling. Secondly, he recognized completely the danger to the royal prerogative stemming from the power of the House of Commons, a fact which none of his predecessors had fully understood. It is true that on several occasions the Commons had denied him money he needed just as it had refused to grant supplies to his father. But Charles saw that he had to be firm with them even if it meant sacrificing financial assistance. Because he had secured a permanent revenue at the beginning of his reign, because both Customs and excise duties (first introduced during the Commonwealth period) expanded in their yields with the growth of commerce and industry, and, to a lesser extent, because he enjoyed French subsidies, and finally because, after 1674, he kept out of wars, Charles was able to defy his parliaments and in the end to manage without them.

Though Charles was always ready to take strong action when he felt that he had to, he did not see why he should not have some pleasures in life; he believed that God would pardon him for a few venial sins. In England he had a variety of mistresses, most of whom he treated generously, but they had little or no influence, any more than had the buffoons who sometimes entertained him at Court. In his last years a French lady, Louise de Kéroualle Duchess of Portsmouth, cared for him more like a wife than a mistress, much as the less atractive Madame de Maintenon behaved towards his cousin, Louis XIV.

Charles was not a connoisseur of all the arts, as his father had been, but he interested himself in architecture, both domestic and naval. He carried out improvements at Windsor castle and planned a new palace at Winchester. He loved walking, riding and horse racing, but was not such a keen huntsman as the other Stuarts. He dabbled in scientific experiments and was the official founder of the Royal Society. During much of his reign his kingdom prospered: it was an era of economic, scientific and philosophical progress, heralding the British triumphs in all spheres achieved in the eighteenth century. Charles neglected Scotland because he could never forget the way he had been humiliated there when he was a young man. But England has had many worse kings.

My detailed account of the life of Charles II is set out in my book, *Charles II: the Man and the Statesman*, first published in 1971 and revised and corrected for Panther Books (paperback) in 1973. A selection of Charles's letters was edited by Sir Arthur Bryant, first published in 1935. Charles II's early life up to his restoration to the throne is described by the late Hester Chapman in her book, *The Tragedy of Charles II* (1964). Antonia Fraser's biography was published after this book went to press.

[15]

James II – the Last
Catholic King of England

THANKS TO CHARLES II'S devotion to his dynasty, his brother James entered upon his reign in England without any trouble or confusion, even though he was an avowed Roman Catholic about to rule over a Protestant realm. In his earlier days he had been highly regarded as a brave and handsome soldier when he was serving as a volunteer first in the French and then in the Spanish armies; during his brother's reign he had held the appointment of Lord High Admiral and twice fought gallantly and victoriously against the Dutch in two naval wars. In character he was very different from his brother. He was always conscious of his dignity; he took himself extremely seriously; he did not stoop to any kind of buffoonery; he remodelled the Court at Whitehall, sternly forbidding drunkenness; and he was happily married to a young Italian wife. Virtually the only characteristic the two brothers had in common was an obsessive love of sex. But whereas Charles thought this was pardonable by a merciful God, James, at any rate in his later years, confessed that he had long lived 'in almost a perpetual course of sin' and warned his son about the grave dangers of 'deceitful pleasures'.

After James came to the throne he made it clear that he was going to be bold and tough. He promised he would always take care to defend and support the Church of England of which, though himself a Catholic, he was the Supreme Governor. But his aim was to abrogate the penal laws and Test Acts that denied equal political rights to Christians who did not adhere to the Anglican Church. On several occasions he repeated how much he disliked any kind of persecution and how deeply he believed in the importance of liberty of conscience. He blamed his brother for withdrawing his two declarations of indulgence. At once he demonstrated his own convictions by ordering the release of Quakers from prison and also of Catholics who had failed to pay fines for not attending the services of the State Church.

On the wrong assumption that it was James's immediate intention

forcibly to Catholicize England and therefore provoke the bulk of his
subjects, his nephew, the Protestant Duke of Monmouth, landed in Dorset,
after sailing from Holland, at the end of May 1685 with the purpose of
rallying all anti-papists against the King, while three weeks earlier the
ninth Earl of Argyll tried to collect a rebel army in the west of Scotland for
the same purpose. Neither of these invasions was a success – for, after all,
judged by his first speeches James's religious policy was unexceptional –
and both Monmouth and Argyll were caught and executed.

Although the House of Commons that met immediately after the new
King's accession had asked him to enforce the penal code and had resented
his haughty attitude towards its members, it was natural that these two
rebellions, even though they had been overcome fairly easily, should decide
the English Parliament to stand firmly behind James II. It voted him an
extra income to reinforce his army, with the ironic consequence that he was
given a big enough revenue, amounting to about £2,000,000 a year, to
manage without parliaments. But at the same time the House of Lords held
a debate in which some speakers dilated upon the dangers of a standing
army, officered by Roman Catholics, being employed to overthrow the
Church of England. That was certainly not James's objective, although he
undoubtedly wanted to allow Roman Catholics to become or remain army
officers; some had been enlisted to defeat Monmouth. With the memory of
the Popish Plot seven years earlier fresh in their minds, members of both
Houses insisted that the Test Acts and the penal code must be completely
retained. James's reply was to prorogue and later dissolve this parliament.
No other parliament was to meet during the course of his short reign.

During much of the following three years James concentrated on pursuing an egalitarian policy aimed chiefly at freeing his co-religionists from
legal disabilities. In a test case in the Court of King's Bench it was ruled by
eleven out of the twelve carefully selected judges that the King had the
right to use his prerogative to dispense with the laws, for they were the
King's laws; therefore he was entitled to absolve Catholic officers from the
penalties imposed by the first Test Act. In 1687 and 1688 James published
declarations of indulgence in which he suspended 'the execution of all and
all manner of penal laws in matters ecclesiastical, for not coming to Church
or not receiving the sacrament or for any other nonconformity to the
religion established'; in the same declaration he said, 'We cannot but
heartily wish . . . that all the people of our dominions were members of the
Catholic Church.' Obviously this alarmed the Anglicans; they were further
provoked when the King ordered that his declaration of 27 April 1688
should be read out from the pulpits of all the English churches. The aged

Archbishop of Canterbury and six other bishops thereupon drew up a petition to the King asking him to withdraw his order since, as it had been clearly demonstrated during the reign of his brother, the suspension of penal laws and the Tests by prerogative had been condemned in Parliament as illegal; that was why Charles II had cancelled his declarations of indulgence.

James II was much less flexible than his brother; indeed he prided himself on being tenacious and resolute. When the bishops came to see him in May, he exclaimed: 'this is the standard of rebellion!' After some hesitation he ordered the protesting bishops to be sent to the Tower of London there to await their trial by the Court of King's Bench for publishing a seditious libel, since their petition had been printed and widely distributed, though it is not known for certain who had arranged this.

The bishops, with whom public opinion in London was obviously sympathetic, were to James's surprise acquitted, but he remained unabashed. During June 1688, the month in which the trial took place, his wife gave birth to a son, who was promptly baptized according to the rites of the Roman Church. The Pope agreed to become one of the godparents. Thus it looked as if a Roman Catholic Stuart dynasty would from then on be fastened upon the British people. The spirits of the Whigs, who had been crushed during Charles II's reign, after the petering out of the alleged Popish Plot and the failure of Parliament's efforts to exclude Catholics from the throne, now rose from the ashes. But James had an army and navy, while in the last resort he thought he could depend on French assistance if civil war threatened. Nevertheless he realized that it would be difficult for him to sustain liberty of conscience and equality of opportunity for all his Christian subjects unless these were approved by Parliament. From the beginning of 1688 James launched a campaign, sycophantically managed by the third Earl of Sunderland, his chief Minister, and George Jeffreys, his Lord Chancellor, both of whom were Protestants in name, to pack a House of Commons with a majority committed to the repeal of the Test Acts and penal code. How far such a campaign might have succeeded has been disputed by modern historians. In any case the campaign soon proved irrelevant; for in the autumn of 1688 the rebellion, that James had dreaded ever since the 1670s, became a reality.

Even before the refusal of the seven bishops to endorse James's claim to suspend the laws of the land, he had angered the Church of England by rushing too fast towards his goals. Early in 1687 he had dismissed the two most prominent of his Protestant Ministers, his uncle, the second Earl of Clarendon, and his brother, the Earl of Rochester, from his service on the

ground that all his Ministers must give full support to his policies. He had
established an Ecclesiastical Commission with the duty of preventing
Anglican preachers from attacking the tenets of Roman Catholicism, such
as transubstantiation, and armed it with the power to suspend clergy from
their functions and appoint others in their places. He had used his authority
in the universities to appoint heads of colleges who were either Catholics or
crypto-Catholics. Making a liberal use of his dispensing power, he
appointed Roman Catholics as admirals, colonels and privy counsellors.
When the campaign to pack a House of Commons was in full swing in the
spring of 1688 large numbers of Anglicans were dismissed for one reason or
another from membership of borough councils and replaced by Catholics or
nonconformists. Thus, however well meaning were the King's intentions
(after all, what he sought was finally granted in the reign of Queen Victoria)
and however admirable his motives, his actions were bound to estrange
members of the Church of England, who had enjoyed a monopoly of offices
in Church and State ever since the second year of Charles II's reign.

James's foreign policy was mainly concerned with sustaining his domestic policy. He was far too proud a man to be as obsequious to the King of
France as his brother had been. And at the beginning of his reign he had
actually annoyed Louis XIV by renewing treaties with the Dutch. Since the
Dutch had successfully defied the French in the 1670s, James's nephew,
Prince William of Orange, who had married James's daughter, Mary, had
exerted great authority and influence in the United Netherlands. James had
been anxious to obtain their acquiescence in his attempts to secure the
repeal of the Test Acts and the penal code. At first his relations with his
son-in-law were pretty friendly, for William as Captain-General of the
United Netherlands had agreed to send over the English and Scottish
regiments in Dutch service at the time of Monmouth's rebellion and had
actually offered to command them himself. But Princess Mary was an
enthusiastic Protestant and her husband wanted to protect her right to
succeed her father on the English throne. William had agents and friends in
England who kept him fully informed of everything that was going on. He
came to realize that his father-in-law was pressing far too hard in his policy
of winning equality of opportunity for all his Christian subjects by the
employment of his dispensing and suspending powers. Consequently when
in 1687 James begged him and his daughter to give their open approval to
this programme, he received a dusty answer. They made it known that
while they approved of 'papists' exercising their religion in private and of
modifying the severity of the penal laws against them on account of their
religion and also of granting full liberty of conscience to dissenters 'they

could not consent to the repeal of those laws that tended only to the security of the Protestant religion'.

The reply shattered James's hopes. But he was consoled and cheered by the birth of a son, for that meant that Princess Mary had ceased to be heiress presumptive by dynastic law. William, who was a pretty unscrupulous politician, retorted by claiming that James's son was an impostor, smuggled into the Queen's bed in a warming pan. His wife, relying on the information she received from her sister, Anne (who was not present at the birth), came to believe this, but it is doubtful if William really did.

Apart from his special relations with the Dutch and the French, James was anxious for peace to prevail in western Europe. Like several of his Scottish ancestors, he favoured a Crusade against the Turks and and was delighted when, after an Ottoman invasion had been defeated before the walls of Vienna in 1683, the Holy Roman Emperor's armies had launched a counter-offensive that had driven the Turks out of Hungary, while the Venetians had captured Athens. James was disturbed, however, by Louis XIV's quarrels with the Papacy and tried hard to mediate between them. With the growing resentment of his Protestant subjects at his religious policies James fully realized that he must not get involved in a European war since peace was essential to his position. Although he had managed to build up a sizable army, deliberately neglecting the militia in favour of professional soldiers, he needed to keep it in England to maintain his own authority. He even attempted to recall the six British regiments in Dutch service, after having failed to persuade William of Orange to accept a Catholic commander over them; and he tried hard to persuade Louis XIV to pay a contribution towards the cost of bringing them home to enlarge his army.

That attempt further antagonized his son-in-law when he learned about it; it also aroused the suspicions of the Dutch States-General in which the foreign policy of the Republic was determined. Little did James realize during the eventful summer of 1688 that six peers of the realm together with the Bishop of London, who had been suspended from his functions by the Ecclesiastical Commission, had written a letter to William of Orange (framed at William's request) pledging themselves to rise in rebellion against their King if William would bring over an amphibious force to sustain them.

In fact, ever since April, William had been contemplating an invasion of England. He was aggressively anti-French and was determined, if he could, to put a stop to Louis XIV's effort to thrust his troops forward across the Rhine and extend his authority into Western Germany. What William feared was either that James would conclude (or had concluded) an alliance with the French, as his brother had done before him, or, even worse from William's point of view, that James would provoke his subjects to such an extent that a civil war would break out and thus render England impotent in European affairs. In actual fact James had for the reasons already discussed not the slightest intention of making war on the Dutch or allying himself with the French King. But his unsuccessful attempt to recall the six regiments from the United Netherlands, his negotiations with the French for subsidizing an increase in the size of his army, and an offer by Louis XIV, that subsequently became public knowledge, to give James protection by adding a squadron to his navy created such profound suspicion among the Dutch that they became willing to allow the Prince of Orange to carry a force over to England with the aim of compelling his father-in-law to alter his policies.

French intelligence was first to learn that William of Orange was preparing an expedition to cross the North sea and bring his father-in-law to his senses. James, however, was hard to convince that he was in peril. It was not until the last fortnight of September that in order to repel such an invasion, which the King still felt was unlikely to be successful because of the inclement weather in the late autumn, he began equipping and reinforcing his army and navy, abandoned the work already done to pack a new parliament, and, to pacify his Protestant subjects, put his entire domestic policy in reverse.

Throughout his reign James had persuaded himself that however extravagantly he behaved himself towards the leaders of the Church of England and towards the Anglicans entrenched in Oxford and Cambridge universities, their passive acceptance of the divine right of the Stuart kings to govern them would always induce them in the last resort to rally around the throne and defend the monarchy against all its enemies. But after they had put up with James's various methods of weakening the power of the Church of England, from bringing Catholics into his Privy Council to ordering the reading out of his indulgences from the pulpits, these leaders had grown tired of being browbeaten. When James sent for the Archbishop of Canterbury, who had been forbidden to come to Court ever since he had refused to sit on the Ecclesiastical Commission, and the Bishop of London, whom that Commission had suspended from his office, they were naturally tepid about helping him out of his difficulties. What James required them to do in return for vague assurance was to publish a declaration patriotically abhorring William of Orange's now known intention of invading England from abroad.

The bishops were not to be satisfied with soothing generalities. In order to enlist their moral and material help James had to agree to abolish the Ecclesiastical Commission, to reinstate Anglicans who had been extruded from borough councils and lord-lieutenancies in the counties, to reverse his policy of introducing Roman Catholic Fellows into Oxford and Cambridge colleges, and to ban Roman Catholics from teaching in schools. In response to all these concessions the bishops undertook to draw up prayers for the King and kingdom's safety. That was far less than James had hoped for. He therefore turned to trying to persuade the Dutch that he never had the slightest intention of making war upon them in alliance with France, as his brother had done sixteen years earlier, while he reopened negotiations with the French for the loan of warships. Neither of these steps led anywhere. The States-General had already given their approval to William's expedition, although they treated it as a private venture on the Prince's part aimed at protecting his wife's claim to the succession to the English throne. As to the French, Louis XIV believed that if the Dutch attacked James's navy and army a prolonged war would result: then his invasion of Germany, which he was launching that same September, would not be interfered with either by the Dutch or the English. Thus James was thrust back on his own resources.

Historians have debated the reasons for James's volte-face in the autumn of 1688. How was it that the Stuart King, who had distinguished himself both as a soldier and a sailor, who prided himself on his strength of character, had overthrown the Duke of Monmouth, had defied the House of Commons, and had boldly used his prerogative powers to assist his co-religionists, now showed himself to be both defeatist and cowardly? One explanation that has been offered is that he had contracted a form of syphilis which palsied his nerves. But if that were so, would his wife have been able to give birth to a healthy son? Moreover, although James panicked and refused to take command of his army or navy, relying instead on Protestant commanders who in fact failed him, he did in the following year assume personal charge of an Irish army and fought with it in a last desperate effort to regain his thrones. It is more likely that he was shocked by the reluctance of the English Church, of which he was, after all, the Supreme Governor, to be zealous in his cause. He had long laboured under the delusion that however outrageously he had behaved in trespassing on the preserves of Anglicans, thus offending great men like the Earl of Rochester and the Marquis of Halifax, who had been loyal servants to his father, in the last resort, they would support their anointed King in the event of an invasion from abroad. The last straw came when, after William's troops had disembarked in south-west England without meeting any opposition at all and had advanced upon London, James learned that even his second daughter, Princess Anne, and her Danish husband had deserted him to join William.

By now James was resigned to his fate. He ordered his baby son to be brought back from Portsmouth, where he had been sent for safety, with a view to his being carried to France, if necessary. But George Legge Lord Dartmouth, his highly incompetent admiral, who had been one of James's few Protestant friends, refused to obey his orders on this matter. So the Prince of Wales was brought back to London by Lady Powis, the child's Roman Catholic governess. Then Queen Mary of Modena took charge of her son and escaped from England disguised as a laundress, reaching Calais on 11 December. James himself, after throwing up a smoke-screen by sending commissioners to treat with William, left Whitehall in the early hours of the following day, but was caught by a party of mariners out hunting for papists in Kent. Ignominiously he returned to Whitehall, but William, who had no wish to be saddled with his father-in-law as a prisoner, deliberately gave him another opportunity to escape. On Christmas day James landed near Calais. Later he was welcomed as an honoured guest and equal by Louis XIV who placed at his disposal the palace of St Germain, where his mother had lived and died forty years earlier.

James never really recovered from his bloodless defeat. His army had been nearly three times as large as that of William of Orange, while his navy, anchored near Harwich, had proved incapable of intercepting the troop transports, guarded by Dutch warships, which sailed safely through the straits of Dover with all their lights aglow. After James had inspected his army, based on Salisbury, it refused to fight for him, gradually disintegrating through desertions. In the north of England the Earl of Danby, once on friendly terms with James before the Exclusion crisis, made ready to rebel, as did also Lord Delamere, who had been acquitted of helping Monmouth in 1685. The undoubted fact was that William was generally accepted as a saviour at all levels of society. James's belief that he could in November 1688 have opened a parliament favourable to his policies, had it not been for the invasion, was a pipe dream. A parliament (technically a 'convention') that was freely elected without any pressure from William in January 1689 voted that the throne was vacant and offered the Crown to William and Mary jointly. That meant in effect that William would rule; all that Mary was required to do was to act for him whenever he went abroad. But it has to be remembered that William himself was a Stuart. His mother had been Princess Mary, daughter of Charles I and granddaughter of

James I. His wife, Mary Stuart, was also his cousin. Were they to have any children, they would have been royal Stuarts.

Once settled in France, James grew more and more reconciled to his overthrow. He would have been perfectly content to enjoy the comforts of St Germain and other palaces belonging to Louis XIV, to which he was invited, such as Versailles, where he admired the paintings, china and glassware that he saw. He came to understand that the Catholic rulers in Europe were far too immersed in their own affairs to spare him any material help, although he told Pope Innocent XI on his first arrival in France that he had 'no small hope that divine Providence would shortly restore his fortunes'. Yet he needed to be prodded by his host and his Queen into at once venturing into Ireland so as to create a sideshow that might distract the new King William from taking an active part in the Grand Alliance that he had formed to resist continued French aggression in Germany.

Thus history repeated itself with differences. Like Charles I and Charles II, when he was in exile, James had some reason to believe that he might be able to strike back at England with assistance from Ireland or Scotland. He reached southern Ireland with some French military advisers in March 1689, where he was joined by the Duke of Tyrconnel, who was his Lord Deputy there. But James did not take to Ireland, especially as the Protestants in Ulster were Orangemen; moreover Tyrconnel and the French did not get along happily together. James's plan was to land in Scotland or England as soon as he possibly could. But his commander in Scotland, Lord Dundee, who raised an army in the Highlands, was killed and later this army was overwhelmed, while in Ireland James himself was beaten at the battle of the Boyne by King William III, who arrived in Northern Ireland in the spring of 1690. Once again James showed himself to be pusillanimous and once again William was careful not to take him a prisoner. Without difficulty James returned gladly to France.

Although the Catholic Irish held out for James for another year or two and the Jacobites, as his followers were called, plotted on his behalf in England, the exiled monarch ceased to deceive himself with illusions of a swift restoration. He was nearing the age of sixty; and whether he was afflicted with syphilis or not (his wife gave birth in 1693 to a daughter, Louise, who lived to the age of twenty), James was constantly in ill health during the last six years of his life. It is true that the death of his daughter, Queen Mary II, in 1694 temporarily rekindled the aspirations of the Jacobites, but by now Louis XIV was too deeply involved in his war against the Grand Alliance to offer them much assistance. James appreciated that his deprivations had been imposed upon him by God because of his sins: he therefore gave his humble thanks to the Lord for taking his kingdom away from him. 'He lives always surrounded by his friars,' noted a contemporary, 'and talks of his misfortunes with indifference.' Periodically he plunged into austerities at a monastery presided over by a remarkable Frenchman, the Abbé de la Trappe, who assured him that 'we must suffer in the world and humiliate ourselves before God to recognize our feebleness'. He was consoled by the Abbé's insistence that one need not be an anchorite in order to become a saint. He told his wife that he wanted to die; his wish was granted on 5 September 1701.

James II's life is fully documented. Many of his letters have survived; his memoirs, which he compiled assiduously, especially during his youth, were embodied in an official history commissioned by his son. His papers of devotion throwing light on his feelings during his last exile are also extant. The reason for his insignificance as a king was that he allowed himself to be overpowered by his conversion in his middle age which plunged him into fanaticism: this induced him to favour his fellow religionists too blatantly after he came to the throne, though his belief in liberty of conscience for all was undoubtedly sincere. To lose his throne within four years after all the lengths to which Charles II had gone on his behalf required some doing. One may sympathize with his intellectual difficulties, but unquestionably he was the least able or attractive of the Stuart monarchs.

The Life of James II, written by William Dicconson about 1710–15 and edited by J. S. Clarke in 1816, was based on six volumes of the King's memoirs (no longer extant) and on his letters to his brother Charles II and others. I have discussed the authenticity of this nearly contemporary biography in my book on James II, which was published in 1978, and contains my detailed appraisal of his character. (Since I wrote this a detailed article in the *Innes Review*, vol. xxviii, also deals with James's memoirs.) I also consider James II's relations with William III of Orange in my book, *The Glorious Revolution of 1688*, which I revised as a paperback in 1968. An earlier biography by F. C. Turner, published in 1948, is less sympathetic than mine.

King Charles II (1660–85): a painting attributed to E. Hawker.

Whitehall palace seen across the river Thames: an engraving. The palace was the site of the royal Court, but was burnt down during the reign of King William III.

King James II (1685–8) by Sir Godfrey Kneller.

The coronation of King William III (1688–1702) and Queen Mary II (1688–94): a contemporary print.

The battle of the Boyne, where William III defeated his father-in-law, James II: William troops are seen crossing the river.

Queen Anne
(1702–14) with her
son, the Duke of
Gloucester: a
painting after
Kneller.

Prince James Francis
Edward
(1688–1766), son of
King James II,
known as the Old
Pretender: a portrait
painted in his youth
by François du Troy.

Prince Henry (1725–1807), the younger brother of Charles Edward, also painted by Antonio David in 1732.

Prince Charles Edward (1720–88), the Young Pretender, painted by Antonio David in 1732.

Above. The battle of Culloden (1745) where the Young Pretender was defeated by the Duke of Cumberland, who is seen in the foreground.

The palazzo Muti in Rome: one of the papal palaces where the Old Pretender lived and died.

IACOBO·III
IACOBI·II·MAGNAE·BRIT·REGIS·FILIO
KAROLO·EDVARDO
ET·HENRICO·DECANO·PATRVM·CARDINALIVM
IACOBI·III·FILIIS
REGIAE·STIRPIS·STVARDIAE·POSTREMIS
ANNO·M·DCCC·XIX

BEATI MORTVI
QVI IN DOMINO MORIVNTVR

The monument by Canova to James III, Charles III and Henry IX, the three Pretenders,
in St Peter's cathedral, Rome.

16

William III and Mary II

WILLIAM III was the most heroic of all the Stuart kings. But in his blood flowed also the genius of the House of Orange. His great-grandfather, known as William the Silent, had led armies dedicated to wresting independence from the Spanish monarchy for the seven Dutch provinces that came to comprise the United Netherlands. His great-uncle, Maurice, possibly the best of all the Dutch generals, fought the Spaniards tenaciously for over forty years while William's grandfather, Frederick Henry, had carried on the war for another twenty-two years from 1625 to 1647. His father, William II, had died young from smallpox in 1650: William III was a posthumous child. All his ancestors had been extremely wealthy, rejoiced in the title of prince (Orange was a small enclave in southern France) and were exceptionally energetic and capable. They had been given two elective offices, that of Captain-General of the Union and Stadhouder of some but not all of the Dutch provinces. The Stadhouder was responsible for law and order and wielded more influence in fact that he did on paper.

After the death of William II a reaction against the House of Orange had set in, largely because the country was exhausted and strove after prosperity in peace. By an Act of Seclusion, passed in 1654, when he was a child, Prince William III was banned for life from becoming either Captain-General or Stadhouder in Holland, the richest and most populous of the seven provinces; by a Perpetual Edict in 1667 the office of Stadhouder was abolished altogether in Holland, though this edict envisaged that the Prince might become Captain-General when he was twenty-two. In fact once his country was in peril he was appointed Captain-General at the age of twenty and quickly won his spurs; although he had no military experience whatever, he assumed the command of the Dutch army and successfully defied the might of the King of France when without warning the United Provinces were assaulted in 1672.

In the course of this war, which lasted for nine years, William earned the reputation of being the outstanding Protestant general of his time. He also proved himself as a diplomatist, recognizing that the relatively sparsely populated Republic could not withstand the power of the French monarchy without allies. One potential ally was England. 'It is from England', he once declared, 'that the salvation of Europe must come; without England she must fall under the yoke of France.' It was because he was anxious to induce England to side with him against France that on 4 November 1677 he married his sixteen-year-old cousin, Mary, niece of Charles II and elder daughter of the future James II. William had much strength of character, but was too withdrawn and serious to get along easily with strangers. He told Charles II and his brother James that the marriage must first be agreed before any other questions were discussed. Mary, a pretty and charming girl, at first shied away from this humourless and ungracious Prince, but she grew to admire his qualities, shared his perplexities, and told him that he must love her whatever happened 'and be assured I am yours till death'.

As a child William had been thin, frail and asthmatic, while in character reserved and aloof except with a few intimates. Educated as a strict Calvinist, he believed firmly in predestination. Within him glowed a flame that determined him not only to be the recognized leader of the Dutch Republic but also the Protestant champion of Europe. To serve his ends he was at times exceedingly ruthless. When John de Witt and his brother, Cornelis, the two statesmen who were mainly responsible for the French alliance, which Louis XIV abandoned to attack the Republic, were both murdered by an indignant mob, William, though he admitted that they were guiltless of treason, made no attempt to discover their murderers and actually gave a pension to one of the men who instigated the assassinations. William also did not hesitate about plotting against his English uncle and father-in-law, but of course his original intention when he was preparing to invade England in 1688 was not to seize James II's throne, but to force him to enter the anti-French camp. As has already been noticed, after his victory William gladly allowed James to escape into exile.

Princess Mary had settled down fairly happily to her married life in Holland. In 1678 she had two miscarriages and another one later. By 1680 she discovered that her husband was having an affair with one of her Maids of Honour, Elizabeth Villiers, who was no beauty, as Mary was, but was witty, intelligent and excellent company. Mary resigned herself to this misfortune after she had vainly tried to send Elizabeth back to England, for she had become so devoted to her husband that she was eager to help him forward in any way she could. When her half-brother, James Edward, was born, she soon convinced herself that he was a changeling. For that she relied upon some pretty revolting and dubious information supplied by her sister, Anne. At first prayers were said for the new-born child in Mary's chapel, but suddenly they ceased. Anne told her that she could never be satisfied whether James II's son was true or false – ' 'tis possible,' she added, 'it may be our brother, but God only knows . . . 'Tis possible . . . but where one believes it, a thousand do not . . . I shall ever be of the number of unbelievers.' That was why Mary ordered the prayers to be stopped. Later she heard from Anne that the baby was ill and might soon be 'an angel in Heaven'. William himself was too astute and unscrupulous to refrain from taking advantage of these unfounded rumours about the birth. In the proclamation that he published before sailing to England in 1688 he announced that 'all the good subjects in England, Scotland and Ireland do vehemently suspect that the pretended Prince of Wales was not borne by the Queen'. When the Queen of England wrote to Mary, whom she called 'my dear Lemon', protesting about the ending of prayers for the Prince, Mary gave her an evasive answer, assured her that it was an accident, and that she would order that the prayers be resumed.

From then on Mary was in her husband's full confidence, but she grew agitated when she learned that it was his intention to exert pressure upon her father to compel him to stop favouring his fellow Catholics and to make him acknowledge her right to succeed him. With tears in her eyes she begged William to see that no harm befell James. Before William left her in October he told her that if anything happened to him, she must marry again. But Mary replied: 'I have never loved any man but you and I should never know how to love another.' She also said that 'having been married for many years without it having pleased God to bless me with a child, I believe that is enough to prevent me ever thinking of what you propose'.

Once James was safely in France and the Convention elected and summoned, the question arose who was to govern England. The Earl of Danby, who had been prominent in promoting William's expedition, favoured Mary taking the title of Queen with her husband as consort. Mary would not hear of that; she had already been taught by Dr Gilbert Burnet, who was later to become Bishop of Salisbury, that she must be contented with being William's wife, 'and engage yourself that you will give him the real authority as soon as it comes into your hands'. So she rejected Danby's proposals with indignation; later, although the Convention agreed that she and William should reign jointly, the actual administration was left entirely to him.

Mary did not come over to England until the beginning of February 1689 when her husband told her to look cheerful instead of being miserable over the way that her father had been ousted. Obediently she played her part, though she overacted. But by her graciousness and charm she soon offset William's boorishness and habitual reserve with his English subjects. On 13 February they accepted the offer of the Crown after a Declaration of Rights, listing at length all the illegal deeds committed by James II with the aim of 'subverting and extirpating the Protestant religion and the laws and liberties of the kingdom' had been read out to them. Two months later they were crowned in Westminster abbey (where William thought very little of what he called 'those silly old Popish ceremonies') and then the new King was able to turn to his main objective of fighting the French.

On 4 May 1689, after the House of Commons had voted supplies for military action, war was declared. William sent over an army under the command of John Churchill Earl of Marlborough to the Spanish Netherlands, but he himself had first to see to the conquest of Catholic Ireland. While William was winning the battle of the Boyne, Mary with an advisory council of nine, known as the Lords Justices, was left in charge in England. Much to her dismay, the day before the battle of the Boyne, the English fleet was beaten by the French off Beachy Head; Mary had given orders to the admiral, Lord Torrington, to fight at all costs. After his defeat he was deprived of his command, arrested, imprisoned in the Tower of London and put on trial but acquitted. The country was in a panic, fearing a French invasion. On William's return he had to restore confidence. Two years later the French navy was crushed at the battle of La Hogue. In fact English sea power contributed notably to the eventual loss by the French of a war that lasted nine years.

From 1690 onwards William's routine was divided into three phases. In the spring of each year he visited Holland and then went on campaign against the French in the Spanish Netherlands. After the campaign ended, usually in September, he allowed himself two months' holiday which he spent hunting at his country houses of Dieren and het Loo (he bought the latter estate in 1686) which lay conveniently near one another. Then he returned to England, where he remained during the late autumn and winter. He recognized how important Parliament was in England, for it met every year during his reign.

William aimed at non-party government or government above party. To begin with, he had the Earl of Danby (whom later he created Marquis of Carmarthen) as Lord President of the Council and the Marquis of Halifax for Lord Privy Seal. His first Secretaries of State were the Earl of Shrewsbury and the Earl of Nottingham. Danby and Shrewsbury had belonged to 'the Immortal Seven', who signed the invitation asking William to come over to rescue England; Halifax, known as 'the Trimmer', and Nottingham, called 'the Dismal', had not done so, although they knew all about it. William placed the Treasury, the Chancellorship and the Admiralty in the hands of commissioners. He never had a single leading Minister. Danby had less influence under William than he had possessed under Charles II. William was in fact his own Prime Minister. He interviewed departmental Ministers or commissioners individually, discussed problems with them and gave them his orders. Thus although he also attended weekly meetings of the Cabinet Council and the Privy Council when he was in England, these meetings were largely formal. As his biographer, Stephen Baxter, has pointed out, 'in general, it may be said that the King kept policy in his own hands and used the heads of departments as if they were clerks'. The fact that he only completely trusted the Dutch advisers who came with him to England, that he spoke English hesitantly and never wrote in English tended to antagonize his subjects and make them feel unfairly treated and insufficiently relied upon. It was because of the King's unpopularity that several English statesmen took out an insurance policy by secretly communicating with the exiled James II. William knew all about it, but did not much care.

In spite of his domination over his Ministers, as William spent about half the year abroad, some central machinery of government in England was essential. Queen Mary did her best with the advice of the Lords Justices, whom she both disliked and mistrusted. Before her death on 28 December 1694 William established a small war committee. This got around the difficulty that too many Ministers wanted to attend the Cabinet Council for it to be an effective administrative body.

Recent research has shown that during William's reign party nomenclature was important and elections were beginning to be fought along party lines. The Whigs, who claimed to have brought about the revolution of 1688, were determined to pare the powers of the monarchy; their manifesto was the Declaration of Rights, which was converted into an Act of Parliament. The Tories respected the royal prerogatives, but their loyalties were mixed; some of them would have welcomed the return of James II upon conditions or a Regency in the name of his son rather than having to obey a Dutch prince, who was more concerned with events on the continental mainland than with the welfare of England and Scotland. They were also, for the most part, strict Anglicans, whereas the Whigs sympathized with the nonconformists. On the whole, William preferred the Tories. He was not perturbed by their flirtations with his exiled father-in-law. Moreover once the Bank of England was founded in 1694, in which such statesmen as the Earl of Marlborough invested their money, it provided a material reason for the King's belief that the English aristocracy would not initiate a counter-revolution.

William's relations with his parliaments were pretty amicable except towards the end of his reign, as he took immense trouble over the speeches he made to it and the messages he sent. Because the Commons held the purse-strings, when big sums of money needed to be voted to pay for the war and since Mutiny Acts had to be passed from time to time to secure discipline in the English army, parliaments had to be called regularly. In 1689 the Commons provided William with a modest Civil List of £700,000 a year and appropriated other sums for the use of the armed services. So William had to work with his parliaments as best he could. In spite of the Bill of Rights he retained substantial prerogative powers: he could and did prorogue his Parliament and he could and did veto some of their Bills.

William had wanted Parliament to pass a comprehension Bill which would have enabled some at least of the nonconformists to re-enter the Church of England; he was also willing to allow Protestant dissenters to be employed in public offices. His first parliament (the Convention was converted into a parliament after the coronation) much to his disappointment was only willing to enact a Bill permitting nonconformists who promised loyalty to the Crown and believed in the Holy Trinity to attend their own services in their own chapels after notifying the local authorities. William vetoed two Place Bills that would have prevented Ministers of State and other officials from sitting in Parliament. He also twice vetoed Triennial Bills that required parliaments to be called regularly whether he wanted them or not; he eventually gave way over this in December 1694. He also vetoed a Bill about the tenure of judges; by it they were to be entitled to retain office as long as they behaved themselves, that is to say they could not be removed merely by the exercise of the royal prerogative, as had been done during the reign of James II. William did not object to that; indeed he never interfered with the judiciary. What he did not like was being held responsible for the payment of their salaries out of his own revenue. William also had major differences with his later parliaments, first over the size of the army and secondly over the grants he gave to some of his Dutch favourites out of confiscated Irish lands. Understandably enough, a parliament which was elected in 1698 and contained a Tory majority thought that since by then the war against France was over, a standing army of 7,000 men was big enough for the country's needs. It also refused to reduce the national debt. William considered it 'a miserable session' and was with difficulty dissuaded from resigning the Crown and returning to his beloved Holland.

Whereas William had his perplexities in England, they were nothing compared with his problems in Scotland. He never went there himself and is said to have expressed the wish that it was thousands of miles away. James II, on the other hand, had been familiar to the Scots as Charles II's royal commissioner there and after the revolution had a number of faithful supporters including James Graham of Claverhouse Viscount Dundee and the Roman Catholic Duke of Gordon, who for some time held Edinburgh castle on his behalf. Moreover although the Scottish Presbyterians were even more virulently anti-papist than the Anglicans, among the Highlanders many Roman Catholics were to be found.

William could spare few troops to garrison Scotland; his principal military officer there was Major-General Hugh Mackay, who had at his disposal the three Scottish regiments long in Dutch service. William made the third Duke of Hamilton his commissioner while in 1691 John Dalrymple Master of Stair became one of his two Secretaries of State. In 1689 the Scots, like the English, had summoned a Convention to meet in Edinburgh, but it was not until three months later than in England that the decision was taken to offer William and Mary the Crown. Even then the point was made that James overstepped the rights of a constitutional monarch to become a despot; he had therefore forfeited not abdicated his throne; and the new monarchs were elected in his place. Thus the Scots maintained that they had the right, if they wished, to choose a different ruler from England, a precedent with far-reaching consequences in the following reign. The offer of the Crown had been accompanied by a Claim of Right, which included a clause stating that episcopalianism was a grievance: this meant in effect that the Scottish authorities were asking that a Kirk, governed by Presbyterians, as envisaged by John Knox and that had held sway in the middle of the century, should now be fully restored.

The Jacobites, led by 'bonny Dundee' were soon defeated, although the Highlanders fought heroically for the exiled King. Had James, instead of landing in Ireland, gone straight to Scotland, that kingdom might have been as big a thorn in the side of the new English monarchy as it had been in the Middle Ages. As it was, the necessary military precautions were taken including the establishment of a fort, named after King William, at Inverlochy, while William himself aimed at an enlightened and tolerant policy. When he accepted the Claim of Right he insisted that he would not be a persecutor of 'heretics'. He advocated a legislative union with England, such as had been set up at the time of the Cromwellian Protectorate. He also allowed a freely elected General Assembly to meet without interference from outside and he assented to the final abolition of the Scottish bishops.

But two episodes soured William's relations with his Scottish kingdom. The first arose out of unrest in the Highlands where Jacobite sympathizers were encouraged by the distractions of the Nine Years War in Europe to attempt a rising on James II's behalf. The Government tried to keep the clans quiet by distributing several thousands of pounds in bribes and demanding that the chieftains took an oath of loyalty to their King and Queen by 1 January 1692. The chieftain of one clan, MacDonald of Glencoe, for various complicated reasons failed to take the oath in time. Dalrymple, who was in London, then decided that an example should be made of the MacDonalds and induced William to sign an order that they should not merely be punished but 'extirpated'. Soldiers from Fort William, mostly Campbells, thereupon massacred the MacDonald chieftain together with thirty-three clansmen, two women and two children. There is hardly any doubt that William signed the order without reading it; to that extent he was responsible. After the massacre became known and was exaggerated by Jacobite pamphleteers, a commission of inquiry was appointed by the King. Dalrymple was dismissed from office, but otherwise no one was punished. Thus William, though twenty years older, behaved in much the same way as he had done after the murder of the de Witts.

The other episode related to the foundation of the Darien trading company. It has to be appreciated that Scotland was still a poor country with a population even smaller than that of Ireland. Though it had enterprising merchants, they needed to compete with English trading companies, notably the East India Company, which enjoyed monopoly rights. An Act was passed by the Scottish Parliament in 1693 permitting the foundation of a company to trade with countries with which the King was not at war. Half the capital for the trading company of Scotland was subscribed in England. But the establishment of the company caused great indignation, stimulated by the East India Company, and the English investors withdrew their capital. An attempt by the Scottish company, to plant a colony in the gulf of Darien on the north coast of South America proved a complete fiasco; moreover, as William was the ally of the King of Spain, who had joined him in the first Grand Alliance against France, he could not countenance such a project. He dismissed the Ministers who had procured his assent to the foundation. As a wise statesman, he realized that the best solution of Scottish economic problems at that time was a union with England.

It was scarcely surprising that William had little leisure to spare for Scottish affairs. After his return from Ireland in 1690 he had to concentrate on winning a war in which almost the whole of Europe was engulfed. This Nine Years War has also been called 'King William's war'. That did not mean that he had provoked it. On the contrary, it was Louis XIV's decision to act aggressively in the Rhineland and his declaration of war on the United Netherlands, when William was away in England, that started the conflict. Louis had hoped that he could win influence and gain territory in the Rhineland while the Holy Roman Emperor, Leopold I, was still absorbed in the long war against the Turks that had begun in 1685. The Grand Alliance, which William fashioned, therefore included not only the Emperor, but most of the German states, the Dutch, the English and the Spanish and later the Duke of Savoy, whose possessions included Piedmont in north-west Italy. Sweden and Denmark did not take part, but furnished mercenaries. William had hoped that the Emperor would conclude peace with the Turks and concentrate on defending Germany from the west. But in October 1690 the Turks recaptured Belgrade and the Emperor relied largely on his allies to defend Germany against France.

The French had virtually no allies, but depended upon their large and experienced armies under capable generals to wage a defensive war upon inner lines which would ultimately exhaust their enemies. William was the heart and soul of the resistance. As soon as he had expelled James II from Ireland he left for The Hague where he gathered the allies together to concert the campaigns. Indeed each year the strategy of the war was discussed and planned in Holland. William himself was commander-in-chief of the English and Dutch armies. He realized that the best place to confront the French and defend the United Netherlands was in the Spanish Netherlands. He was also able to apply pressure on France by the use of sea power, since the Anglo-Dutch navies outnumbered those of France. It has been argued that William misconceived the use of sea power, employing it merely where his enemy could not be reached by land. Nevertheless it cannot be doubted that the dispatch of English warships to the Mediterranean – he kept an English squadron there throughout the winter of 1694–5 against the wishes of his English Ministers – helped prolong the resistance of the Spaniards to a French army besieging Barcelona.

English historians have tended to be rather caustic about William as a general during the Nine Years War. But at first he laboured under many disadvantages. It took time to train a sizable English army and to find adequate commanders; it was also not easy to weld together the troops that had been hired from the Danes or Germans. A war of attrition rarely leads to clear-cut victories. Yet William held his own. After the losses of the fortified towns of Mons and Namur, the drawn battle of Steenkerk pre-

vented the French from advancing along the Meuse valley and menacing the
Dutch frontiers. As the French at that date outnumbered the allies and were
commanded by the best of the French generals, the Duke of Luxembourg,
that was no mean achievement. Similarly the battle of Landen in the
following year impeded French progress and prevented them from capturing either Liège or Brussels. In 1695 William recaptured Namur, which
had been fortified by the famous French Marshal Vauban, defying an army
under Marshal Villeroy that attempted to distract him by bombarding
Brussels. In the words of Professor Baxter, 'perhaps the strongest place in
Europe had been taken in the face of an army of nearly 100,000 men which
did not dare to come to the relief of the fortress'.

Through the tenacity of William, Louis XIV was in the end compelled to
conclude peace on humiliating terms at Ryswick – for though the French
King put a bold face on it, he himself knew that this long war had gained
him nothing. He was obliged to give up all his conquests since 1678 except
for Strasbourg, which had been an independent imperial city. He recognized William as the legitimate King of England, Scotland and Ireland and
promised to give no further help to the Jacobites. William agreed to let
James II remain at St Germain where, as has been seen, the previous Stuart
King was absorbed in religious melancholia. For a second time William had
successfully defied Louis's effort to become supreme in Europe.

One reason why Louis had reluctantly consented to the treaty of Ryswick
was that the death of the feeble King Carlos II of Spain was known to be
imminent. As he had no direct heirs, claims through marriages could be
made both by Louis XIV, whose troops stood ready to cross the Pyrenean
frontier, and by the Emperor, whose long war with the Turks was at last
drawing towards its close. William fully understood that the succession
question might lead to another long-drawn-out European war and upset the
balance of power in the civilized world. He therefore took upon himself the
role of mediator: he had no specific interests of his own either for the Dutch
or for his English subjects. By the treaty of Ryswick the Dutch had been
allowed to man a barrier of fortresses in the Spanish Netherlands, while all
the English wanted was ports of call in the Mediterranean and for commercial reasons they were anxious lest that ocean should become a French lake.
Exhausted by the war, Louis XIV agreed to diplomatic negotiations with
the Maritime Powers; he accepted a partition treaty which provided that the
bulk of the Spanish empire should go to the five-year-old son of the Elector
of Bavaria, who was married to a niece of Carlos II.

When in the following year the potential King of Spain died at the age of
six – poisoned, some thought – a second treaty was negotiated and signed in

March 1700. By this fresh treaty a second son of the Emperor Leopold I, by name Archduke Charles of Austria, would acquire Spain, the Spanish Netherlands and the Spanish overseas possessions, but the French monarchy would obtain directly Sicily, Naples and Tuscany and by an exchange of territories Lorraine, which was still nominally independent of France. But both these treaties were doomed from the start. For the Emperor, especially after he concluded the Turkish war, was not prepared to agree to them; neither was the dying Carlos II, who did not wish his empire to be divided. In the end he made a will bequeathing all his possessions to Philip Duke of Anjou, a grandson of Louis XIV.

An English historian has claimed that 'the conclusion of the partition treaty was the most unconstitutional act of William's reign'. Certainly it was condemned as such by the Tories, who had a majority in the Commons after the general election of 1698, because it had been negotiated in secrecy, mainly by the King's Dutch friend, William Bentinck Duke of Portland, and neither the Privy Council nor Parliament had been consulted; also, because it might lead to another expensive war. But, after all, by precedent foreign policy was a royal prerogative: none of the Stuart kings of England had ever yielded on this point, though they had at times persuaded the Commons to go along with them since diplomacy needed to be backed by threats of war if it were to be effective, and the costs of wars had to be met by votes in the Commons.

In any case all William's altruistic efforts proved vain. To his fury Louis XIV repudiated the second partition treaty and accepted on behalf of his grandson the will of Carlos II, who at last died in November 1700. At first English public opinion was not unduly disturbed. The general belief was that the Crowns of France and Spain would be kept separate and the commercial classes much preferred the Mediterranean ports to remain in Spanish hands and not to be under the sovereignty of France or Austria. But a series of provocative acts by the King of France, including the recognition of James II's son as legitimate King of England in defiance of the treaty of Ryswick quickly changed English feelings. Some of Louis's actions were defensible because he knew that war with the rival claimant to the Spanish throne, the Archduke Charles, was almost unavoidable. French troops therefore thrust the Dutch out of the Spanish Netherlands and made ready to march into northern Italy. William was then driven to the conclusion that he would have to face another war, which he had tried so hard to avert, in order to maintain the balance of power in Europe. So he set to work to form a new alliance embracing the English and Dutch, the Emperor and several German States, though he was not prepared to concede the claim made by the Archduke Charles to the entire Spanish heritage. William took the Earl of Marlborough with him to The Hague to arrange this new alliance and then concert plans for military strategy if Louis XIV insisted on accepting the will of Carlos II instead of agreeing to a partition of the Spanish possessions with the Austrian Habsburgs. The main treaty was duly signed in August. A general election at the end of the year produced a House of Commons which approved of the alliance and was ready for another war against France. The formation of this second Grand Alliance was the last important public act of William III.

The enormous pressures to which William had been subjected from the time when he invaded England are sufficient to explain his comparatively early death at the age of fifty-two in 1702. The nature of his ill health has been exaggerated. It is true that he did not like living in London, but this is hardly surprising for much of the city, including Westminster, was smelly, dirty and unpleasant. That was why he preferred to reside at Hampton Court and then built himself a palace in Kensington. But he undertook to visit Whitehall once a week when he was in England. He suffered from asthma and had a chronic cough, but the evidence that he was a consumptive is slight. The strains from which he suffered were largely psychological. He regarded the death of Mary as 'an irreparable loss' and never seriously contemplated marrying again, especially as his cousin, Princess Anne had seemingly given birth to a healthy boy in 1689. He was distressed by the setbacks he experienced in the early part of the Nine Years War while opposition to his military plans from English politicians upset him so much that he threatened to resign.

William had few self-indulgences. He did not eat or drink to excess. Evidently he had a strong head for drink; he is said to have been capable of drinking anyone under the table. He deliberately did so on occasion in order to persuade others to do what he wanted at the time, for example, the Earl of Marlborough. After the death of Mary he was accused of being a practising homosexual. So numerous were the rumours circulated to this effect that William Bentinck Duke of Portland, long his most trusted friend and adviser, who was about his own age, wrote to him candidly about his relations with another Dutchman, Arnold Joost van Keppel, a handsome youngster in his early twenties, who had been one of the King's pages since he was thirteen. William indignantly repudiated the suggestion that he was a homosexual; it is indeed much more likely that his feelings towards Keppel, whom he created Earl of Albemarle, were paternal, Keppel taking the place of the son William never had.

Since the death of Mary, William had never been popular with the

English ruling classes; but when a murder plot against him was disclosed in 1696 it was generally realized that they would be at a loss without him. An 'Association' was circulated and signed on the model of that introduced in the reign of Elizabeth I by which the subscribers avowed their loyalty and promised to avenge his death if he were assassinated. They were soon to discover that their next ruler would be a childless Queen. The hopes that William had nursed about the Duke of Gloucester were shattered when he died of smallpox in 1700. At the King's request Parliament in 1701 passed an Act of Settlement providing for Anne's succession (she had earlier waived her claim to the throne in favour of William) and after her death the Electress Sophia of Hanover, who was a granddaughter of James I. The House of Commons took advantage of the opportunity to lay down rules for future monarchs which amounted to overt criticism of William's career. Thenceforward any future monarch must join the Church of England; he must not go to war in defence of dominions or territories not belonging to the English Crown; moreover no such monarch should be allowed to leave the realm without the permission of Parliament. It was also enacted that no person who held an office or place of profit under the Crown could become a member of parliament. Thus the Commons tacked on the Place Bill which William had twice vetoed. The Act also provided that the judges could not be removed from office except on an address from both Houses of Parliament. Had this enactment taken full effect England would have seen the separation of the powers of the executive, legislature and judiciary which was to prevail in the United States of America.

William was not unduly worried over these constitutional changes. His anxiety was that the contest against the overweening power of France should be continued after he died. This raised personal issues. While Mary was alive, Princess Anne and her friends, the Earl and Countess of Marlborough, had intrigued against William, partly motivated by xenophobia. But after Queen Mary's death a reconciliation was effected. Marlborough, who had once been sent to prison on Queen Mary's orders, was taken back into favour: William recognized that he was a good general, though he had not enjoyed many opportunities of demonstrating his skill. By associating the Earl with him in the formation of the second Grand Alliance William hoped that French supremacy in Europe would be overthrown after his death. On 9 March 1702 William died of pneumonia, not as the direct result of a fall from his horse caused by a molehill. His death was a relief to a majority of members of parliament, who, although they valued him as an opponent of popery, felt him to be a foreigner with foreign advisers who were more worried over the protection of the Dutch Republic than with the welfare of England and Scotland. In her first speech Queen Anne boasted of her 'entirely English heart'. But it is hard to escape the conclusion that William III was the greatest of the Stuart kings.

There are two excellent biographies in English of William III by Stephen Baxter (1960) and Nesca A. Robb (1966). Hester Chapman and Elizabeth Hamilton wrote biographies of Mary II (1953 and 1972).

17

The Obstinacy of Queen Anne

QUEEN ANNE, who was thirty-seven when she came to the throne in 1702, was the last Stuart monarch to reign and the first entitled to call herself the lawful ruler of Great Britain, although her great-grandfather had assumed that title without any warrant for it. Her mother, by birth Anne Hyde, the mere daughter of a lawyer, had died when her younger daughter was only six; James II, although he was an excellent father, had not seen much of his second daughter except when he and his second wife, Mary of Modena, were exiled in Brussels and then in Edinburgh.

Anne's childhood was spent, as was that of her father, in Richmond palace. Here she received an introduction to a beautiful girl, five years older than herself, Sarah Jennings, who was to become her second bosom friend – her first having been Frances Apsley who was twelve years her senior and whom she nicknamed Semandra. Sarah Jennings was appointed Maid of Honour to James's second wife: so she frequently saw Princess Anne and a passionate friendship of a perfectly proper character developed between them. When Anne was twelve, her elder sister, Mary, married William of Orange and departed with him to Holland. While for some time Anne's relations with her stepmother were amicable, once she had grown old enough to take religion seriously – her uncle, Charles II, had insisted that she should be brought up as a Protestant – she was alienated by Mary of Modena's strict Roman Catholicism and blamed her for converting her father to this faith, although in fact it was Anne's own mother, who, as much as anyone, had been responsible for that.

As there seemed little expectation that Anne would succeed to the throne, her education other than in religion, where her chief tutor was Henry Compton Bishop of Oxford, was somewhat neglected. She read little because, like her sister Mary, she suffered from sore eyes. She learned music and dancing, but spent a great deal of time playing cards, which she continued to do after she became Queen. By the time she was fifteen marriage was contemplated. She had a platonic love affair with John

Sheffield third Earl of Mulgrave, a poetic character, who wrote songs in her honour and was exiled from the Court for his pains. Prince George of Hanover, son of the Electress and the future George I of England, came over — so gossip had it — to inspect her, but then snubbed her, possibly because her mother had been a commoner. Anne never forgot the way she had been treated by these two gentlemen. As Queen she was to make Sheffield Lord Privy Seal and create him a Duke; on the other hand she did her utmost to prevent George's son visiting England when he had become Duke of Cambridge, to take his seat in the House of Lords. Anne did not easily forget kindnesses and nursed animosities. In 1682 she was married to Prince George of Denmark, a simple man without much ambition but with an enormous appetite which made him fat: he was said to love gossip, his bottle and his wife. Anne became devoted to him, tried hard but vainly to bear him a son or daughter, and was to care for him through his last illness. After his death in October 1708 she was never to be quite the same woman again.

Anne was never healthy; for years she suffered excruciating pain. Modern doctors are reluctant to hazard a guess about the nature of her ailments. She had a mild attack of smallpox when she was a child. After her marriage she endured seventeen pregnancies and miscarriages, the last when she was thirty-five. Afterwards she was racked by what contemporary doctors called 'gout' in various parts of her body. When she became Queen she was often unable to walk: she had to be lifted into coaches and carried up stairs. No one who reads about Anne can fail to admire the courage with which she faced her constant ill health. Like William III, she always attended meetings of her Cabinet Council, presided over her Privy Council, and listened to debates in the House of Lords. Her sense of public duty was paramount. She was altruistic and generous, contributing from her own revenues to the cost of the war, to that of raising the salaries of poor clergymen, and to enhancing the incomes of her personal friends. She was a patriot: in 1706 she was to say: 'I have no interest, no end, no thought but for the good of my country.'

Sarah Jennings was married to John Churchill, created by James II Baron Churchill and by William III Earl of Marlborough, some two or three years before Anne herself married. That did not affect their close friendship; indeed Anne was allowed to employ her as her principal lady-in-waiting. Anne's character was for a long time painted by historians and biographers with Sarah's brush. We have virtually only one side of the story because Sarah told Anne to burn all the letters she wrote to her. Moreover the Duchess of Marlborough, as she was to become in 1702, not only wrote her devastating autobiography known as an *Account of her Conduct*, but left behind several drafts of it on which recent authors have been allowed to graze. Sarah was a handsome woman when young, had an extremely forceful personality and was more caustic than witty. During the reign of William and Mary she was a bone of contention between the two Stuart sisters. Mary had good reason to believe that Marlborough, after distinguishing himself as a military commander at the outset of the reign, was plotting against William in the army and corresponding with the exiled James II. Because of this he was first dismissed from all his offices and then imprisoned in the Tower. Under the circumstances Mary felt that Anne ought not to retain Sarah in her service. When Anne refused to dismiss her, Mary ordered her sister to leave the Cockpit, that part of Whitehall palace which had been assigned to her as her residence.

Queen Mary was also annoyed because the Marlboroughs had sought to obtain for Anne an allowance voted by the House of Commons instead of accepting a gift of the same amount from William out of his Civil List. Owing to these rows the two Stuart sisters were completely estranged. Anne was not even allowed to see Queen Mary when she was dying of smallpox. After Mary's death, as has already been noticed, William became reconciled to Anne, hoping that her son, the Duke of Gloucester, might ultimately become his successor; Marlborough, a man always ambitious for himself, his wife and family and extremely fond of money, was pardoned and appointed ambassador extraordinary and commander-in-chief. Until then, influenced by Sarah, Anne found her reserved brother-in-law distasteful in his ways and spoke of him in private as 'the Dutch abortion'. As soon as she became Queen she emphasized that she was completely an Englishwoman (even though her husband was Danish), that she would be unshakably loyal to the Anglican Church, and was confident that Marlborough would retrieve the honour of England, thus denigrating William's prowess as a soldier.

Throughout her reign Anne chose all her own Ministers, though she was often obliged to submit to the needs of party politics. But, unlike all previous Stuart monarchs in England, she never acted as her own Prime Minister. To begin with, her choices largely coincided with national necessities. She confirmed Marlborough in the post of Captain-General besides creating him a duke and conferring upon him the appointment of Master-General of the Ordnance, a lucrative office. It was through Marlborough's influence with her that Sidney Godolphin became Lord Treasurer. Godolphin, now aged fifty-seven, had long been at the centre of public affairs, having served Charles II, James II and William III with equal assiduity. His knowledge of public finance was profound. He lost his wife, Margaret Blagge, after he had been married to her for only three years: she had died after giving birth to their only child, Francis, who was to marry the Marlboroughs' eldest daughter. Godolphin never married again, but indulged in two hobbies, the breeding of horses and gambling. He was not at all enthusiastic about resuming public office, but felt it his duty to comply with his friends' wishes. As a rule, he got along well with women. He had been devoted to Mary of Modena, now in exile in St Germain, and he was on the easiest terms with Sarah. To begin with, Anne liked, trusted and depended upon him. As Marlborough was to spend much of his time fighting the French abroad, Godolphin was in effect Prime Minister.

Godolphin and Marlborough have been justly described as Queen Anne's joint 'Managers'. They aimed to establish a broad-based Cabinet dedicated to winning the war against France, but in fact most of the other Ministers were Tories, some of them extreme Tories, headed by Anne's uncle, the Earl of Rochester, though one or two Court appointments were held by Whigs. Anne called Godolphin in her correspondence with John and Sarah Marlborough 'Mr Montgomery'; the Marlboroughs themselves were 'Mr and Mrs Freeman'; and Anne, since the death of the Duke of Gloucester, referred to herself as 'your poor unfortunate Mrs Morley'. Sarah was made Groom of the Stole, Keeper of the Privy Purse and Mistress of the Robes, offices which she treated extremely seriously. To this group Anne appeared to be entirely devoted. In 1703 she wrote: 'We four must never part till death mows us down with his impartial hand.'

But Sarah tried too hard to exploit her friendship with the Queen for party political objectives. She was soon begging Anne to admit into office members of the Whig Junto, a powerful group during the reign of William III including her son-in-law, the third Earl of Sunderland, who particularly annoyed Queen Anne by opposing in the House of Lords a Bill for the benefit of Prince George. Jonathan Swift was to state later that Sarah's influence with the Queen actually began to decline during the first year of her reign. That this was so is confirmed by a significant letter that Anne wrote on 21 November 1702 in reply to a letter from Sarah. In it Anne rejected Sarah's criticisms of the opening address she made to a parliament, elected in August and summoned in October: in this speech the Queen had claimed that the Church of England had been in danger during the reign of William III. She added that she would not answer other things in Sarah's letter 'since everything I say is imputed either to partiality or being imposed upon by knaves and fools'. That was hardly the way to speak to one's superior. Anne loathed being told she was incapable of making up her own mind.

To start with, Anne distinctly favoured the Tories. By her saying soon after the beginning of her reign that her principles must always keep her entirely firm to the interests and religion of the Church of England 'and will incline me to countenance those who have the truest zeal to support it' many of her subjects were induced to vote Tory. Most Whigs had nonconformist sympathies. Anne particularly disliked the way in which some of them took the sacrament in church once a year simply in order to qualify for offices. The parliament elected in the first year of the reign passed a Bill condemning such occasional conformity. Anne insisted that the Managers should vote for it in the House of Lords, but it did not become law because amendments unacceptable to the Commons were added to it.

For their part the Tories, though impeccable as far as religion was concerned, were critical of the involvement of England in the war on land where huge armies, consisting in part of hired mercenaries, had to be paid for. They wanted the Government to concentrate its exertions on sea power, as in the reign of Elizabeth I. They therefore magnified the achievements of British admirals – for example in capturing a Spanish plate fleet, defeating the French and the Spanish in Vigo bay, and occupying the rock of Gibraltar in 1704, contrasting them with Marlborough's costly victories in Flanders.

Thus Anne had to be persuaded gently and gradually by her two Managers that what was necessary was a broadly based Ministry whose members were single-minded in the aim of overthrowing French supremacy. But it was with considerable reluctance that she let High Tories like Rochester and Nottingham resign from office and it was with even greater misgivings that she accepted William Cowper, a very moderate Whig, as Lord Keeper. By 1705 she was finally converted to the idea of having a coalition government; by then she began saying that she did not want to be 'in the hands of a party' and that she detested the names of Whigs and Tories. In a notable letter she wrote to Godolphin:

All I desire is my liberty in encouraging and employing all those who concur faithfully in my service whether they are called Whigs or Tories, not to be tied to one nor the other, for if I should be so unfortunate as to fall into the hands of either I shall not imagine myself, though I have the name of Queen, [to be] in reality but their slave . . .

Anne wrote in these terms after the Whigs, strong supporters of the war on land against France and Spain, had been victorious in a general election in 1705 and could therefore argue that their leaders must be taken into the Government. Her two Managers recognized this political fact and were highly embarrassed by the success of their own earlier teaching of the Queen. Vainly Sarah Marlborough attempted to exert her influence on behalf of the Whigs now loudly clamouring for offices. But Anne took little notice of Sarah. On the contrary, she began to be impressed by the attitude of Robert Harley, first Speaker of the House of Commons and then senior Secretary of State, who with Godolphin and Marlborough was reckoned to be a member of the Triumvirate really ruling the country. For whereas his two colleagues began pressing the Queen to admit the Whig Junto into the Ministry, Harley was talking the language that they had abandoned and urged her to resist the infiltration of extreme Whigs, just as she had ousted the extreme Tories earlier. Harley, though with a nonconformist background, was arguably never either a Whig or a Tory. At any rate he went on pressing the theme of a queen above party. For that reason Anne became perfectly willing to dismiss Godolphin and put Harley in his place. But she found herself unable to do so because Marlborough had won such magnificent victories abroad, at Blenheim, Ramillies and Oudenarde, that he had become a national hero and an irreplaceable commander. When he threatened to resign if Godolphin was removed from office, it was Harley who had to go.

Anne had been obdurate. It was Harley, not she, who crumpled. She resented being compelled to part with him. Above all, she was angry at being bludgeoned into taking the Junto Whigs, headed by Sunderland, into her Cabinet Council; and she hated the way in which Sarah badgered her into making more and more Whig appointments. Moreover she was becoming convinced that the war had gone on long enough. After Oudenarde she exclaimed: 'when will all this dreadful bloodshed cease?' The breakdown of peace negotiations in 1709 and the heavy loss of lives in Marlborough's last victory at Malplaquet appalled her. She refused (on the excuse that she was in mourning for her husband, who had just died) to appear at the thanksgiving for what was at best a very expensive victory.

There was in fact no real reason why the war should be continued after Louis XIV, recognizing that he was beaten, became willing to negotiate. It was with difficulty that England's chief allies in the war, the Dutch, had been persuaded to go on fighting in order that the entire Spanish empire could be acquired by the Austrian Habsburgs, a commitment to which Marlborough had unwisely agreed in 1703. In 1710, without consulting either of her two Managers, Anne brought the Duke of Shrewsbury, an extremely moderate Whig, into her Cabinet, dismissed first her bête-noire,

Sunderland, and then Godolphin, and recalled Harley to office. Thus Anne showed her independence and exercised her authority fully.

In the general election of the autumn the Tories, who, like the Queen, were now eager for peace, won a sweeping victory. This victory was largely influenced by the cry that the Church of England was still 'in danger' after a clergyman named Henry Sacheverell had been impeached by the Whigs for an indiscreet sermon they thought seditious. Queen Anne herself considered it a bad sermon and that Sacheverell should be punished for it. The idea that she had 'High Tory' sympathies has little basis in fact, although undoubtedly she was deeply religious. Her main preoccupation at this time was not over the Church but over the need to bring the long and costly war to an end. After her abrupt dismissal of Godolphin before the election the only ministerial opposition to peace negotiations with France was to be expected from Marlborough. Anne was quite prepared to be tougher with him than Harley wanted her to be. At the beginning of 1711 she insisted on relieving the Duchess of Marlborough of all her posts at Court, even though her husband grovelled before the Queen on his wife's behalf. Anne warmly approved of the separate diplomatic discussions with the French being kept secret from the Duke. Moreover she convinced herself that Marborough wanted to prolong the war, a conviction that was by no means baseless.

When towards the end of the campaign of 1711 Marlborough's capture of the fortified town of Bouchain on the river Meuse opened the way to a direct invasion of France, which the Duke advocated, Anne wrote to Harley: 'I think the Duke of Marlborough shows plainer than ever by this new project his unwillingness for peace, but I hope our negotiations will succeed and then it will not be in his power to prevent it.' She took the deepest interest in what she called 'the great affair' and was quite ready to recommend that some of the conditions put forward by the English envoys should be waived because she had 'this business of peace' so much at heart.

The unilateral negotiations provided that England should retain Gibraltar and Minorca, thus giving the navy predominance in the Mediterranean, that Hudson's bay, Newfoundland and Nova Scotia should become British (thus paving the way towards the acquisition of Canada), and that British merchants should be given commercial advantages in South America. In return it was agreed that Philip of Anjou should be recognized as King of Spain and the Spanish Indies provided that the Crowns of France and Spain were kept separate. This was a partition of the Spanish possessions such as William III had agreed to and was in tune with the Grand Alliance treaty signed by Marlborough in 1701. It was a not unreasonable attempt by the Queen's Government to sustain the balance of power in Europe. For in 1711 the Habsburg Emperor had died and was succeeded by the very Archduke Charles whom the Allies had promised should replace Carlos II as ruler of the entire Spanish empire. Had that happened, the Austrian Habsburgs would have become supreme in Europe as well as in South America. As it was, the treaty of Utrecht, which finished the war in 1713, enabled the British to expand their first empire, the Austrians to become dominant in Italy, the Dutch to obtain their fortress barrier in Flanders, and Louis XIV's grandson to become King of Spain.

Though the preliminaries of peace had been concealed from Marlborough, he naturally got to hear of them and was determined to oppose them. In order to undermine his popularity as a consistently victorious general charges of peculation were preferred against him to damage his reputation. The Queen was not responsible for these charges, but allowed herself to be persuaded that they were true: indeed she thought they were 'prodigious'. When Marlborough came to visit her at Hampton Court in November 1713 she received the impression that he was 'dejected and very uneasy about this matter of the public accounts'. Anne was perfectly prepared to dismiss him in the same ruthless way as she had dismissed Godolphin, although she lived to regret it. When she opened Parliament on 7 December she informed it that a place and time for opening a treaty of peace had been agreed 'notwithstanding the arts of those who delight in war' – an obvious hit at her commander-in-chief. Marlborough then seconded an amendment to the Queen's address to the effect that no peace would be honourable to Great Britain or Europe if Spain and the Indies went to the House of Bourbon. That amendment was carried by a majority of five votes in the House of Lords. Although the doctrine of joint Cabinet responsibility did not then prevail, it was plain that Marlborough could not be retained in his posts if the Queen and her other Ministers were determined upon concluding peace on terms of which he disapproved.

Queen Anne had no hesitation over dismissing this great soldier, who had once been her close friend. She did not send for him but wrote him an ungracious letter, which he promptly burnt. In much the same way she had in the previous year dismissed Godolphin, telling him not to come to her and hand over his staff of office, but to break it himself. This procedure smacked of cowardice. Moreover it reflected the manner in which all the Stuart rulers of England except William III behaved towards their loyal servants – as instanced by James I's treatment of Bacon and Middlesex, Charles I's betrayal of Strafford and Laud, Charles II's dismissal of Clarendon and Danby, James II's handling of Rochester and Sunderland. The Stuarts cannot be noted for their gratitude. Still, it can be argued that had

Marlborough been sent back as commander-in-chief and allowed to invade France, the war might have been indefinitely prolonged; for, as the battle of Malplaquet had shown, in the last resort Frenchmen were willing to fight and die for their aged King.

Besides the victory over Louis XIV and the foundation of the first British empire the most important achievement in Queen Anne's reign was the union of England and Scotland.

As compared with England, Scotland remained a poor and sparsely populated kingdom. The population was not more than a million, while Edinburgh, the largest town, housed only 40,000 people. Feudalism lingered on; agriculture was backward; little enclosure had taken place. Infields consisting of arable land consumed all the manure that was available. Outfields were devoted to pasture, but as little or no fodder was grown, most cattle had to be slaughtered before winter. The export trade was modest: the goods offered were meat and corn, some coal, wool and linen. Outside the Highlands whisky was drunk only as medicine. Lack of overseas markets and inadequacy in shipping chiefly accounted for commercial failure. The last years of William III's reign had witnessed a succession of bad harvests; starvation was not unknown.

Yet, paradoxically enough, the reign of William was a period of constitutional advance. The Stuart monarchs had tended to neglect their smaller kingdom. Once settled in England, James I had been content to rule it from afar; Charles I had antagonized it by his policy of religious conformity; Charles II never went there once he had been restored to his thrones and had harboured distasteful memories of the Presbyterian Elders. James II was far too occupied during his short reign to think about it a great deal; William III never went there at all, but relied upon his Dutch friend, the Duke of Portland, for advice about how it should be governed.

This neglect enabled the ruling classes in Scotland to strengthen their constitutional independence. First, they had insisted that William and Mary had been accepted as their King and Queen only on specified conditions, thus claiming that Scotland was an elective monarchy. The Convention, which had been called there after the revolution of 1688, sat right throughout the reign and since the Lords of the Articles, who planned public business when a parliament was not in session, had been abolished after the revolution this parliament wielded more authority than any before it.

Although the Highlanders were shocked by the massacre of Glencoe and the Lowlanders were angered by the failure of English capitalists to back the scheme for an indigenous trading company, the Scots thus found themselves in a position to promote their national independence. It is true that the Convention or Parliament ratified the succession of Queen Anne in 1702, but when a new Scottish parliament was elected in 1703, it passed three significant Bills. The first was a Bill of Security, which provided that unless concessions were made to Scotland's economic needs, the next Scottish monarch should not be the same as Anne's successor in England. The second aimed at maintaining the established Protestant religion without any bishops. The last took away from future monarchs the right to declare war without the consent of a Scottish parliament.

William III, like Oliver Cromwell, had advocated the union of England and Scotland; Anne in the very first speech of her reign had announced her wish for union. In England the Whigs and the moderates favoured it, but not the High Tories, who were infuriated by Scottish recalcitrance. But since the Tories were defeated in the general election of 1705 the political climate favoured the negotiation of union. The Queen's Ministers were alarmed at Scottish assertions of independence for two reasons: first, they feared lest the French should land an expeditionary force in eastern Scotland; after all, the French had been for many years the traditional allies of the Scots, while Jacobitism was rampant in the Highlands. Secondly, Anne's health was never good. Were she to die the Scots might opt out of obedience to the Dual Monarchy since it had only been loyalty to the Stewarts, who had reigned over them for over two hundred years, that bound them to England. Consequently Queen Anne and her Ministers had no wish to alienate the Scots: that was why Anne was persuaded reluctantly to give her consent to the Act of Security. The English Parliament was less submissive. It reacted to the Act of Security by passing an Alien Act which provided that if the Scots broke the family union between the two Crowns or refused to accept the succession as laid down in the Act of Settlement, all Scots would be treated as aliens and Scottish exports would be admitted neither into England nor Ireland.

Yet what appeared to be a constitutional impasse was quickly overcome. After the election of 1705 in England it was decided to reopen negotiations for union, which had broken down in 1703 because of anglophobia in Scotland and Tory obstruction in England. Even then negotiations might have proved fruitless had it not been for the fact that James Douglas fourth Duke of Hamilton had succeeded in carrying a snap vote in the Scottish Parliament on 1 September 1705 that the nomination of the Scottish commissioners (as well as of the English commissioners) should be left to Queen Anne. This was remarkable. For the Douglases had long been the most distinguished nobles in the Scottish Lowlands, had intermarried with the Stewarts, and could themselves well have been candidates for the throne of an independent Scotland. Even today it is not certain why he acted as he did since he had before been one of the most vehement opponents of union. Perhaps he realized that fresh negotiations could not be avoided and therefore he wanted to be one of the commissioners himself. Indeed he had been secretly assured of this by the Duke of Argyll, who was Anne's third Royal Commissioner in Scotland.

Anne herself was throughout an enthusiast for union – 'for putting the two nations on one bottom in all posterity': the thirty-one commissioners she appointed for England were mostly Whigs, while with one exception the commissioners she named for Scotland were already resolved in principle in favour of union. In only just over three months after the commissioners first met the articles of union were agreed. The Scots were to be represented both in the House of Commons and in the House of Lords; there was to be free trade between the two countries and Scottish merchants were to have access to the English colonies overseas. The Scots were compensated for having to share the burden of the English national debt, which was created by the heavy costs of the two wars against France, with a financial grant or 'equivalent' much of which was to go to the Scottish investors who had lost money over the Darien scheme. The Scottish Parliament ratified the treaty of union by 110 votes to 57 in January 1707. Three days before the treaty became effective the last parliament to meet in Scotland was dissolved.

Nevertheless the treaty was certainly not popular in Scotland. Whereas ninety addresses against the union were presented in Scotland, not a single one was put forward in its favour. The General Assembly of the Kirk refused to order a fast while it was being negotiated. Riots broke out in Edinburgh and Glasgow. It has since been recognized by historians that the political nation in Scotland, if not blatantly bribed into agreeing to it, was at least subjected to political pressure, promise of office, and other indirect financial inducements. But the discontent of most ordinary Scotsmen at their subjection to the Auld Enemy was so plain that Louis XIV thought it worth his while to allow James II's son, the Old Pretender, to accompany an expedition, consisting of 5,000 French soldiers, escorted by a naval squadron, which sailed to Scotland in the spring of 1708 with a view to heading a rebellion against his sister, for he was convinced that many Scottish Jacobites would rise on his behalf. In fact English sea power thwarted the plan.

What to an English historian is mysterious about the Act of Union is that the concept of a federal rather than an incorporative union was not seriously considered by either side. No doubt one reason was that the long time it then took to drive or sail from Edinburgh to London and the slowness of communication between the two capitals made it look impractical. Moreover the idea of a federal union was relatively new: such a constitutional scheme for English-speaking peoples had to await the emergence of the United States of America. But, after all, the neighbouring United Netherlands had built a confederation that had survived every kind of vicissitude over a period of nearly 150 years. And the Duke of Hamilton at any rate had leant towards this solution. It has only been revived in modern times. But whatever the majority of Scots thought about the incorporation and the loss of political independence, Queen Anne was delighted: it thrilled her at least as much as Marlborough's victory at Blenheim. On 1 May 1707 she drove to St Paul's cathedral 'to give thanks for the greatest of all the victories with which God had graced her reign'.

The character of Queen Anne has encountered various transformations in the writings of historians. She once used to be described as stupid and uneducated and putty in the hands of a succession of favourites, first Sarah Marlborough, then the red-nosed Abigail Masham, and finally the Duchess of Somerset, known as 'Carrots'. Though first Godolphin and then Harley did the real work of government, they had to obtain Anne's approval for their decisions and at times had to wear down her resistance. Certainly she was no nonentity. Sir Winston Churchill called her grandiloquently 'one of the strongest personalities that have ever reigned in these islands'. Professor George Trevelyan regarded her as a second Elizabeth I. One living historian has attributed the triumphs of her reign – the victory over France, the treaty of Union and the treaty of Utrecht as 'essentially personal to her'. That is going rather far. She was of course conscientious and patriotic, but her outstanding characteristic was obstinacy, especially in personal matters, a trait she inherited from her father. Towards the end of her life she was to write to Harley: 'I desire you would not have so ill n opinion of me as to think that when I have determined anything in my mind I will alter it.'

It is likely that Anne herself was confused about her exact constitutional position. It was not the same as her father's. The Bill of Rights and the Act of Settlement, both passed in the previous reign, had substantially reduced the royal prerogatives. Furthermore the Triennal Act had limited, though not abolished, the Queen's right to call, prorogue and dissolve parliaments. In spite of all this, it has been argued that the monarch's powers were still far-reaching: George III was to believe this and demonstrate it. If modern historians differ about the nature of eighteenth-century monarchy, it is hardly surprising if Anne herself was puzzled over it. She was, however, sufficiently realistic to accept that she did not govern by divine right, even though her grandfather and great-grandfather were sure they did.

Anne was more concerned about people than ideas. She had violent likes and dislikes: she could not stand the third Earl of Sunderland; she was reluctant to appoint him Secretary of State and got rid of him as soon as she decently could. She was furious when the second Duke of Queensberry, who, after he had been dismissed as Royal Commissioner in Scotland in 1704 had headed the opposition to her Government, was restored to office by Godolphin in 1706: 'it grates my soul', she wrote, 'to take a man into my service that has not only betrayed me but tricked me several times'. In spite of pressure from her two Managers to discharge Mrs Masham from her post as bedchamberwoman because she was a friend of Harley, Anne refused to do so. She never cared for the profligate Henry St John Viscount Boling-broke, who negotiated the treaty of Utrecht, and refused to give him an earldom or appoint him Lord Treasurer. The only politician she trusted over a long time was Robert Harley whom she created Earl of Oxford; his views about government above party, as has been noticed, coincided with her own. When at the end of her reign she dismissed him it was because of his mental and physical collapse which prevented him attending to business or being sufficiently respectful to her. But differing from the way in which she had treated Godolphin and the Marlboroughs, she actually sent for Oxford and talked to him for two hours before asking him to surrender his staff of office. Two days after that painful interview the Queen died in Kensington palace on 31 July 1714. She was mourned by the public as Good Queen Anne.

The best biography of Queen Anne to date is that by David Green (1970). This should be supplemented by Professor George Holmes's penetrating book, *British Politics in the Age of Anne* (1967) which is invaluable: I have borrowed the phrase 'the two Managers' from this book.

Most of Anne's letters have been printed by historians who have had access to the Blenheim archives, which have recently been sold to the British Library. Sir Winston Churchill's *Marlborough: his Life and Times* and G. M. Trevelyan's *England under Queen Anne*, though written nearly fifty years ago, still make excellent and largely convincing reading. Recently much has been written in Scotland about the Act of Union. Besides the balanced account given by David Daiches's book referred to in Chapter 1, Mr William Ferguson has discussed it in his *Scotland 1689 to the Present* (1968) and in *Scotland's Relations with England* (1977). Perhaps most important is his article on 'The Making of the Treaty of Union of 1707' in *S.H.R.* xliii (1964).

[18]

The Pretenders

JAMES EDWARD, 'the Old Pretender', who was recognized by Louis XIV as King James III of England after his father's death in 1701, was a model character but an unlucky prince. Thirteen years old when his father died, he was devoted to his memory and actually tried to follow the letters of advice which James II in his pious old age had copiously compiled for the instruction of his only legitimate son. James Edward also loved his mother dearly; it was significant that the first girl to whom he offered marriage was Mary of Modena's niece, a fact that has been held to show that he had a mother fixation. He adored both his sons and his sister, Louise. Always courteous, he was seldom haughty or angry and he took after his father in his constant attention to business. He wrote hundreds of letters, drafting them himself when he had no secretary. On the whole, he was politically cautious, trying to avoid unnecessarily risking other men's lives in his service. He was entirely honourable. Had it not been for his inflexible Roman Catholicism, he might have made an excellent constitutional monarch in succession to his half-sister, Queen Anne.

But that handicap proved insurmountable. So he was destined to suffer a series of misfortunes. They began in 1708 when, taking advantage of Scottish hostility to the union, the French, at war with Anne, sent him with a fleet and an army to head an insurrection in Scotland. Before he left he caught measles and had to be wrapped up in a blanket as he was carried on board ship. He wrote to his mother: 'the body is very weak, but my courage is so high that it will sustain the weakness of the body. I hope not to write to you again until I write from the palace of Edinburgh.' But the French ships were rebuffed by a British squadron and tossed to pieces in a gale, whereupon the French admiral decided to make for home. He refused to allow James to land in Scotland. James's half-brother, the Duke of Berwick, who had already made a name for himself as a marshal in the French army, thought that had James Edward disembarked, 'all Scotland was ready to take up arms in his favour' while 'England was . . . entirely denuded of troops'. It was a measure of the Old Pretender's ineffectiveness that he had not insisted on being put ashore.

After fighting bravely in the French army both at the battles of Oudenarde and Malplaquet – the Duke of Marlborough is reputed to have described him in hyperbole as being 'of excellent capacity, one of the best bred, best natured, and bravest persons upon earth' – James had to await the death of Queen Anne before being given another chance to lead a rebellion in Scotland. The coming of the Hanoverians with the accession of King George I, who could not speak English, was not enthusiastically welcomed in Great Britain, especially not in Scotland. On the other hand, by September 1715 Louis XIV was dead and the Regent for his successor, the five-year-old Louis XV, was in no way committed to the support of the exiled Stuarts. In fact although John Erskine Earl of Mar raised James's standard at Braemar, it was not until late December that the Old Pretender managed to reach Scotland; he had been expelled from France in accordance with the terms of the treaty of Utrecht and after sheltering in Lorraine, passed through France in disguise to embark at Dunkirk in an eight-gun ship. Before he landed, Mar had fought an indecisive battle against the second Duke of Argyll, who commanded the Hanoverian forces, and withdrew to Perth, while another Jacobite contingent had been crushed at Preston in Lancashire. Once again James proved himself ineffective. After reaching Perth he retreated north to Dundee. It was mid-winter, the worst possible time for fighting, but James was able to establish a base at Aberdeen, ready to resume battle in the spring. Mar, however, persuaded him that the situation was hopeless. Berwick, who had refused to accompany his half-brother to Scotland (on the ground that he was a naturalized Frenchman and France was no longer at war with Great Britain) wrote in his memoirs that James's precipitate return to France with Mar was 'only because of the too great deference paid by the young Prince to the advice of others'. His sister, Anne, could not have been accused of that.

When James got back to France he did at least take strong political action. He dismissed Henry St John Viscount Bolingbroke, who, fearing impeachment after Queen Anne's death for secret dealings with the Jacobites, had fled to France and became James's Secretary of State. It was Bolingbroke who was responsible for organizing James's expedition to Scotland in 1715; James evidently believed that he had betrayed the plans to his enemies. The Old Pretender was then obliged to leave France for fear of arrest by the Regent, who was seeking an alliance with the Hanoverian King. He first went to Avignon and then travelled by way of Modena and Bologna to Rome. The Pope, Clement XI, was James's only real friend, for most of Europe had no wish to annoy the victorious British Government by offering refuge to the Jacobites. Clement XI put a palace at Urbino in the Papal States at James's disposal and paid him a pension. It was at Urbino that the Old Pretender learned to his disappointment that the Duke of Modena would not allow him to marry his young cousin. In this isolated fastness of Urbino James's fortunes plunged to their lowest ebb. He determined, however, on one positive step. Having failed to win the girl he loved, he aimed to marry a rich heiress: that would at least enable him to help his fellow exiles. In this he was triumphant. On 1 September 1719 he married Clementina Sobieska, the granddaughter of the great Polish King, John Sobieski; she was one of the richest prizes in Europe. They settled down together in the palazzo Muti in Rome, a grey building where they were protected by a papal guard. The Pope also assigned to them the palazzo Savelli at Albano, eighteen miles from Rome, as a country residence. There James went regularly every spring and autumn. On the last day of 1720 his first son, Charles, usually known to history as 'the Young Pretender', was born in Rome. Four years after he was born (on 6 March 1725) Clementina had a second son, Henry. Charles was called the Prince of Wales and Henry the Duke of York.

James had not met his wife before he married her. At sixteen she was an extremely pious and plain Roman Catholic princess, whose delicate health was not improved by constant fasting. She was attracted by the idea of becoming a queen, and was a sufficient catch to induce the British Government to try to prevent the marriage. Pressure was brought to bear on the Emperor Charles VI, who was her cousin, to have her arrested as she crossed Austria on her way to Italy. Placed in prison in Innsbruck, she was rescued and smuggled out by one of James's young Irish officers, but did not arrive at Rome until nearly a year after she had set out from Silesia.

The marriage was not a success apart from the birth of the two sons. Writing on 6 April 1725 from Rome, the proud father described the birth of his second son as 'a great blessing and will, I hope, soon be followed by many others'; he told the Earl of Seaforth that 'we must all look forward now and by a strict union among ourselves become formidable to the adverse party and capable of pursuing what we all wish'. But the Queen became jealous and hysterical. She objected to her son being given Protestant governors; she also took a violent dislike to John Hay, who had replaced the Earl of Mar as James's Secretary of State and to his wife, Marjory, both of whom were Protestants. In March 1725 they were created Earl and Countess of Inverness: it is clear that Clementina believed, entirely wrongly, that the Countess was her husband's mistress. Eight months after the birth of the Duke of York Clementina left the palazzo Muti and retired into the convent of St Cecilia.

James was appalled. He told her by letter on 9 November 1725 that her departure was a public outrage which exposed him to unhappiness and shame; he blamed his enemies for 'taking advantage of her youth and the feebleness of her sex' and insisted that he must be 'the master of his own affairs and his own family'. Two days later, realizing her jealousy, he wrote 'il est certain, Madame, que je vous ai toujours uniquement aimée' and added that though it was his right to give orders about the upbringing of their children, she had no other reason to complain of him and he offered to receive her back tenderly. He also wrote protesting to his father-in-law and later told the Duke of Ormonde that he had learnt that his wife had been contemplating this step for some time in order to force him to dismiss Inverness. When the Pope, Benedict XIII, tried to effect a reconciliation James stood on his dignity. He told his friend, Francis Atterbury, the exiled Bishop of Rochester, that 'I had no occasion for the Pope's concern in an affair that concerned my private family'. It was almost the only occasion in the life of the Old Pretender that he asserted himself.

Eventually Clementina, under pressure from the Pope, returned to her husband, joining him in Bologna, but things were never to be the same again. When the King took the Prince of Wales to a ball in January 1728 the Queen refused to accompany them. He told Inverness, who had resigned office at his own request, that the Queen lived 'a most retired life, though I have encouraged her to alter it, I don't think she will '. After they returned to Rome she lived in seclusion in the palazzo Muti where her health steadily declined. She was to die in January 1735 at the age of thirty-four. From then on James faced a lonely middle age. One of his biographers believed that Clementina had done more damage to his cause than any of the spies maintained by the British Prime Minister, Robert Walpole, ever did.

Since the death of Louis XIV and the failure of the rebellion of 1715 James realized that the only hope of his restoration to the thrones of his ancestors lay in positive help from one of the Great Powers. He was to discover that the Spaniards were willing to make use of his nuisance value when they were twice at war with Great Britain. Philip V's second wife, Elizabeth Farnese, was anxious to secure principalities for her two sons in Italy. This chimed in with Spanish resentment at the loss of their Italian possessions by the terms of the treaty of Utrecht. So in the year before his marriage James left Italy for Spain, was splendidly received in Madrid and granted a pension. The chief Spanish Minister, Alberoni, was in James's debt because he had prevailed on the Pope to make him a Cardinal. So everything for the moment looked rosy.

After Spanish armies had occupied Sardinia in 1718–19 and the British Government had joined the French in resisting this violation of the treaty of Utrecht, expeditions against England and Scotland on behalf of the Jacobites were optimistically planned, but, as usual with James, everything went wrong. The Spanish fleet was scattered by storms, a British squadron appeared off the west coast, and although a Spanish force actually succeeded in reaching northern Scotland, where it was joined by a thousand Highlanders, they were soon defeated. After that the Spaniards wanted to get rid of James as quickly as they could. He himself was disillusioned, for he recognized that he and the Jacobites were simply pawns in an unsuccessful war.

The second war between Spain and Great Britain began in the autumn of 1739 – it is sometimes known as the War of Jenkin's Ear – and arose out of disputes between British merchants and the Spanish authorities over smuggling and piracy off the West Indies and Central and South America. Once again elaborate preparations were made for a Jacobite invasion, but nothing came of them. By now James had reached late middle age; he was disappointed by the fact that he had ceased to received his Spanish pension; and he concentrated his energies on writing diplomatic dispatches, trusting that his two sons, growing to manhood, would uphold the Stuart cause if suitable opportunities presented themselves.

By the late 1740s James, whose health was rarely good and who frequently suffered from dyspepsia, became a hypochondriac as well; he was ageing prematurely and, in the words of one of his biographers, had 'sunk into the pious recluse who passed much of his time in church and the rest in writing interminable letters'; the English Whigs called him 'Old Mr Melancholy'. One by one those whom he trusted most died: his former Secretary of State, the Earl of Mar in 1732, his half-brother, the Duke of Berwick was killed at a siege in 1735, and his nephew, Berwick's son and heir, died of consumption five years later. The Earl of Inverness passed away in 1740, while James's own wife had perished in 1735.

But James had justifiably high hopes of his sons, for in them were mingled both the blood of their once martial grandfather, James II, and that of their great-grandfather, John Sobieski. As their portraits reveal, they were both handsome young men. They were also charming and fairly wealthy, for their maternal grandfather had left them all his money, jewels and estates. Charles was the more high-spirited of the two; though he never learned to spell or be grammatical and was a dunce at Latin, he was a fine horseman and shot and seemed destined to be a soldier. When he was thirteen James allowed him to go in the care of his cousin, the first Duke of Berwick's son, to join in the siege of Gaeta near Naples, which had been undertaken by Don Carlos, the elder son of Elizabeth Farnese. Henry Duke of York, who was then nine, was envious, but he himself was studious, religious and hard-working and his father's favourite. When in 1744 war was about to break out between Great Britain and France Charles, now twenty, was sent off in disguise to Paris. James was content to stay in Rome with his younger son and had optimistically appointed Charles Edward as his Regent in England, Scotland and Ireland. The young Prince moved off on a black horse into the January night with two or three servants, managed to reach Antibes, and arrived in Paris in mid-February. Father and son were never to meet again.

Charles had an adventurous journey from Rome to Paris, but when he reached the French capital he was disappointed at his reception. Although in the previous year a French army (supporting the King of Prussia) and an Anglo-Hanoverian army (supporting Queen Maria Theresa of Austria) had fought a battle at Dettingen in the Austrian Netherlands, the two countries were not officially at war. Thus when it became known that Prince Charles was in Paris the British delivered a formal diplomatic protest. Neither the King of France, Louis XV, nor his Ministers would see the Prince, who wrote to his father: 'Nobody knows where I am or what is become of me; so that I am entirely buried as to the public and . . . am obliged very often not to stir out of my room for fear of somebody's noting my face.' However, by March Louis XV plucked up his courage. He sent his best general, Marshal Maurice de Saxe, to Gravelines; there Charles was told to join him. Together they moved to Dunkirk where 7,000 French soldiers were embarked and a French naval squadron assigned to escort them to England. But heavy gales blew up, the transport ships were damaged, and an English fleet which had sailed across the Channel inflicted a defeat on the French warships.

This was a terrible disappointment to Charles's hopes. But he refused to return to Italy and contemplated sailing to Scotland in a skiff or enlisting as a volunteer in the French navy. For a time he lived under the name of Chevalier Douglas, but then moved back to Paris where he emerged at times from his hiding place to attend the opera. Gradually he built up a Jacobite following, consisting chiefly of Irishmen, and managed to collect sufficient funds to hire ships and buy weapons. James of course warned him that he should not undertake any enterprise unless he obtained definite backing from the French Government. But Charles took no notice; he pushed on with preparations to land in the Scottish Highlands. Undoubtedly the French must have known or guessed what he was doing, but they did not interfere.

Eventually in July 1745, nearly eighteen months after he had arrived in France, Charles embarked with seven friends on a frigate of forty-four guns called the *Du Teillay* (or *Dutelle*), loaded it with muskets and swords and set sail from St Nazaire. On 12 July he wrote to his father and his brother to let them know that after waiting a week in Belle Isle, he had been joined by a larger escort ship, the *Elizabeth*, which carried sixty-six guns and 700 men. He added that he was already a little seasick and expected to be more so, but 'it does not keep me much abed. I find the more I struggle against it the better.'

On the voyage the *Elizabeth* was lost. A British warship, sailing to join its squadron in the Bay of Biscay, ran into it by accident; in the fight that ensued the *Elizabeth* was so badly damaged that it had to return to France to refit. Charles, who wanted to join in a naval battle, had to be almost forcibly restrained. His companions, older and more experienced men, then urged that the *Du Teillay* should go back to port as well. But on that Charles was adamant. He showed himself a stronger character than his father, who had not been allowed to land in Scotland after the rising of 1708 and had been persuaded to leave quietly in 1715.

On 25 July 1745 Charles disembarked on the west coast of Scotland. His first stepping stone was a small island, Eriska in the Hebrides. The island was inhabited by fishermen who spoke only Gaelic. His welcome there was far from warm. The local laird was away, but his uncle, MacDonald of Boisdale, at once visited the ship at its mooring to assure Charles that not a single chieftain would rise on his behalf unless he brought French troops and arms. Then the chieftain himself, MacDonald of Clanranald, was found and entertained with choice French wines. Even that did no good. But one of the younger MacDonalds swore that he would follow Charles till death. Charles then moved to the mainland, where with difficulty he managed to persuade Donald Cameron (whose father had fought in the 1715 rebellion) to enlist his clan in the Stuart cause. Soon after that Charles sent back his ship, from which the arms and stores had been unloaded, to France. He hoped that the news it would carry of his safe landing in Scotland would inspire the French to help him since he was in effect opening up a second front against the British Government. But by doing so he forfeited a life-line for himself. He was left marooned in Scotland.

On 19 August Charles raised his standard at Glenfinnan, some twenty-five miles from the military base of Fort William, where he was joined by

150 MacDonalds and 700 Camerons. Thus he had the nucleus of an army. He had already written to his father: 'I am joined here by brave people, as I expected . . . We, whatever happens, will gain the immortal honour by doing what we can to deliver our country in restoring our Master or perish with sword in hand.' The Prince was evidently a romantic orator with a genuine gift for persuasion. At Glenfinnan he read out a manifesto, given him by his father before he left Italy, and his own commission as Regent; then he delivered a stirring speech, declaring that his righteous cause must triumph.

Having collected his miniature army, Charles was anxious to move forward into central Scotland while the iron was hot. The British Government, headed by Thomas Pelham-Holles first Duke of Newcastle, a politician who became extremely nervous when he heard of the rising, put up a reward of £30,000 for the capture of the Young Pretender. Sir John Cope, the military commander-in-chief in Scotland, who was stationed at Stirling, was ordered to dispose of his forces as he thought fit, to secure the forts along the waterline in the Highlands and to take his dragoons' horses from grass. Cope, who was said at the time to have 'no shining abilities and no experience and no forces', was in fact a reasonably competent regular officer, but some of his soldiers were newly raised recruits and the size of Charles's army was wildly exaggerated.

Charles was eager to fight; he aimed to ambush Cope in the Corryarrick pass through which the enemy would have to advance if he moved north to attack the Highlanders in the region of Fort William. Aware of what was happening, Cope thought that discretion was the better part of valour and moved north-east to Inverness, where he intended to increase the strength of his forces with Highlanders loyal to the Hanoverians. Charles was disappointed at the failure of his manoeuvre, but Cope's refusal to attack immediately raised the Prince's prestige and opened the way for a move south. He took the opportunity at once; first he went to Blair Atholl, where he was lavishly entertained by William Murray Duke of Atholl, who had come with him from France. On 4 September he occupied Perth, where he stayed for a week and even contemplated a coronation at Scone, and was joined by a number of distinguished Scotsmen. He appointed Lord George Murray, an extremely well qualified officer aged fifty-two, and James Drummond Duke of Perth as his two lieutenant-generals, then marched by way of Stirling, Falkirk and Linlithgow to Edinburgh, which he reached on 17 September. The Prince made no attempt to occupy the formidable castles at Stirling or in Edinburgh, but met with little resistance in the capital. He was able to sleep comfortably in Holyroodhouse, the palace of his Stewart ancestors.

In Edinburgh Charles learned that Cope had sailed from Aberdeen to Dunbar and was ready to fight him. The Jacobite Highlanders, who were accustomed to wielding the claymore or the dirk rather than the limited number of rifles that were available, attacked Cope's forces on the plain of Prestonpans, a few miles outside Edinburgh, at dawn on 21 September. Cope's soldiers were panicked by the ferocity of Charles's Highlanders, who killed horses as well as men and plundered the dead as well as the living. Charles was shocked: he ordered all the wounded to be cared for. So he returned to Edinburgh blooded but not elated. Here on 14 October he was greeted by a French envoy, sent by Louis XV, who, even before the news of the victory of Prestonpans reached him, had ordered the Scots Royal regiment, which served in the French army, to be sent to Scotland. Charles wrote to tell his father that he now had an army of nearly 8,000 infantrymen and 300 cavalry with which he planned to march into England. He added that he wished to God he would find his brother Henry had landed in England by the time he himself entered it.

Apart from Sir John Cope, defeated at Prestonpans, the only British officer in the north capable of stopping the Jacobite advance was Field-Marshal George Wade, who was in his seventy-fifth year, and was stationed at Newcastle with 10,000 men. Charles wanted to fight him before pushing on south. However, Lord George Murray, his second in command, would not hear of it: he urged Charles and his Highlanders to take the western route, thus avoiding Wade, unless he chose to cross the Pennines and attack them, and enabling the Prince to recruit more volunteers in Lancashire and Wales, both reputedly Jacobite in sympathy. Charles gave way; armed with broadswords and pistols and wearing white cockades on their hats, the Highlanders marched into England. Carlisle, the capital of Cumberland, was quickly captured; after a short rest the Jacobite army pushed on to Derby, less than 130 miles from London, where they arrived on 4 December.

Having gone so far and meeting little opposition, Lord George Murray and most of the Highland chieftains decided that they wanted to go back home. The arguments for doing so were that it was nearing mid-winter, that few Englishmen – a maximum of about 200 in Lancashire, mostly Roman Catholics and later described as 'a set of the most hardened wretches ever met with' – had joined the invading army, and that it was known that the Duke of Cumberland, the younger son of the reigning King George II, a capable officer and administrator, had been recalled from the war in the Austrian Netherlands with most of his troops and was advancing towards Scotland with a sizable army. At the same time no news had been received of any French contingent, accompanied by the Duke of York, arriving to assist them. Charles had originally meant to march on London, but the Council of War accepted Lord George Murray's arguments against attempting it. Charles and the rank-and-file were thunderstruck. Dejectedly Charles rode back with the rear guard. He insisted on leaving a small garrison behind at Carlisle, persuading himself that they were retreating *pour mieux sauter* later. In January 1746 he laid siege to Stirling castle, always a key point in Scottish military operations, for, as has been noticed before, it guarded the main route from the Lowlands into the Highlands.

It has been contended that Charles should have overruled his subordinate commanders at Derby, trusting in the élan which had been created by the victory at Prestonpans and the quick surrender of Carlisle to startle the British Government and overthrow the Hanoverians. But that was a daydream. By then the Hanoverians had been in power for over thirty years; a new generation had grown up in England with their future fortunes invested in a stable and prosperous régime. The traditional fear and dislike of the Whigs who comprised the King's Ministries both for the French (with whom they were now at war) and for the papists, headed by the Old Pretender, a pensioner of the Vatican, were still aglow. Moreover all the precedents were against a successful march south: the Scots army under the first Duke of Hamilton, fighting for Charles I in 1648, had been destroyed by Oliver Cromwell in Lancashire; King Charles II, like his great-nephew, had failed to recruit many adherents in Lancashire or Wales and had been crushed at Worcester before he was within sight of London.

Thus before the spring of 1746, when good campaigning weather might be expected, the steam had gone out of the rebellion. Meanwhile the young Duke of York had done all he could to help his elder brother. Towards the end of August 1745 he had left Rome and, although taken ill at Avignon, had arrived at Paris in October, employing the title of Duke of Albany, and succeeded in meeting Louis XV, his son, and his Ministers. It was then agreed that he should be the nominal leader of a French expeditionary force, consisting of at least 10,000 troops, to be convoyed in transport ships from Dunkirk or Bologne to some point on the coast of England. But the news of the retreat from Derby reached the French Court about the end of 1745; after five million francs had been spent on organizing such an expedition, it was at once abandoned.

Back in Italy James III, more cautious and realistic than his elder son, always recognized that neither England nor Scotland could be won over to his cause without the assistance of the French. When Charles had set out without official French approval from Belle Isle in July 1745 he had done so without consulting his father. Therefore James had written to his representative in Paris, Lord Sempil, to tell him that his son could not possibly succeed in removing King George II from his throne 'except he is vigorously supported by the Court of France'. But, he continued, 'the question is now to look forward and not to blame what is past', and he proceeded to bombard the French Government with interminable letters. He also reluctantly had sent his second son, a youth of twenty, to Paris. Sempil told his master with some asperity that 'there are too many people meddling with your Majesty's affairs with the French Court at this juncture' and that the French should be given information about Charles's activities and then 'they will consider what can be done'. It was of course this information which decided the French to do nothing.

Charles won one more victory before his campaign collapsed. Without consulting anyone he took the resolve to besiege Stirling castle, hoping that this would allow the Jacobites to retain their hold on Scotland while another advance into England was attempted. By now the Hanoverian troops in Scotland had been reinforced with veterans from Flanders and put under the command of a martinet, General Hawley. Moreover the Duke of Cumberland was known to be on his way north. Once Charles learned all this he decided he must take action quickly before Cumberland could join Hawley. So another battle was fought. Again through their undisciplined ferociousness the Highlanders overcame a stronger enemy who had more cavalry. The contest, to be known as the battle of Falkirk, was all over in twenty minutes; though the losses on both sides were relatively small, Hawley told the Duke of Cumberland 'we are quite beat'.

For the second time Prince Charles was persuaded by Lord George Murray that he must retreat. They were both aware that the Duke of Cumberland had already occupied Edinburgh with a fine army. The decision was therefore taken to retire into the northern Highlands, where it was hoped that a delaying action against Cumberland could be fought while hoped-for reinforcements from France were arriving. In February 1746 Charles entered Inverness, but spent most of March in Elgin where he was seriously ill. Meanwhile Cumberland, a tough character who, like Lord Montgomery in our own time, believed in tying up all loose ends before launching a battle, was making his way from the Lowlands into the Highlands. He was not happy over his reception by the Scots and complained that he could obtain no intelligence from them, but was delighted that he was allowed without any interference from his enemy to cross the river Spey, which winds its way south across the route that runs from Aberdeen to Inverness.

For his part Charles was fully informed about the Duke of Cumberland's movements. He was aware that after crossing the Spey he had encamped at Nairn, fifteen miles north-east of Inverness and only nine miles from where the Jacobites were posted in the park surrounding Culloden house. It was also known to the Jacobites that it was Cumberland's twenty-fifth birthday which was being celebrated in his camp on 15 April. A Council of War was held at which it was determined to surprise Cumberland's army by a night attack directed from two different angles. After all, Charles's Highlanders knew the country far better than did the Hanoverian general. Who actually made this proposal is obscure, but it was probably the best chance of winning a victory. Another Stuart, the Duke of Monmouth, no mean soldier, had thought the same at Sedgemoor. However, the Jacobites were short of food and the march, beginning at dusk across the boggy ground in the dark, was so hazardous that the whole force was unable to move quickly enough to get to Nairn before dawn. Once again Lord George Murray counselled retreat. The exhausted, half-starved soldiers returned to Drummossie moor, east of Culloden house. Most of them were able to snatch only an hour or two's sleep before being ordered to draw up in battle formation on the moor.

The reason for the haste was that Charles had learnt that the Duke of Cumberland had broken camp and was advancing against him with an army of some 9,000 men. Perhaps he was over-anxious because his enemy was coming slowly, as was necessary owing to the weight of Cumberland's artillery. Though outnumbered, the Prince was determined that he would stand and fight rather than retreat into the northern mountains to wage guerrilla warfare. He remembered the heroic fierceness of his Highlanders who had frightened and crushed their foes at the battles of Prestonpans and Falkirk. But the circumstances of that spring day could hardly have been worse for him. Many of his soldiers had deserted their posts and gone into Inverness in search of food. The site of the coming battle on the moor contained little cover except for a four-foot-high wall behind which the right wing was drawn up. Finally the Jacobites were distributed on slightly lower ground than the Hanoverians, who because of the desertions by their enemy, had twice their strength and had superior cavalry and artillery.

The battle opened in the early afternoon with such a heavy cannonade that the Highlanders, who impatiently awaited the order to charge in their usual uninhibited fashion, were held back. In the end the Jacobite right and centre surged forward without receiving any clearly given command. At first their impetuosity carried them on to their enemy, but soon they were mown down by musket and bayonet. Charles could hardly believe his eyes;

he had never seen his men so completely routed. As the course of the battle turned against him, he decided or was persuaded not to die heroically on the field, as he had promised. Though shaken to the core, he was induced to seek for personal safety in the belief that he could recruit another army and fight another day. From the refuge he found he wrote a letter to the chiefs of the clans telling them that he would make for France so as to induce the Court there to intervene in the war or at least 'procure for you such terms as you would not procure otherwise'.

But that was self-delusion. The Duke of Cumberland's men exacted terrible retribution from the rebels. Those who were rounded up after the battle were executed without trial; some were thrust into overcrowded prisons and suffocated; others were sent on prison ships to London to be tried for treason, over a thousand of whom were sentenced to transportation. The western Highlands were devastated, many villages being set on fire. All this earned Cumberland the title of the Butcher. But that kind of punishment is the risk that all rebels run, even in our more civilized world today.

The Stuart cause perished on the field of Culloden. Contemplating the might-have-beens of history, all one can say is that conceivably a Stuart or Stewart kingdom might have been carved out of Scotland had the Old and Young Pretenders gone about that task cautiously and carefully. There was never much enthusiasm for the Hanoverians in Scotland or even for the Act of Union under Queen Anne. Prince Charles was blamed, particularly by his second-in-command, Lord George Murray, for setting up his standard in the first place without obtaining a guarantee of maximum assistance from France. But it was, after all, unlikely in the extreme that the English Government would have allowed the Auld Alliance to pave the way for an independent Scottish kingdom. In any case superior sea power would have been decisive, even as it was in the dark days of 1940.

After many adventures, chiefly in the Hebrides and the island of Skye, to which the legendary heroine, Flora MacDonald, took him, disguised as a woman, Charles found his way back to France just as his great-uncle, Charles II, had done before him. It was a proof of the loyalty of the Scots that no one betrayed him despite the prize of £30,000 offered for his head.

In Italy James III anxiously waited to learn what had happened to his elder son. 'We are always without the French post, my dearest Carluccio . . .' he wrote, 'I live always in the hope of receiving at least some news of you . . . But I trust God that Providence will always protect you and soon take you out of the power of your enemies. Till it please God that happens I cannot have a quiet moment.' When at last James was assured that Charles was safe and well in Paris, he tried hard to persuade his son to be patient and prudent and not to resent his treatment at the Court of France or to be cross with his brother, Henry, with whom he was reunited there. The Duke, James wrote, 'desires to be your friend, as he is your brother'.

But Charles was completely demoralized by the tragic end of his adventures; he soon ceased to write regularly to his father and he quarrelled with his brother, who finally returned to Rome in April 1747. Having been angered by what he called his 'scandalous treatment by the French', Charles tried vainly to solicit help from Spain. He insisted that the only way of behaving towards the French was 'to be laconic with them'. James was upset by his behaviour to Henry before he left him and on 3 February 1747 wrote him a long letter of reproof. He told Charles that he was misled and deluded by 'wicked men'. 'Were you never so irreligious a libertine,' he continued, 'the name of Catholic will still stick to you. *Enfin*, my dear child, I must tell you if you don't alter your ways I see you lost in all respects.' He added that he blamed him for his bad relations with the French Court, for not accepting a pension that had been offered him, and for his silence since his return from Scotland. But Charles was not in the least repentant and was by no means mollified when he was informed later that his brother, Henry, after his return to Rome, had at the age of twenty-two been elected a cardinal. He replied it was a disagreeable shock and 'a dagger thrown at my heart'.

The last years of the three Pretenders have often been described: they are fully documented and entirely distressing. After the peace was concluded between France and Great Britain in April 1748 Charles was arrested outside the Paris opera house and obliged to leave the city. He wandered around France, Italy and Austria and even paid a secret visit to London where he declared himself to be a Protestant. Henry, after taking priest's orders, became richer and richer. He received high appointments in the papal hierarchy and was also created Bishop of Frascati. Until he went there, he lived in the palazzo Muti with his father, who grew querulous and quarrelsome. But Pope Benedict XIV scolded the new Cardinal for his unfilial behaviour. James did not share his younger son's interest in music, art and science and took a dislike to an abbot who was Henry's close friend. This quarrel was made up and Henry returned to Rome from Bologna. In 1759 James, weakened by dyspepsia and even more by senility, took to his bed, while Henry, after his elevation to his bishopric, had to leave Rome for Frascati. His father died on 1 January 1766 at the age of seventy-eight and was buried in St Peter's cathedral.

Charles proclaimed himself King Charles III of England, Scotland, Ireland and France. But nobody recognized him as such, not even the Popes, although he had apparently returned from his brief flirtation with Protestantism to the Catholic faith. Charles was not highly sexed; early on he liked women to nurse and comfort him. It was not until he came back to Paris from Scotland that he was fortunate enough to be taught the facts of life by an extremely beautiful and cultivated woman, Marie-Louise Princesse de Talmond, who was ten years older than he was. When he left France after his wanderings he recalled a rather plain and homely Scottish girl, named after his mother Clementina, one of ten daughters of a Jacobite father named Walkinshaw; she had nursed the Prince when he had influenza before the battle of Falkirk. He invited her to join him in Ghent, where they set up house together in 1752; next year she bore him a daughter, named Charlotte, who took after her mother in being plain and homely. This affair came to an end after eight years when Clementina and her daughter retired into a convent, seemingly paid for by Cardinal Henry.

It was not until he reached the age of fifty-five that Charles married. James III had always pestered him to do so, but six years had passed since his father's death before he decided it was his duty to perpetuate the Stuart line. The girl chosen for him was a minor Princess, Louise of Stolberg, with an impeccable ancestry but no money. Charles was really no catch, for by now he was bloated and alcoholic. However, Louise fancied the idea of being a queen, if in name only, and mixing with the best Roman society. The marriage foundered after eight years when her husband started beating her. They had no children. Louise disappeared into a convent. In 1784 a legal separation was arranged. Charles then invited his illegitimate daughter, Charlotte, whom he had forbidden to marry but had given birth to three children by the Archbishop of Bordeaux, to come and live with him in Florence, which she did. Later they moved into the palazzo Muti in Rome. She became known as the Duchess of Albany. When Charles died on 30 January 1787 he left her all he had. He was buried in his brother's cathedral at Frascati. Charlotte did not long survive him. She made Henry her heir, understandably, because he had always looked after her and her mother.

The Cardinal of York, as he is generally, if confusingly, known, was in many ways the most attractive of the three Pretenders. On his brother's death he assumed the title of King Henry IX. He took sufficient interest in his Stewart ancestry to institute an inquiry into the papal dispensation granted for the first marriage of the first Stewart king, Robert II, because (as was pointed out in Chapter 3) it was claimed that his eldest son, who became King Robert III of Scotland, was born out of wedlock so presumably Henry IX, the last Stuart to call himself a monarch, was satisfied he was the lawful descendant of the first Stewart King of the Scots.

Henry IX was reputed to be the wealthiest of the cardinals of his time. But though he had forty or more servants and lived in style, he spent much of his riches on charity and the arts. Poverty and distress were said to have been unknown in his see of Frascati, while he always took care of the needs of his father, his brother and his brother's dependants. A studious and scholarly man and sincerely religious, like his father and grandfather he carried out his ecclesiastical and administrative duties conscientiously and assiduously. But a new Europe was coming into being. Two years after his brother's death the French revolution broke out, of which the heir was Napoleon I, whose troops overran the papal territories. Henry left Rome and first moved to Florence, and then to Venice. All his wealth evaporated in these days of upheaval. King George III of England was persuaded to bestow upon him a pension of £4,000 a year for life.

In fact Henry's last years were peaceful and happy. He died on 13 July 1807 and was buried in the crypt of St Peter's along with his father and mother; Charles III's remains were brought from Frascati to be laid alongside them. On a plain stone their names were carved – Jacobus III, Carolus III, Henricus IX. The Hanoverians bore them no grudge. Their empty shadows stretched into a distant past. King George IV was fascinated by them and purchased many of the historical records relating to King James II and the three Pretenders. They are to be found today, lovingly preserved, in the Round tower at Windsor castle.

The extracts from letters quoted in this chapter are taken from the originals or copies among the Stuart papers at Windsor castle by gracious permission of Her Majesty the Queen. The Jacobite literature is enormous. For a general survey see G. H. Jones, *The Main Stream of Jacobitism* (1954). The latest biographies of the Old and Young Pretender are respectively *James* by Peggy Miller (1971) and *The Rash Adventurer* by Margaret Forster (1973), which is extremely readable. There is a discursive and rather unsatisfactory biography of *Henry Stuart Cardinal of York* by Alice Shield (1908). The numerous books on the Jacobites by Alistair and Henrietta Tayler are reliable and entertaining. There is a book on the battle of *Culloden* by John Prebble (1961).

The Fall of the
House of Stuart

HOW IS ONE to account for the fall of the House of Stuart? One obvious reason is that the direct line of the dynasty died out. With one or two exceptions, such as Robert II with his thirteen children and Charles I with his three sons and three daughters they were not very good at producing legitimate offspring who survived into manhood, although they were mostly excellent at the procreation of illegitimate children. Charles II had no legitimate children, James II had only one son and one daughter by his second wife; William and Mary had no children; nor had the unfortunate Queen Anne, who tried so hard to generate them. James III (the Old Pretender) had only two sons; Charles III (the Young Pretender) had no legitimate children from his belated marriage; Henry IX (the Cardinal of York) stuck to celibacy.

The second reason was the Roman Catholicism to which James II and James III were devoted. In the face of the anti-papist emotions of the majority of his subjects, whose hysteria had burned like a furnace in the Popish Plot agitation and the Exclusionist movement, Charles II by sheer political skill had paved the way for the unopposed succession of his Roman Catholic brother, whose ability to govern his kingdoms of England and Scotland without provoking a rebellion he clearly did not trust. That turnabout is indeed one of the striking paradoxes of English political history. Had James II and VII been a wiser man in less of a hurry to secure equality of opportunity for his Catholic subjects he might have averted or postponed his downfall; for it has to be remembered that William III had made up his mind to intervene in English affairs at least a couple of months before the Old Pretender – with the Pope as one of his godfathers – has been christened. Even then, if towards the close of Queen Anne's reign, the Old Pretender had been willing to change his religion, as the Young Pretender was ready to do, the Stuarts might have continued to reign long into the eighteenth century instead of being replaced by the German-speaking Georges.

As it was, the Stewart reign in Scotland (it was James VI and I's paternal grandfather who changed the spelling of his name from Stewart to Stuart) endured longer than the Bourbon dynasty in France, the Romanov dynasty in Russia or the Habsburg dynasty in Spain. Though one is inclined to think of the Scottish monarchs as characters who were normally bullied by their nobility and unable to subdue the Highland clans or border warriors, the fact is that the success of the Stewarts in remaining in authority in spite of a series of minorities was a remarkable record. Most of them, from Robert II onwards, aimed at peace, only now and again being pushed into war through their Auld Alliance with France – yet of course they needed that alliance to protect themselves against the ambitions of the Plantagenets, the Yorkists and the Tudors to absorb their kingdom into England. The English Stuart kings, with larger resources, were more martial in their foreign policies, though James I, until he became senile, aimed to be a peace-maker, as Charles II also did towards the end of his reign.

The overriding objective of the Scottish Stewarts was to effect the unity of their kingdom. After many setbacks, that had very nearly been obtained in the reigns of James V and James VI. As has already been pointed out, had James VI not become King of England, he could well have completed that difficult task. As it was, the Highland clans remained a source of unrest until at least the middle of the eighteenth century.

One other consideration that must not be overlooked in picturing the story of the Stuarts is the romantic sentiments of the Highlanders and the appeal to them of the representatives of the dynasty, an appeal which stretched even beyond the Highlands. As late as 1750 a group of Jacobites fore-gathered at Shrewsbury on the borders of England and Wales, to sing this song:

> *Charley's red and Charley's white,*
> *And Charley is bonny O.*
> *He is the son of a Royal King,*
> *And I love him the best of any O.*
> *When he came to Derby Town*
> *Oh but he was bonny O.*
> *The Bells did ring and the Bagpipes play*
> *And all for the love of Charley O.*

The way in which Bonny Prince Charlie, after landing in the Hebrides with but a handful of friends, succeeded in raising an army of eight thousand men, inflicting two defeats on the English, and marching unopposed into England is evidence of the enduring romantic attraction of the Stuarts. And it had happened before. The Marquis of Montrose himself a Covenanter, without any troops of his own, had, aided by the Highlanders, virtually reconquered Scotland for Charles I in 1645.

The first English Stuart kings had sought peace abroad, James I because he thought little was to be gained by wars that could not be won through diplomacy and marriage, Charles I because he had not the financial means to engage in foreign wars, while Charles II, though he did not much care for them, had at first been reluctant to be pressed into fighting the Dutch. Then francophobia became paramount. Even Charles II, himself a pensioner of France, remonstrated with Louis about his aggressive foreign policy and for that reason Louis never really trusted him. James II, a proud man, defied the French until he was forced into seeking their help to preserve his own throne. Finally, the two Pretenders realized that they could not win their restoration without French military assistance, which would have meant their intervening in a war against Great Britain on the side of its enemies.

The last English Stuart rulers were responsible for three outstanding achievements. The first was helping to establish a balance of power in Europe that lasted for some seventy-five years, though they could not prevent meaningless dynastic wars or the rise of a militaristic Prussia. Still, they did manage to subdue Bourbon France whose aggressive adventures had intimidated the Dutch, the Germans and the Austrians. William III, after expelling his Stuart father-in-law, had virtually forced Louis XIV to his knees by creating a formidable Grand Alliance dedicated to preventing French expansion eastwards. Then, by altruistic diplomacy, William had tried hard to prevent another devastating European war. But Louis repudiated his obligations and it was left to William's Elisha, the first Duke of Marlborough, to carry on his campaign against overweening French supremacy in Europe. Yet it can be argued that at the expenditure of many lives and much money an evil hour had only been postponed; for Hanoverian Great Britain was left to contend with the mightier power of Napoleon Bonaparte.

The English Stuarts could claim credit for two other historic events: the first was the foundation of a British Empire. The earlier Stuarts might be said to have laid that foundation only in a fit of absence of mind. By harassing the Puritans, they induced the braver spirits among them to establish a New England and a New Scotland in North America, while it was Oliver Cromwell who had paved the way for the conquest of much of the rich soil of the West Indies. Marlborough's victories under Queen Anne not only fortified the young British colonies in America and the West

Indies, but by enabling the Stuart Government to acquire Gibraltar and Minorca won for the British predominance in the Mediterranean, which, in the long run, was to contribute materially to the overthrow of Napoleon.

The third achievement of the Stuarts was the union of England and Scotland. From the time when James VI of Scots obtained his heart's desire by becoming also King James I of England and Ireland an incorporative union of the two countries had been advocated. The fact that the Scots fought both for and against Charles I during his reign was a reminder that it was undesirable for the English to have an independent power to their north easily capable of interfering in their domestic affairs. The Scots had demonstrated their military strength in an emphatic way first during the two Bishops Wars of 1639–40 and then on the side of the Parliamentarians during the first civil war. Towards the end of the Interregnum in the middle of the seventeenth century the Lord Protector Oliver Cromwell and General George Monck had actually fashioned an incorporative union, which fell to pieces when Charles II returned home. But both William III and Queen Anne pressed for the revival of such a union, which was at last established in 1707 when England was involved in a world war.

The Scottish people did not very much care for the Union; the loss of a parliament and a royal Court in Edinburgh was by no means compensated by the right of Scotsmen to trade freely throughout the incipient British Empire. Undoubtedly it was the English who gained most from the Union not only in eliminating a danger to its security, but by being able to make use of Scottish military genius, which was to win glory in the world wars of the twentieth century. Even today most historians in Scottish universities take more pride in burnishing the memory of their Stewart kings, who maintained the independence and unity of their country, than in later monarchs and their Westminster parliaments that ruled Scotland from afar.

I found the song quoted in T.S. 11/926 in the Public Record Office. These Treasury Solicitor documents contain much information about the aftermath of the rebellion of 1745. For a conspectus of eighteenth-century warfare reference can be made to my book, *The Age of Absolutism* (1974).

Index